Social Institutions

Social Institutions

Alan Frank Wells

Senior Lecturer in Sociology
University of Glasgow

BASIC BOOKS, Inc., Publishers New York

First American edition: 1971

Library of Congress Catalog Card Number: 73-135567
SBN 465-07882-6

Printed in the United States of America

For Dorothy
Anna and Nicky

Contents

Preface

In a book of this length, a subject such as this must inevitably undergo drastic compression. Some of the treatment will seem unduly simplified, and the author can hardly escape the charge of being arbitrary in his selection of topics, and of using facts to illustrate, rather than to prove.

Such difficulties are unavoidable, and therefore have not been avoided in the present book. All the same, there appears to be a place for a general introduction to the field; all the more because most writers seem to have been more prudent than I, and therefore rather few such introductions at present exist.

I think it might be said that the general themes around which the book is constructed include the following. Firstly, there are problems of concept and methodology. Can the term 'social institution' be given not merely an intelligible meaning, but also an operational meaning, such that institutions can be studied comparatively? Then there are the methodological problems which are involved in the comparative study of societies or their elements. Naturally I also discuss such questions as that of whether terms like 'economic' or 'legal', which refer to relationships of fundamental importance in Western societies, can be applied to some aspects of behaviour or relations in *all* human societies; what the limits of application are; what the common denominator is; what is the range of variation.

I have put forward, and tried to appraise, certain explanatory hypotheses about the nature and development of institutions. But, lastly, I would wish to say that I have tried to be aware that the study of social institutions is a study of *phenomena*, and not of models. The profusion of raw data is such that model-building is not only necessary, but also comforting. But models are only helpful in so far as they truly explain the data; and therefore the data, and the profusion of data, are the things that one must always remind oneself of. History is a relative of Sociology whom some sociologists may disapprove of, but none can disown.

My thanks are due to all who have, in one way or another, helped me. Especial thanks are due to Professor Donald MacRae and Dr Percy Cohen, of the London School of Economics (but they bear no responsibility for anything in the book); to Miss Joan Biggar, who so carefully typed the manuscript; and, not least, to my family, who put up with me while I wrote it. They will know that this last acknowledgment is not mere form.

A. F. WELLS

Social Institutions

1.

Introduction

I

The characteristic endeavour of members of the human species is to kill as many birds as possible with one stone. Their behaviour, and the customs and groupings which regulate it, are multipurpose. Family groups have for their functions the stable satisfaction of sexual needs; the propagation of fully accredited newcomers into the larger social group; the psychological protection of their members through mutual affection; and the fulfilment of human needs for sociability; but they are often also fiscal units, means for determining the inheritance of rights and duties, and sometimes organizations for trading. A business firm no doubt has production or trade as its primary purpose; but it may also be a means to political power for its leading members; it may confer some social status upon its employees; the opportunities it provides for sociability are often a source of attraction; it may, indeed, even be an unofficial marriage-bureau. Few social activities are purely economic, or political, or aesthetic, or religious; but few have not an economic, a political, an aesthetic and a religious side.

These examples may suggest that the characteristic endeavour springs from several roots. In the first place, multipurpose behaviour may, *at times*, be the most effective way of achieving any one of the given ends. Thus the surest way of rearing satisfactory children is, probably, to have them brought up by the group whose purpose is also to provide stable sex-satisfaction and psychological protection for its other members; while the best way of strengthening the bond between a husband and wife is, usually, that they should cooperate in raising children (but not too many). Whether, in any given situation, these multiple purposes do in fact reinforce one another, or conflict, is of course a major topic of sociological inquiry.

But in the second place, much human behaviour is not

merely instrumental, that is, carried on for the purpose of achieving some end outside itself, but is also an Expression: it is done for its own sake. We are told that the Bushmen of the Kalahari Desert, when this group obtained from outside any supply of nuts or berries, would burst into an orgy of mutual donations, Bushman A giving to Bushman B a quantity of berries, and receiving from him a precisely equal quantity. The satisfaction here was hardly an 'economic' one, in the everyday meaning of that word. It took the form of exchange; but it was rather a symbolizing of friendly feelings, a diffuse assertion of solidarity. The Bushmen's orgy of mutual donations served no end outside itself: it was an Expression: the group 'acted friendship'.

It is well-enough realized that this aspect of behaviour is common in all societies. A person talking to another is not merely conveying, or asking for, information, but is also (or often is) 'acting himself' to his audience.

This is individual action, although the 'image' a person desires to convey, and the means he uses to convey it, may be the fruit of social learning. In other cases the action may be social in a further sense. Religious ceremonies, military parades, street demonstrations: the individual participants in these are, while 'acting themselves', also expressing the nature of the collectivity to which they, for the moment, belong.

Patterns of collective activity may be instrumental, or may be expressive. Some may be both instrumental and expressive, as when a street demonstration may be mounted in order to achieve some particular political objective, but may also have the function of expressing the convictions, or indeed the personalities, of those taking part, irrespective of any effect it may have on others.

The behaviour and the relationships which compose what are known as social institutions are thus in some (varying) manner multipurpose, and in some (varying) proportions both instrumental and expressive. In rather formal terms, it may be said that much of the study of social institutions is concerned with the nature and extent of these variations.

II

Social institutions form an element in a more general concept, known as social structure.

The basic idea intended by the term is that societies show comprehensible and relatively enduring sets of relationships. So, when we speak of the structure of some particular element of society ('the structure of the contemporary white Australian family') we mean such things as the number of people who normally compose a family group; the kinds of consanguine or conjugal relationships which are comprised in it; in short, the normal, regular and persistent characteristics of what may be called its 'shape' and 'size'. Secondly, when it is said that anthropologists are concerned with 'the social structure of primitive peoples', this means that they use these normal and persistent characteristics of 'size' and 'shape' as criteria for classifying, and for making general statements about, human societies. Some sort of notion of this kind, whether clearly formulated or not, must be a necessary part of thinking and living.

Firth[1] says that social structure is 'concerned with the ordered relations of parts to a whole; with the arrangement in which the elements of social life are linked together'. Radcliffe-Brown[2] puts essentially the same thing in a different way: he says that social structure is the complex network of actually existing social relations. Here he means 'actually existing' in contrast to 'ideal' or 'right': what takes place, rather than what people say ought to take place. But he means also, not a particular instance—a particular family—but rather the general form of such relations. He distinguishes between 'social relations', by which he means the raw data, and 'social structure', which for him is the general form. Like other terms of sociology, it is designed to give regularity and order to the raw data of observation.

Radcliffe-Brown restricts the term social structure to actual social relations. But, as Firth points out, the study of social structure involves the consideration not only of those patterns of relations which *actually* exist, but also those which people *believe to exist*, and those which they think *ought* to exist.

Indeed, the essence of the concept of social structure, says Firth, is those social relations which seem to be of critical importance for the behaviour of members of the society, so that if such relations were not in operation, the society could not be said to exist in that form. In this sense, we may view social structure as consisting of systems of expectations held by the people in a society about the way things are usually, or ought properly to be, done. Thus Talcott Parsons tells us: 'The essential aspect of social structure lies in a system of patterned expectations, defining the proper behaviour of persons playing certain roles, enforced both by the incumbent's own positive motives for conformity, and by the sanctions of others.' The function of social structure is thus to canalize the varied potentialities of human nature.

Though we may distinguish, as Firth does in *Social Change in Tikopia*, between actual behaviour, expected behaviour, and ideal behaviour, clearly changes in any one of these affect both the others. In any society at any moment, people's ideas of right behaviour will no doubt have an effect, both on what behaviour people expect from others, and on what people actually do. On the other hand, any change in what people actually do will, in course of time, affect their expectations, and probably their ideals as well.

In this notion of social structure, as it stands, something is evidently lacking. We seem to be contemplating something apparently assumed to be rigid, like a human skeleton. But society obviously is not rigid, any more than a physical body. Things never happen twice in exactly the same way. The sociologist, in order to understand completely an alien society, has to start off by seeing it in simple, formal terms. But this is really a first stage in his understanding of such a society. Later, he has to see it as something not rigid, and not simple, but something which is complex and continually in process of change.

Furthermore, action in society is the action of individuals. Thinking in terms of social structure may lead to the danger of overlooking or minimising individual choice. The study of society has, therefore, at some point to take account of accidents and the need for adaptation within even simpler societies. In certain simpler societies there are, among the relationships within family or kin, certain rights and duties between the mother's brother and the sister's son. Such a body of rights and duties is a feature of many matrilineal societies. For instance, among the Dobu of the Pacific, a man will hand down his magic powers (a form of property) to his sister's son. This regulation may be regarded as a part of the structure of that society. But clearly we need to know, for a proper understanding of their arrangements, more than just that. For example, what happens if the mother's brother is dead at the time when he ought to fulfil his obligations? Clearly, the society then has to make some sort of adaptation to a situation which may be called abnormal, but which is far from impossible.

In some such societies there may be some sort of contingent rule, or understanding, that in the absence of the proper relative, another shall take over his obligations. Obviously, this form of adapting (things being as they are) must in reality play a considerable part in societies. Altogether, it is as much a general characteristic of them as is the formal procedure. And no doubt it is an aspect of social change, insofar as some adaptation may 'take on' enduringly. For this process of adapting, the term 'social organisation' was introduced by Raymond Firth, who describes it as follows: 'In the concept of social structure, the qualities recognized are primarily those of persistence, continuity, form and pervasiveness through the social field. But the continuity is essentially one of repetition. There is an expectation of sameness, or an obligation of sameness . . . a structural principle is one which provides a fixed line of behaviour, and represents the order which it manifests. The concept of social organisation has a complementary emphasis. It recognizes adaptation of behaviour in respect of given ends, control of means in varying circumstances, which are set by changes in the external environment, or by the necessity to resolve conflict between structural principles.'[3] Even in a simple society, situations unprovided for by the rules arise, and in resolving them individuals have to make decisions and choices. These may be suggested by chiefs, or by spirit mediums, or others, but usually ultimately have to be accepted by the community. It may well be, on the other hand, that one of the characteristics of a 'modern' society lies in the number of *alternative 'programmes'* available to meet emergent situations.

Thus we might say that the social structure constitutes the rules of a game played by each individual against his environment. He strives in the first place to make use of the 'rules' to further his own ends (which may not, of course, be 'selfish' in the everyday sense). Society, as an ongoing process, involves a double process of altering behaviour in face of rules and of finding crevices in the rules, to be pushed wider apart.

III

Social institutions subserve the normative regulation of human behaviour.

In looking at any human society, an observer is usually able to define a number of general 'objectives' which that society seems to find necessary or important for its existence. The propagation of children into a stable and recognized primary group; the control of deviance and containment of disputes; the maintenance of right relations with some recognized non-human order of existence: these and other objectives may well be inferred by the observer to have their place.

He infers their existence because he observes in the society a number of customs, attitudes and formal or informal regulations, which seem to compose more or less clear patterns of meaning. Looking at some society—Ruritania, for instance—he finds that it is customary to 'get married' before having children: this confers some prestige, or at least averts negative-prestige: it is regarded as 'normal'. People say they want to have children. People generally look after their children as well as they can; but when they don't, they are liable to be officially punished. Husband, wife and children are expected to feel greater obligations to one another than to anyone else: and often do. People are expected to do something for their aged parents: when they do not, the neighbours look down their noses at them. Husband and wife are supposed to live together: if they don't, they feel somewhat embarrassed, and people gossip. They are supposed to live in harmony: if they don't, the neighbours either feel sorry, or else laugh at them.

The observer, who is also a member of a human society, will comprehend one aspect of this behaviour, and will find no difficulty in applying to it such a term as 'Kinship'. Another aspect of it will also interest him, but he will probably have greater difficulty in deciding whether to apply to this second aspect the term 'Law' (or whether to play safe and just call it 'Social Control').

But at any rate it is possible to analyse out, for any society, a number of broad 'objectives', to which patterns of rules, norms, customs and so forth are instrumentally related. It is important to remember that, as was indicated above, any particular rule or custom may be related to more than one objective.

The name of social institutions is applied to these patterns of rules and customs in relation to given objectives. Among the more important instances of these institutions are 'kinship', 'religion', 'politics', 'law'.

We shall use the term institution in this sense. It is necessary to be explicit about this, since the term has sometimes been given other meanings: for example, as an equivalent to 'organization', here meaning a human *group* having a formal and often complex structure. Thus Goffman speaks of 'total institutions', by which he means such things as prisons, monasteries or lunatic asylums. It is a little unfortunate that the two meanings should exist; however in this book we shall use the word not in Goffman's sense, but in that given in the previous paragraph. For sociologists, at least, this seems to be the most familiar usage. Thus Ginsberg[4] defines institutions as 'recognized and established usages governing the relations between individuals and groups'; Talcott Parsons[5] as systems of 'patterned expectations defining the proper behaviour of persons playing certain roles, enforced both by the incumbent's own positive motives for conformity and by the sanctions of others'. For Blau, 'institutionalization involves formalized procedures that perpetuate organizing principles of social life from generation to generation'.[6]

The concept of institution thus has the following characteristics.

Firstly, it contains an obvious normative element, since in general both rules and roles define behaviour which is acceptable, if not explicitly approved. The word normative is perhaps a little ambiguous here: institutions are systems of *expected* behaviour in given circumstances: the 'norm' may be a statistical, rather than an ethical one. However, in human life what is expected becomes customary, and what is customary tends often to become approved.

Secondly, the relationships which we have defined as institutions possess, in any given society, a degree of formal continuity. Thus the institution of kinship involves in every society a set of juridical or quasi-juridical rules designed to bring not only uniformity at a given time, but also consistency over time, into its relationships. Religions also usually possess sets of juridical, quasi-juridical or moral rules defining 'eternally' right behaviour. This conservative tendency is an obvious and vitally important element in social institutions. Equally obvious and important, however, is the tendency to change, adapt or contravene these rules. The balance, or imbalance, of rule and deviation must engage the attention of the sociologist.

The sociologist who sets himself to study the institutions of kinship, law or religion in Ruritania would do well to give his attention to certain significant and easily apprehensible elements of these institutions. For instance, he ought to look carefully at what people in relevant situations or statuses are supposed to do: what is *expected of* a husband, a wife, a father, a judge, a priest. Such aspects of social behaviour are known as *roles*. He ought to find out, secondly, about the structure of relevant *groups*: what is the normal composition of a family, or a church: what distinguishes a member from a non-member. And he should study the normal or proper way of doing things: the right way or ways to find a marriage-partner (and the wrong way or the unconventional way); the right way or ways to conduct a judicial action; or to invoke the goodwill of the deity. To these ways of doing things we shall (since it is as well to have an appropriate term) give the name of *Programmes*.

Roles, groups and programmes are key-elements in the study of social institutions; and we shall devote a little space to discussing them.

Roles may best be defined as the parts which an individual plays in the drama (or farce, or soap-opera) of human social existence. Any individual plays a number of such parts: in some conjunctures that, say, of a father, in others that of a bank-manager (or a shop-steward) in others again that of the treasurer of a charity (or the secretary of an adult education group). Each such part he has, in the main, to play as it is 'written' by the norms of the society, though there is some latitude for interpretation: a bank-manager who is dishonest ceases to be a bank-manager, and a father who is neglectful may be deprived of the control of his children. But the role of a father in twentieth-century Boston differs from the role of a father in second-century-B.C. Rome: he is accustomed, and is expected, to act differently towards others. The differences are, in a broad sense, consistent with the differences between the total societies in which these roles are played.

Southall[7] makes use of the concept of 'role-differentiation'. Broadly speaking, this refers to the degree to which, in any society at any time, roles tend to be specialized. More exactly, the criteria of differentiation are as set out in the table below.

Little Differentiation	*Much Differentiation*
1. Broad role-definition	Narrow role-definition
2. Diffuse roles	Specific roles
3. Overt role-development	Latent role-development
4. Equality in role distribution	Inequality in role distribution
5. Longstanding role-relationships	Ephemeral role-relationships

An instance of *broad role-definition* occurs where the role of 'father' is relevant to the spheres of kinship, religion and law. A narrower role-definition would occur where it was restricted within the field of kinship only.

A *diffuse role* is one in which the expectations are only vaguely defined. An instance is the role of 'friend' in Western societies. The role of 'magistrate' is relatively specific.

A member of an association has *latent role-relations* with all fellow members; though, especially if the association is a large one, some of these may not be actualised. Latency would appear to vary inversely with the proportion of 'face-to-face' contacts in a society, and directly with complexity of organization.

Rules may be *distributed unequally* among the persons composing a society, a member of an 'elite' playing more than the average person.

Lastly, in stable societies, people tend to act in the *same roles* to one another over long periods; whereas in societies subject to change, role-relationships also change relatively quickly.

The concept of role-differentiation is, in Southall's view, a measure of adaptability to change. 'It is', he says, 'certainly the societies that exhibit a positive process of role-differentiation that occupy the centre of the stage of history.'[8] Furthermore, it clearly offers a basis for comparison between societies. We may see it as an example of the way in which the changing nature of role-expectations and role-contents forms an index of change in the character of social institutions.

Groups may be divided into primary and secondary.

A primary group is (to use the convenient definition of Homans) 'a number of persons who communicate with one another often, over a span of time, and who are few enough so that each person is able to communicate with all the others, not at secondhand, through other people, but face to face'.[9] But equally important are the larger aggregations whose members will not all be in regular direct communication with one another (though some will) but which nevertheless have some degree of structure through having common objectives and some degree of commitment to cooperative action. These are known as secondary groups.

Groups will vary according to size, by complexity of structure, by the degree to which their members are commonly in close personal relationship, and also by the extent to which they serve multiple purposes or functions.

The term programme is being used here to mean a known and established procedure by which men, or a specified body of men, in any given society, are accustomed to act in a typical, recurrent situation.

Examples of programmes are the normal procedures for selecting a spouse (which may be more or less formalized, and more or less elaborate, in different societies) or the procedures—formal, partly symbolical, and closely regulated by custom and law—in a Court of Justice; trading procedures, which involve customs or rules of action relating to credit, to the machinery of exchange, and so on; or religious ceremonies; or what seems today partially to take the place of the last: attendance at football matches.

It seems clear that role, group and programme are among the most important phenomena included in the idea of a social institution. If sport were a social institution, it is pretty obvious that one would be a long way towards the sociological understanding of it if one could study carefully the roles of professional footballer, sports editor . . . the nature and development of groups like football clubs or professional tennis teams . . . and the ceremony of attendance at Celtic versus Rangers[10] or at Wimbledon.

Role, group and programme do not precisely exhaust the content of social institutions. In Law, or Religion, or Art, formal rules (like statutes, scriptures or Rules of Taste) have sometimes a significance which cannot be fully appreciated by seeing them acted out in roles or programmes. We shall occasionally need to consider these as well.

IV

Sociology, like all other sciences, arose because men needed and wanted to *understand* what they had discovered through commonsense observation and report. Among these commonplace observations are the two basic ones: human social arrangements vary from place to place, and change over time. More exactly (and it is this which both stimulates curiosity and makes a science possible) variations appear to exist within a general similarity, and change appears to be related in some way to persistence. In any given society, at any given time, a certain kind of arrangement, in respect for instance of the production and the training of new members of that society, is 'normal', in both an ethical and a statistical sense. It is not only usual, but it is approved: usual because approved, but also approved because usual. There are social pressures towards conformity: the arrangement is 'institutionalized'. Nevertheless such arrangements show variation from society to society, and, though usually slowly, they change. Thus the central question of sociology is how can what is 'normal' vary and change? In other words, we are concerned in the first place with the synchronic comparison of social structures (comparative sociology); and in the second, with the general meaning of historical processes.

In this Introduction, we shall discuss these two forms of inquiry, and their application to the study of social institutions.

Comparative Sociology tries to answer two questions: firstly, what is the *range of variation* shown by human societies or their constitutive elements? and secondly, what are the *causes* of these variations? But in these two questions, apparently so simple, there lurk problems, both empirical and theoretical, which we shall have to start off by facing.

Comparison must surely be an essential part of the task of Sociology. The object of this discipline is to make true general statements about the nature of society: and generalization must proceed by way of bringing together numbers of particular instances. The names 'marriage' or 'family', for example, refer to sets of relationships which, in Western countries, can no doubt be partly defined in terms of the rights and obligations which the laws of those countries attach to particular roles; but it is certain that they cannot be completely defined in such a way; and it is also true that, outside these relatively clear prescriptions, what is 'meant' by marriage differs, even within one nation, with differences in period, in region, or in the social positions of those involved. And when we bring together a number of countries, the degree of variation is of course far wider. And yet not only laymen, but sociologists and social anthropologists too, are accustomed to apply the general term 'marriage' over a very wide range of societies.

The variety of bedfellows thus assembled can readily be illustrated. Lecturers on Comparative Social Institutions in Western universities are fond of discussing the Nayars of Malabar.[11] In this polyandrous society it was the custom for a woman to have a husband; but this husband she knew for about three days only, and thereafter had no contact with him. Also, she had a number of recognized, or should they be called 'institutionalized', lovers, some regular, others casual. The begetter of a child born to her was therefore often uncertain; what happened was that any of her lovers who wished to do so could acknowledge paternity by paying the expenses of the child's delivery. But neither this action, nor anything else, gave the husband or any lover any rights over mother or child: these remained members of, and were maintained by, the mother's own lineage. Thus the 'nuclear' family of the type so prominent in, for instance, Western society was non-existent, and parent-child relationships were very different. In the West, the Nayar procedure would be impossible *de jure*, and *de facto* at least highly abnormal. Are we then entitled to apply the term 'marriage' to cover both that arrangement and those of Western Europe or North America? As Leach[12] points out, the propriety of doing so is by no means self-evident. If we do, what is the *significant* similarity between them? If not, what is the significant difference?

With other terms, such as 'religion' or 'law', these difficulties become still greater. The Eskimos, as reported by Hoebel[13] following Rasmussen, had no prisons, no police, no courts or magistrates, no legislature, no legal codes; did they have 'law'? If we say that they did, what do we assert to be the minimum necessary features of a 'legal' system? If we say they did not, what name do we give to the practices which maintained social control in that society?

One of the initial problems of Comparative Sociology is therefore that of the principles or grounds of classification. How do we determine whether to place a certain phenomenon—such as the customary behaviour of Eskimos in the face of an affront to their norms—in the category of 'law-behaviour' or not? The problem is somewhat more difficult than, for instance, that which once faced zoologists, of deciding whether to classify a slow-worm as a snake or a lizard. In the latter case, there is apparently fairly general agreement among zoologists as to the relative importance of certain anatomical criteria. Also a biological species normally maintains its structure unchanged over many generations. Neither of these conditions holds in regard to social entities. The former does not, for the obvious reason that, in general, the subject matter of sociology does not consist of things which are perceptible by the senses or by instruments which aid the senses. Customs, institutions, roles, even groups are constructions of the sociologist, which he arrives at through 'interpretive understanding' (to use Weber's phrase) of the *meaning* of social actions, the intentions of actors. The difficulty here lies not primarily in disagreement among sociologists, but rather in the complexity and fluidity of the meanings put upon their behaviour by the actors themselves.

This problem is not merely an arid and formalistic one. The ultimate concern of the sociologist is, as we said, to make general statements about social reality; classification is an indispensable means to generalization; and to make interesting and significant generalizations demands that the sociologist shall hit upon the most *fruitful* classification for the particular problem in hand.

This discussion we shall return to later on. We now proceed to consider more particularly the purposes of comparison.

The Comparative Method has been used at varying levels of sophistication.

1. It may bring to our attention features of our own society which would be less noticeable if that were the only form of human grouping with which we had acquaintance. Although, from the scientific standpoint, this use may be somewhat naïve, its value in leading to reflection, to hunches, to new insights has obviously been very great. One might add that it has sometimes had political motives; thus French writers of the eighteenth century, such as Voltaire, contrasted what they understood to be the institutions and customs of the Chinese with those of their own country in order to arouse indignation about the faults of the latter.
2. It has been held that comparison enables us to discover general or universal elements which underlie variation. Thus, in the words of Radcliffe-Brown[14]: 'a study of kinship systems all over the world by this method reveals that while there is a very wide range of variation in their superficial features, there can be discovered a certain small number of general structural principles which are applied and combined in various ways. It is one of the first tasks of a theoretical study of kinship to discover these principles by a process of abstractive generalization based on analysis and comparison.' But the sociologist distinguishes and defines 'general structural principles' in terms of the aims, intentions and meanings which he, from his analysis of a given society, infers that its members hold. Thus the 'principles' which should be sought are those which will assist our understanding of society to the greatest degree.
3. It has been asserted that the use of the comparative method enables us to seek for those factors which are causally associated with the emergence, existence or change of given elements or forms of social structure.

Mill, in Book III of his *System of Logic*[15] discusses what he calls the 'Joint Method of Agreement and Difference' and the

'Method of Concomitant Variations'. If we find that the presence of some element A is always associated with that of another, B, and the absence of A with the absence of B, other things remaining unchanged, this would tend to support the hypothesis that A and B are causally connected, directly or indirectly. Or if, in cases where A and B can be given cardinal measurements or ordinal rankings, a variation in a particular sense in A is always associated with a variation in a particular sense in B, other things remaining unchanged, this again would tend to support the hypothesis of a causal connection.

But, as Mill was at much pains to emphasize, such a conclusion is only acceptable if we can assume that any given effect has one cause and one only, and that any given cause has only one effect. In no sphere is this more wide of the truth than in the social sciences. The system of human interactions is influenced by innumerable factors; and what affects one part of it will, by doing so, also affect, directly or indirectly, the other parts.

Since Mill's day the development of statistics has enabled social scientists to use more and more sophisticated techniques in order to demonstrate more and more complex relations between measurable, or rankable, factors. But of course this fact in no way invalidates what Mill said. It increases the number of possible causal connections which can be hypothesized; but it neither exhausts them, nor by itself identifies the causal processes which may operate.

Furthermore, in spite of the obvious successes which the use of statistical methods has brought, it can generally be said that their power as means ancillary to explanation has been greatest where the entities dealt with are simple. Whatever the causes of population increase or decrease are, the *facts* of change can be ascertained and demonstrated fairly clearly. But to many of the most important entities which sociologists have to be concerned with, it is difficult to attach any numerical index at all, or even to distinguish them from other entities in such a way as to examine them in isolation. It is possible, at least in principle, to count the number of families in a given area, but it is not possible, with any hope of real success, to *measure* the strength or nature of ties within such families; yet it is probably the latter, rather than the former, which is the more interesting sociologically. Similar remarks could be made about religious activities, or even many economic ones. And, as was suggested earlier, this is partly because human behaviour in the real world is multipurpose to an extreme degree.

The question therefore arises of the nature, and of the means, of sociological explanation: more generally, of the *use* of sociological inquiry. The comparative method in sociology is, in principle, an application of the statistical operations of classification and correlation. We want to know whether a certain entity is present, absent, or present in varying degrees, in different societies; and, further, whether differences or changes in its incidence are associated with differences or changes in other entities: 'the standard canon of research that differences are explained by other differences'. But how is all this, or any of it, to be done?

This procedure of classification and correlation is of respectable antiquity. In 1889 E. B. Tylor communicated to the Anthropological Institute a paper 'On a Method of Investigating the Institutions applied to the Laws of Marriage and Descent'. In the ensuing eighty years a vast amount of material, psychological as well as sociological, has strengthened the conviction that the social and cultural environment in which a man lives has profound influences upon his behaviour, and that therefore comparative studies of different societies and cultures are an essential means to the understanding of human behaviour.

It is nevertheless true that the difficulties in the way of developing an adequate comparative method in sociology are formidable. Following Naroll[16] we may indicate six methodological problems: (1) how to define the societal units which are to be compared; (2) the problem of sampling bias; (3) that of the reliability of data; (4) that of diffusion; (5) the problem of defining one's categories; and (6) the problem of explanation.

1. *Definition of the Societal Unit.* If we are comparing, for example, the marital institutions of different societies, what counts as a society? Is Britain one society, or three, or four, or how many? Do Gosforth (the Westmorland village studied by Williams), and Bethnal Green, and Banbury (the subject of Stacey's *Tradition and Change*), form three units, or three parts

of one unit? How many are there in the United States, or Nigeria, or Malaya? One short answer might be, that it depends what problems you are concerned with. For some purposes, this would be an adequate retort. But it is clearly not a completely satisfactory one. In the first place, if a cross-cultural survey is to satisfy the statistician, we must be able to make a complete and precise enumeration of the units of the 'population' of societies to be studied, and therefore the rules of definition should leave no room for ambiguity. Secondly, in order that adequate sociological conclusions should be drawn from the comparison, it appears necessary that the units should be defined according to some intelligible uniform principle.

Naroll has proposed a principle for distinguishing and defining societal units (which he calls *cultunits*). A cultunit is defined as 'people who are domestic speakers of a common distinct language and who belong either to the same state or the same contact group'. There are thus two forms of cultunit identification: through a linguistic boundary, or through a communication-link formed either by political allegiance or by social contacts, direct and indirect. A cultunit boundary is formed by either of these boundaries, whichever is the *least inclusive*. An English-speaking man in Bristol is in a different cultunit from an English-speaking man in Connecticut, because they are in different states. A native of Oxford and a native of Glasgow live (in 1969) in the same state, but they are in different cultunits, because at home they speak mutually unintelligible languages. (Naroll offers Ayrshire in place of Glasgow, but this example seems less persuasive.)

Naroll distinguishes, and names, four types of cultunit (named, it should perhaps be said, after indigenous American peoples): the *Hopi* type, in which people belong to no state, but are linked by a common distinct language, and inter-connected by successive contacts; secondly, the *Flathead* type, comprising peoples who belong to a state all of whose members speak a common distinct language; thirdly, the *Aztec* type; this is found *within* a state in which mutually unintelligible dialects occur, and it would comprise those people whose domestic dialect is intelligible to speakers of the official language of the state. An example of the Aztec type would be the Malay community in Malaya. The fourth is the *Aymaran* type, which also is found within a state in which mutually unintelligible dialects occur; but an Aymaran type of cultunit is composed of people whose common and distinct domestic dialect is *un*intelligible to those speaking the official language of the state. The Chinese minority in Indonesia would comprise several instances of the Aymaran type, according to the number of distinct Chinese dialects to be found there.

It will be noticed that the concept of cultunit is not entirely free from ambiguity. It turns upon such debatable matters as what constitute mutually unintelligible dialects. Nevertheless, if employed uniformly, it does appear to provide a standardised means of defining and enumerating societal units. As Naroll says, it offers one means of answering two question of fundamental importance in comparative sociology: firstly, when you count societies, just what are you counting? and secondly, if you take a sample of societies, what is your sampling universe, and what are the units that have a stated chance to be picked for the sample? We shall discuss later whether this uniformity is obtained at the expense of other important requirements.

2. *Sampling Bias*. Hitherto, most of the raw material of comparative sociology has been taken out of monographic studies of individual societies or parts of societies. Such a society would be selected by (or for) its investigator on various grounds. He happened to be interested in the form some institution, custom, process or the like took in that society; he was interested in some theoretical problem, and believed it could fruitfully be studied there; his university had special contacts with that part of the world; some administrative body wanted a survey done, for policy reasons; or he just happened to be there. All these are respectable reasons, even the last, for making studies of particular groups; but when these studies are considered in the light of their comparability, several consequences become apparent.

First, there is no reason to suppose that those societies of which accounts have been compiled are representative of all societies. Societies whose structure offers interesting theoretical problems; those which themselves constitute practical 'problems' to administrators; 'visible' groups rather than less visible ones, are likely to be chosen. The consequence is that it is difficult, from the material available, to select a sample of 'the population of societies' which would satisfy statistical principles.

Secondly, valid cross-cultural comparison would surely require that each society should be reported on in a standardized fashion, following as it were the lines of a uniform schedule of headings and subheadings. This is most certainly not done, and for good reason. Most studies of societies are built round some single issue, theoretical or practical: kinship-structure, social mobility, or the like; the rag-bag kind of survey, into which anything was shoved, is no longer of interest. But a study concentrating upon kinship may need to say little about economic activity; and a student of a society's political structure may find it is sufficient to be brief about its religion.

Thirdly, for reasons discussed earlier, no agreed sampling universe of societies has been defined.

As a result, there is every reason to apprehend that no random sample drawn from available ethnological materials would be representative of the totality of societies, or even of all contemporary societies. What appears to be chiefly done by those anthropologists and statisticians who have concerned themselves with the matter, is that 'purposive samples' are drawn up, that is stratified samples the members of which are selected so as to represent (in the investigator's judgement) the significant characters of the universe. Thus Murdock's *World Ethnographic Sample*[17] proceeds by three steps. In the first step, the world is divided into six great regions, having a certain general unity. (They are those of the five continents, except that the Central Mediterranean Basin is regarded as a distinct region.) In the second step, each of these six is divided into ten smaller areas, 'recognizing boundaries between cultures as far as feasible'. Lastly, from each of these sixty areas, between five and fifteen cultures are selected: more for the larger or more heterogeneous areas than for the smaller. The principles of selection are stated by Murdock in some detail: he took (a) the most populous society; (b) the best-described one; (c) 'an example of each basic type of economy, and of each major rule of descent'; (d) one example of each linguistic stock; and (e) 'additional cultures which appeared for any reason to be relatively distinctive within the context of the entire area'. Furthermore, the author states that in choosing societies, he avoided geographically contiguous areas, and those characterized by mutually intelligible languages, because, he says, care must be taken to prevent multiplication of examples of any one particular type.

Murdock states his reasons for favouring this procedure, rather than random sampling, in the following passage.

> Random sampling of all the world's known cultures must unfortunately be excluded for several reasons. In the first place, this would result in the inclusion of many cultures for which the descriptive information is very incomplete, and in the exclusion, through chance, of a substantial proportion of the richest and most dependable ethnographic literature. In the second place, it would yield only a percentage of all the world's cultures without reference to their distribution by types. Areas like Europe and the Far East, with a few large and culturally homogeneous nations, for example, would tend to be heavily under-represented as compared with areas like aboriginal Australia, with hundreds of discrete but not notably divergent tribal cultures. Thirdly, purely random sampling would inevitably omit many of the truly unique cultures of the world, each the sole known representative of a distinctive type. A truly satisfactory ethnographic sample . . . must give representation to every distinct cultural type and sub-type for which information is available, even when these include only a single known example.

Much of what Murdock says here is sound, though it is largely concerned with the difficulties of defining societal units. Equally good objections could be levelled against his own principles of selection: if an example of each type of economy is taken (and how does one define a 'basic type of economy'?) why not one of each basic type of polity? How can one hope, by deliberate selection, to 'give representation to every distinct cultural type or sub-type', of which it is possible to distinguish innumerable species? Can any purposive sample be, in the circumstances, other than quite arbitrary?

It seems clear that no completely satisfactory sampling procedure is feasible, or is ever likely to be so. It becomes a question of what advantages one will settle for, in choosing between different procedures. In fact, much of what seem the most fruitful comparative studies have been instances of what Duverger calls 'close comparison', that is to say, comparisons within a set of societies known to show a high degree of similarity. Examples of these are comparative studies of family-structure in Britain and the U.S.A.; of legislative bodies in Western Europe; of family-structure[18], political systems[19] and markets[20] in Africa; and of capital and credit organization in peasant societies[21]. In effect, this bears some degree of resemblance to the experimental procedure: some factors are known to be common to all the societies composing the group studied (a high level of industrialization in Western societies; or undercapitalized subsistence agriculture in peasant ones), and these can therefore be regarded as constants in seeking for associations and correlations. But the conclusions derived from comparison of each 'narrow range' should themselves as a second stage be brought together (capital-raising in industrial societies with capital-raising in peasant societies; markets in Africa with markets in Latin America): by this means it is possible to proceed to wider though controlled generalizations. Some work of this 'second-stage' kind has been done, but not yet enough.

3. *Reliability of Data.* Nothing is better known in sociology or anthropology than that to do reliable fieldwork needs aptitude, training, care and time. Most of the reports written prior to the nineteen-twenties, and a number written since, were done by people who lacked some, and occasionally all, of these requirements: missionaries, government officials, traders or travellers. What is lacking is not necessarily care or intelligence; adequate sociological fieldwork can only come after immersion in sociological theory. This, of course, is so because all observation, and certainly all observation of social phenomena, is at the same time a process of assessment and interpretation of observations. The object of a theory is to form a framework of explanation for a series of observations; but at the same time a theoretical training should make clear to the investigator that these explanatory systems are only satisfactory in so far as they consistently and completely account for the facts. Theory is at the same time an explanation of the facts and an incentive to find out what the facts really are.

Two practical problems arise. The first is that, if we are to exclude all reports which are judged unsatisfactory, information will be entirely lacking about some areas or societies. Is it possible, while throwing away the undesired bathwater, to retain at least some portions of the baby? And secondly, how are we, not ourselves acquainted with Society X, to judge whether the reports on it are complete, accurate, insightful?

Naroll has proposed a method which he calls Data Quality Control. In substance, this consists in a number of principles or procedures for the critical evaluation of sources. How long did the investigator spend in the field? The longer the time, the more likely (other things being equal) is it that his work will be accurate and comprehensive. Did he know the language, or did he work through interpreters? Did he live *in* the community, rather than near it? How long an interval between fieldwork and publication?—The longer, the more suspect the report. How lengthy is the report?—On the whole, the longer it is, the more likelihood that all important aspects will be covered.

But these precautions are only rough and ready ones, and it is not mere purism to suggest that now, when the volume of studies by persons and institutions of high repute is increasing rapidly, it would be preferable to rely on them as sources, rather than fill in gaps with dubious ones.

4. *The Influence of Diffusion.* On the occasion earlier referred to when E. B. Tylor read to the Anthropological Institute his paper on the comparative study of marriage and descent systems, Francis Galton, then the Institute's president, gave a warning that 'it was extremely desirable, for those who may wish to study the evidence of Dr Tylor's conclusions, that full information should be given as to the degree in which the customs of the tribes and races which are compared together are independent. It might be that some of the tribes had derived them from a common source, so that they were duplicate copies of the same original'.

What is sometimes known as 'Galton's Problem' is a real one, but it is essential to be clear as to what exactly the problem is. It is, in fact, a statistical problem: let us say we find that, out of a sample of one hundred societies, seven societies, A, B, C, D, E, F and G have a common trait (matriliny, or a peculiar way of decorating horse-ploughs, or what not). But let us say that we also find that Societies A, B, C, D, E and F all borrowed this custom, in recent times, from Society G. Do we say that the incidence of this custom is represented by 7 per cent of the sample, or by one per cent?

This essentially statistical, and, of course, important question must be distinguished from the general topic of diffusion, that is, of the nature, extent and importance of borrowings of cultural traits by one group from another. Three points may be made here. Firstly, it will be one of the themes of subsequent chapters that diffusion has been one of the fundamental and virtually all-pervasive processes of human history. Secondly, diffusion is rarely a mere passive reception: the receiving group adapts, and indeed re-creates, what it has received; so that sometimes the question whether the trait was the result of diffusion or not becomes a meaningless one. An example: in Hong Kong, Chinese film-magnates make highly popular film-serials based on traditional Chinese fairytales. Diffusion from Hollywood, or not? Or another: Britain now has the institution known as 'kingship'. Is this 'diffusion'?

Thus, thirdly, it may be the most fruitful method of procedure, at all events if any trait has existed in a particular society for any considerable time, to treat the question of diffusion as not necessarily relevant to an explanation of its present existence at this time. It *may* be relevant (for instance, if the trait has been received from another country which currently has a predominant influence over the first one) but this is a matter to be decided in the particular case, and should not preclude a study of the functional importance which the trait has assumed in the recipient society.

5. *The Problem of Defining one's Categories*, that is, the problem of deciding whether a given system of relationships, observable in a particular society, is to be called (let us say) 'marriage', is one which has been briefly referred to earlier in this chapter, and will be discussed more fully in later chapters.

The sixth and final problem requires a section to itself.

V

The Problem of Explanation

Although correlation may show that the existence of a causal connection is probable, and indeed, one objective of the invention of more refined statistical methods is to increase the *demonstrable probability* of a causal connection; nevertheless the 'interpretive understanding' of the nature of this connection has to come by other means.

Several general theories, or models, have been used, as explanatory principles, in conjunction with the comparative method.

That method was, for example, used by sociologists of the nineteenth and the early twentieth centuries to demonstrate that the principle of evolution could be applied to human society, as to the rest of animate nature. Thus, for Herbert Spencer, social evolution was the culminating stage of a general process of evolution throughout knowable existence. Social evolution or social development also played the part of a shaping principle in the work of E. B. Tylor, Westermarck, Frazer, and L. T. Hobhouse.

In the work of all these writers, institutions, customs, moral ideas, and so forth, were dependent variables. The independent variable was some conception or other of stages in human development. Thus, with Hobhouse, whose work was perhaps the most sophisticated of these earlier writers, a broad division was made, in the first place, between what were known as 'simpler peoples' and civilizations; the former in their turn were divided into certain stages: the lower hunters, the higher hunters, three stages of agricultural peoples and two stages of pastoral peoples. All these were marked by an increasing degree of control over their material environment. In his book, *The Material Culture and Social Institutions of the Simpler Peoples*, Hobhouse claimed to have established a correlation between these stages, that is to say, general trends towards greater control over the environment, and general trends in the development of politics, religion, justice, and other social institutions. It is clear, however, from a reading of his later works, *Morals in Evolution* and *Social Development*, that these stages were not merely analytical categories, but historical stages through which the human race was believed to have successively passed. In these books Hobhouse continued this theme through the study of the development of ancient and later civilizations. As a result of these investigations, he claimed to have established that historical development has been marked by certain general characteristics: by increases in Scale (the general size of the human societies); in their Efficiency, as means to the carrying out of their objectives; in the degree of Freedom enjoyed by members; and in the degree to which cooperation or partnership in seeking the ends of the society was institutionalized ('Mutuality'). Hobhouse made it clear that development was to be seen as a balanced increase in all four of these conditions, not in one or two at the expense of the rest.

To the methods and assumptions of these writers, objections of various weight were levelled by later scholars, which rendered them for some time unfashionable. Firstly, there were objections to the nature of the evidence presented of unilinear development.

The contemporary 'savages', upon whom reports were being accumulated during the nineteenth century, were then regarded, in what appeared to be their weird uncouthness, as survivals, showing to us stages of society which resemble, and therefore illuminate for the scientist, those stages which societies now 'civilized' had passed through. E. B. Tylor, perhaps the greatest of nineteenth-century anthropologists, wrote near the beginning of his book *Primitive Culture*:

> This hypothetical primitive condition [of mankind] corresponds in a considerable degree to that of modern savage tribes, who, in spite of their difference and distance, have in common certain elements of civilization, which seem remains of an early state of the human race at large. If this hypothesis be true, then, notwithstanding the continual interference of degeneration, the main tendency of culture from primaeval up to modern times has been from savagery towards civilization.[22]

The notion of savage survivals would not be fully accepted today. But we should note the caution with which Tylor phrases these sentences; some of his contemporaries were more rash. It is very important to see that Tylor was putting this idea forward as a hypothesis; and whether this hypothesis is proven or provable (it is unlikely to be) it was, with Tylor, a method of inquiry, an heuristic device, which enabled him to bring together, to order and clarify, the accessions of data which were then becoming available. Further, it enabled him to see the theme of the nature of human society as a special case of the great scientific paradigm of the nineteenth century: the theme of Evolution. This, at the time, can only have been to the good of Sociology, even though it led to the commission of errors. Certain ideas have, at certain times, a special creative power: they seem suddenly to offer golden keys. Some of the rooms thus opened are dark, and some of the doors have booby-traps; nevertheless the experience is a liberating one. The concept of Social Evolution (which has not been disproved) helped to liberate Comparative Sociology.

More serious was the liability of some writers to confuse the concept of evolution with that of progress: to confuse an ethical conception with one which, at least in biology, is ethically neutral. With Hobhouse, it is true, there was no confusion here. He was quite aware of the issue, and put forward explicit arguments to support his assertion that social development did show a tendency towards moral progress. But the answer one gives to this question depends on the criteria of progress which one uses, and quite different ones could be proposed on equally reasonable grounds. (While writers such as Hobhouse were inferring ethical progress from the facts of history, other writers contemporary with them, such as Spengler, were using the data of this same historical development to demonstrate cyclical change or decline.) A certain degree of arbitrariness is thus imported into what is supposed to be a scientific demonstration. Further, the more positive attitude of sociology in the twentieth century made for the view that it was desirable that social science and ethics should be distinguished clearly.

These are criticisms of a particular application of the theory of evolution, and not necessarily levelled against the idea of social evolution as such. While this idea did go out of fashion, it is doubtful whether it could ever become obsolete; and in the work of Talcott Parsons and other writers, another version of it has returned to the forefront of sociology.

Lastly, a danger which Spencer, Westermarck, and Frazer did not escape was that in their huge and encyclopaedic works, the ethnographic material was not only obtained at secondhand, but was accepted uncritically from sources of various value, and without due regard for the real significance of any item in the total life of the society from which it was reported. With the growth of knowledge about, and of opportunities for study of simpler peoples, the unsatisfactory nature of this became obvious.

The most important reaction against these writers was what is called the 'structural-functional' approach. This was no new discovery; it had been used in anthropology by Tylor. But possibly the first systematic use of 'function' as a general principle of sociological interpretation was made by Durkheim. One of the objectives of Durkheim's work was to establish explicitly sociological explanations of social events, rather than to be content with seeing them as the result of universal mental characteristics of the human species. Durkheim held that psychological explanations of social phenomena were inadequate, for the reason that society precedes the individual and moulds his development. Sociology had therefore to seek explanations within its own sphere. One such approach lay in the use of the concept of function. To ask what the function of any phenomenon is, said Durkheim[23], is to seek for the *need* which it supplies. The term function implies a correspondence between the phenomenon and the need, as when we speak of the 'function' of respiration as being the introduction of necessary gases into the tissues for the sustenance of life. And Durkheim himself studied, for example, the needs to which the social division of labour corresponded.

The British anthropologist Radcliffe-Brown proposed that the concept of function implies the contribution made by some element to the 'on-going' of a social system. One of the clearest definitions of the meaning of 'function' is given in the Introduction which he wrote to *African Systems of Kinship and Marriage.* Here he says:

> For any particular system as it exists at a certain time we can make a study of how it works. To do this we have to consider how it links persons together by convergence of interest and sentiment

> and how it controls and limits those conflicts that are always possible as the result of divergence of sentiment or interest. In reference to any feature of a system we can ask how it contributes to the working of the system. This is what is meant by speaking of its social function.[24]

Thus (as he says elsewhere in the same Introduction) 'a system of kinship and marriage can be looked at as an arrangement which enables persons to live together and cooperate with one another in an orderly social life'. For a system of kinship and marriage consists of a number of inter-related customs or rules, which prescribe, for example, whom one may marry or should marry, or must not marry; and lay down the rights and obligations of the parties (individuals or kin groups) in respect of the marriage. They may prescribe to what kin group the members of an elementary family shall belong, or where they shall reside; what general links there are between one member of a kin group and the rest; what special links between any particular pair of persons; and so forth: these prescriptions, recognized by the community as a whole, set out differentiated roles which make for what Durkheim would call organic solidarity. It seems reasonably clear that orderly society could not exist without bodies of prescriptions such as those governing kinship. And it is reasonable to hold, too (taking another example), that role differentiation, the social division of labour, is necessary for an orderly and efficient society. Further it is plausible to see the particular form which such regulations take as, sometimes at least, consistent with the needs of the particular society in which such a variant is found. These institutions may therefore be said to play a part, to do a job, or to have a function.

A neat and elegant presentation of the functionalist approach is given by A. L. Stinchcombe,[25] who sees the following elements in a 'functional' explanation:

1. The existence of an *end* or *consequence* which tends to be maintained (let us say, for example, the maintenance of an orderly society, with provision for the rearing of the young).
2. Causal forces, tensions or difficulties, which tend to upset (1). (Following the example, let us include in them sexual aggressions and jealousies which, if uncontrolled, might prevent the fulfilment of (1).)

3. Some social structure, behaviour-pattern or the like, which tends to maintain (1). Following Radcliffe-Brown, we may take as an example the institution of kinship and marriage, with its regulations for the choice of marriage partners, its socially-enforced prohibitions on incest, and the like.
4. A causal process, which causes those structures (3) maintaining the end (1) to be selected and reinforced.

While elements 1, 2 and 3 *define* the functional relationship, element 4 *asserts its effective existence*. Obviously, discussion of the first three would be futile if the existence of the fourth could not be presumed; but much of the argument over functionalism is about the *extent* of the presumption.

Radcliffe-Brown held a functional explanation to be essential. To the anthropologist in the field, the evolutionary approach was useless, he held, because the history of the primitive peoples whom he studied was unknown. What passes for history was, in Radcliffe-Brown's view, merely conjecture. When observing his primitive societies, therefore, he must have a different principle of explanation. To explain the existence of a custom, a myth, a norm, we must, said Radcliffe-Brown, ascertain what part it plays in that society—how it assists in the ongoing of the society: we must uncover its 'function'. Ideally, the study of a society should consist of careful detailed study of the functions of the elements of that society, each society thus being revealed as a network of functionally inter-related parts.

Both Radcliffe-Brown and the other founder of modern British anthropology, Malinowski, made functionalism the basis of their system of analysis. Malinowski, in revolt against chair-bound anthropologists, asserted that no social action can be adequately studied in isolation. Its meaning is given by the part which it plays in an interacting system; and what this 'part' really is can only be known through a detailed exercise of observation.

Thus his classic work, *The Argonauts of the Western Pacific*[26], is a study of the Kula, a form of social transaction practised by the Trobriand Islanders of Eastern New Guinea, and involving the exchange, according to certain rules, of particular kinds of bead necklaces and shells. While the transaction appeared superficially to be a case of economic exchange, Malinowski's detailed examination of its working shows it to have wide and interpenetrating functions, political, status-giving and ceremonial, in the life of the society.

'Function' meant for Malinowski the contribution made by the custom, institution, myth or what not, to the satisfaction of needs, both social and biological. One may note here that the concept of 'social need' is not altogether satisfactory. Such a need is presumably either one which is *expressed* by individuals in the society, in which case it is likely to be the need of some, rather than all its members; or else the word refers to some condition or state which the sociologist postulates as necessary. (Perhaps he may even infer the 'need' from the existence in the society of an institution or process which is held to supply it.) Now while the number of possible 'needs' of a human society is indefinitely large, the number of indisputable ones is very small, and these must be expressed in very general terms. Talcott Parsons, Aberle[27] and others have put forward a list of 'functional prerequisites of society'; that is, of the generalized conditions necessary for the maintenance of the system concerned. These include such conditions as the following: provision for the recruitment and protection of members of the society; role-differentiation and means of role-assignment, so that the activities rendered necessary by these prerequisites may get done; means of communication; an adequate degree of consensus in interpreting the environment; a shared set of goals; a set of rules prescribing how ends are to be achieved; socialization; and controls over disruptive forms of behaviour. It would be hard to deny that socialization, communication and population are necessary to the existence of a society. But a list such as this is a mere scheme. What is more interesting, and more difficult, is to compare, *in different societies*, the means whereby such ends as these are secured. That 'socialization' is necessary is no discovery; the real problem is, why, or in what sense, is the Trobriand custom of socialization through the authority of the *mother's brother* (instead of through the father) a 'need'?

The functionalist approach is, up to a point, a commonsense, almost commonplace one: the question which in everyday life we tend to ask about anything, when we seek to find an explanation of its presence, is: what sort of job is it doing? What ends is it fulfilling? What, however, is often lacking (and indeed often difficult to supply) is rigorous demonstration. Thus, if it is asserted that the element A exists because it is functional, in that it makes possible the end X (the existence of noses is because they are functional, in that they make possible the existence of spectacles, which are essential . . . etc) it would have to be shown (a) that the end X *is* in fact essential; the assertion that A has a 'function' is not merely the assertion of a cause and effect relation between A and something else, but the assertion of a relation between A and something which is highly important to the existence of society. (b) It would secondly be necessary to demonstrate that the causal connection between A and X did in fact exist. (c) Furthermore, 'function' as an *explanation for the existence of A*, would cease to be cogent or to be anything but trivial if the end X could be supplied equally well by a considerable number of other elements in the society.

We may illustrate all this by a discussion of Radcliffe-Brown's explanation[28] of the existence of what are known as 'joking relationships'. In a number of societies people standing in certain relationships to one another (a husband to his wife's sisters among the Dogon of Africa, for example) are licensed, and also required, to behave to one another with joking, ridicule and horseplay which they must not resent. This peculiar custom Radcliffe-Brown asserted to have a functional explanation. Some social relationships can be regarded as involving both attachment and separation. In many societies, that of the husband to his wife's family is of this kind. His position in the social structure, the majority of his rights and duties, are, in most societies, determined by his birth into a certain family, lineage and clan. Before his marriage, his wife's family are outsiders to him, and this disjunction is not destroyed by the marriage. Nevertheless he is now married to his wife, and her kin still maintain ties with, or at least interest in, her. 'Social disjunction implies divergence of interests and therefore the possibility of conflict and hostility, while conjunction requires the avoidance of strife. How can a relation which combines the two be given a stable, ordered form?' One way is by maintaining extreme mutual respect and limited personal contact: this is shown, in many societies, in the relation of son-in-law to parents-in-law. But, while the relation between contiguous generations is normally one of respect (and is so to an extreme degree in the relation just mentioned) that between alternate generations, or between members of the same generation, is usually one of ease and familiarity—and again is so to an extreme degree in those relations mentioned earlier. The joking relationship is one in which there is an obligation not to take insults seriously: one which, 'by means of sham conflicts, avoids real ones' which might easily, and to the great damage of the society, arise between persons so related.

Radcliffe-Brown has given here an explanation at the level of plausibility, rather than of rigorous proof. He has asserted that certain relationships involve the danger of socially damaging conflict. He has asserted, secondly, that in a large number of societies these relationships are associated either with an exaggerated attitude of respect, or with an exaggerated attitude of familiarity; and that these attitudes have the function of preventing the hostility inherent in the relationship from taking effect. Certain criticisms seem in order. First, while it is possible to 'understand' that avoidance will alleviate the consequences of hostility, it is not so easy to feel convinced that joking and horseplay will: in some circumstances they might be supposed to have the opposite effect. Hence it cannot be deduced from their nature that they would have the function imputed to them. If, on the other hand, it could be shown empirically that in all relationships of potential hostility, where 'licensed joking' is present, actual hostility is absent, and in all such relationships where licensed joking is absent, actual hostility is found—if this could be shown, it would at least provide strong statistical evidence for Radcliffe-Brown's theory. This evidence would be very difficult to find, and it may be said at once that he has not attempted the task.

It may also be noted that there are other societies where the potential hostilities of the kinds referred to are not alleviated by avoidance, licensed joking, or any other observed means; yet the societies endure. How serious is such 'hostility' after all? If it is not, then the functionalist explanation is empty.

It may seem unfair to criticize on the basis of two very brief chapters in a book of scattered essays. But these serve to illustrate the point that, all too often, a functionalist 'explanation' consists in pointing to the existence, in a small number of arbitrarily chosen instances, of a particular social element, then asserting that a given effect follows from its existence, and thirdly offering this consequence as a general explanation of the existence of such an element.

It may be useful here to distinguish between the concepts of 'function' and 'functionalism'. To assert that some, at any rate, of the elements of society have a function, that is to say, do a particular job in society as it is at the moment, is plausible, useful and somewhat trite. But on the other hand, to attempt to explain the existence of all elements by their supposed functions—that is, to use 'functionalism' as a general explanation—is dangerous. It is to enlarge the presumption in Stinchcombe's element 4 too widely. It is possible that most writers intend only the former use. But it is facile to slip from one to the other, and this is dangerous.

For, in the first place, 'functionalism', as a general explanation, explains too much. If 'functional' is defined as what makes for the continued existence of a society, then since we can only observe societies which exist, there is a *prima facie* case, and one hard to rebut, for saying that everything in them must be, *in some sense or other*, functional.

Putting it the other way round, functionalism also explains too little. Thus it fails to explain how it is that many practices, or processes, which have manifestly destructive effects do continue to exist. For example, war, for the majority, is harmful; nevertheless it continues to exist. Are we to say, in this case, that war goes on because it is 'functional for somebody'? Such a defence would reduce functionalism to something which is essentially untestable.

Furthermore the fact that a thing is functional does not mean that it is necessary. Capitalism in our own society has clear economic functions; but these can be carried out by alternative means. Merton's[29] concept of functional alternatives is a valuable clarification of the concept.

The relation between functional and so-called conflict theories needs a brief reference. By the latter are sometimes meant those explanations which see the origins, or the existence, of institutions or stages of society as consequences of tension, conflict, or revolution. More generally, the name of conflict theory may be given to those models of society that refuse to make an assumption which structural-functional theory is held to contain: the assumption, that is, that societies tend towards a state of equilibrium. Now conflict can be seen as itself having a function. Gluckman[30] has interestingly developed the view that in some forms of society rebellion (of subjects against ruler) is an essentially functional custom, since it is a means of changing the incumbent of an office, while maintaining the structure of the society in which that office exists. But a good deal depends on what kind of conflict we are thinking about; and while some forms (better perhaps called 'competition') make for structural stability, others will tend to disrupt existing structures.

The student of sociology should, in short, be clear about the purpose for which he uses the idea of 'function'. If he is thinking of it as a *theory* about society, then it would appear to combine ambiguity and triteness to a singular degree. But when, as Radcliffe-Brown[31] once suggested, he sees it as being in the nature of a working hypothesis, which brings up for examination a large number of fruitful questions, then it would seem to be, at any rate, a useful starting-point for research which may lead in some cases to its rejection as an adequate explanation for the continuance or change of institutions.

VI

Sociology, while its aim is to enunciate true statements of some degree of generality, has a uniquely close relation to History. This is because human actions are themselves unique events, in a sense that collocations of inanimate objects are not. Thus Sociology is deeply concerned with elucidating the development and the diffusion of institutions.

A functional explanation does not, of course, render superfluous the search for explanations in terms of historical causes. The fact that Radcliffe-Brown used functional explanations in place of 'conjectural history' should not be taken to mean that functionalism is inconsistent with historical explanations. In fact, as Evans-Pritchard[32] has stated, the question whether any given element of society is functional can only be decided by a study of its existence and consequences over a period of time.

All students of Sociology know the term 'Industrial Society'.

We are aware that it denotes a type of social system which is represented in such nations as the United States, Canada, Britain and Japan. We are also aware that this type of social system is characterized by certain fairly easily distinguishable features. Thus it is based upon large-scale manufacture, which has reached a highly sophisticated degree of organization, and upon an equally sophisticated financial and commercial system. It is distinguished, too, not so much by the existence of towns, as by 'urban dominance': the products, ways of thought and behaviour characteristic of urban life set the pattern for the whole society. There is a relatively high degree of communication and of geographical mobility. And the standard of living is not only significantly higher here than elsewhere, but, in general, tends to continue rising.

These and a number of other well-known traits may be used to distinguish 'industrial' from other types of society. Yet it is equally apparent that the various examples of this type of social system may differ significantly among themselves: in family patterns, in religion, in political system, indeed in economic organization. Thus the character of industrialization does not fully define them. Some of them may indeed share certain features more with 'non-industrial' than with other 'industrial' societies. Thus the technique, and for that matter the meaning, of 'comparison' offer considerable problems.

Industrialism is a historical process, as well as a sociological type. Its development can be traced through successions of inter-related events. There have been influences, whose nature has been traced in detail, of the economic development of one country upon that of another: a complex process of diffusion, which while directly affecting economic organization has more indirect consequences for political, religious and familial institutions also. This is equally true of most 'non-industrial' societies. Often these possess cultures of rich complexity.

'Simpler' societies are not simple. Where historical records are lacking, this does not mean the absence of historical changes; and indeed the more that is discovered about the earlier history of such areas, the more one finds evidence of the contact of many different cultures, migration of peoples, wars, political and economic change.

This process of diffusion has, so far as concerns the history of

Western Europe, been extensively documented: but we may take another, and less well-known example: it is also unquestionably true of South-East Asia, which has for millennia been a main route of cultural contacts. Here, as elsewhere, the movement and contact of different peoples have resulted in a series of social, cultural or political layers one above the other. If it is possible to speak at all about original inhabitants, these are probably represented by the Negritos, the very primitive groups of people living largely in the forests in the inland parts of these countries, and having only slight contacts with the other peoples in the land, or with its political organization. In Malaya, there followed in the early years of the Christian era groups of Malay peoples probably originating, like the Burmans and Thais, as branches of a Central Asian stock. Later, and spasmodically over a considerable period of the present era, there were immigrations of civilized peoples from various parts of Southern Asia, giving rise to the characterization of South-East Asia as the crossroads of that continent. Among these were Indians, mainly from South India, bringing into South-East Asia a monarchical political system, the Brahmanical religion, and a trading economy. At a later time contacts with South Indian traders brought Islam, which now pervades the Malay world.

Thus the Malays, who constitute the largest group both in Malaya and Indonesia, show three culture layers: Animism, Hinduism, and Islam. These cultural patterns have affected not only their religion, but also their political structure and their language.

To this already complex pattern was added an influx, from the fifth century A.D., of Chinese. (Contacts between India and China go well back before this date.) The numbers of Chinese were relatively small until about the beginning of the nineteenth century, when the development of Malaya as a centre of tin-mining brought a very considerable immigration of ex-peasants from South-East China. To a considerable extent, however, the Chinese came as traders, or else took up trade in preference to agricultural activities as soon as they had got there. And during, at least, the nineteenth century and onwards the Chinese have been responsible both in Malaya and Indonesia for a vast amount of inter-regional trade.

We thus have layers of agricultural peoples and of minorities who had recently migrated into the area from outside and constituted the most important element in commerce. The latter are largely to be found in the big cities, having a higher standard of living than the mass of the population. They have introduced alien religions and culture patterns. They have often shown different, and indeed incompatible, political allegiances.

A further layer is shown by the influx of Western traders and colonists. Into South-East Asia came first, in the fifteenth century, the Portuguese. These, having founded some small colonies such as Goa and Macao, failed to keep any important foothold in Asia. Later, in the sixteenth century, came the Dutch to the East Indies; the French colonized Indo-China; and the British, from a base in India, contended with the Dutch over the East Indies, but founded their most profitable settlement in Singapore.

The Westerners brought a 'Roman peace' into what had previously been a highly unstable area, and broke down to some degree the political and economic structures which they had found. They were responsible for a varying degree of exploitation of the colonial peoples. This was not because the standard of living of the latter was not raised: probably, as compared with pre-colonial times, it was. Exploitation occurred in that much of the profit of Western activity in the form of plantations, mining, and the like was drained back to shareholders in the West. Westerners, of course, also introduced their own notions of law and administrative systems.

The cultural complexity of the area is illustrated by the extraordinary confusion of tongues. Malaya shows in an extreme degree what is also the case in other 'under-developed' regions. In Malaya are found, in the first place, the Negrito languages, which on the whole do not form any mixture with those of the other peoples. There is, secondly, the Malay language, which is the political language of the people and lingua franca of Malaya. There is next a group of Indian languages, of which Tamil is spoken by most, the others including Malayalam, Gujerati, and Punjabi. Then there are a considerable number of Chinese dialects, generally mutually unintelligible. These include Hokien, Cantonese, Hakka, Hainanese, Teochew, and several others. Each of these languages or dialects is spoken by some tens of thousands of people. Lastly comes English, an international 'culture', trading and administrative vehicle.

There are to be found a number of distinct socio-economic 'layers' which are largely the effect of movements of people or of cultures. Thus, in the case of Malaya we find as a kind of base, a rural peasant economy, largely subsistence, poor, indebted, and labour intensive. Upon this exists a complex system of local and regional wholesale and retail trading, starting with trading in local produce, and widening therefrom. We also find a pattern of small, family-based industries. Now, while the peasant agricultural system is carried on almost exclusively by Malays, the trading and small scale industrial system is carried on mainly by Chinese, to some extent by Indians, but hardly at all by Malays. (We may incidentally notice here the importance of the alien as a trading entrepreneur: a comparable example is that of the Jews in medieval Europe and the Near East.) Over this again, is laid an economy, international in character, mainly dealing with tin and rubber, organized and owned by Westerners, and having its origin in colonial times. The capital from this comes from the West and is channelled through Western banks. Managerial skill comes also from the West, and is channelled through the organizations known as managing agencies, which are essentially a means to economize in entrepreneurial and managerial skills, and which therefore act so as to inhibit the local development of these skills.

The above rather lengthy account of South-East Asia is given for a somewhat extreme, but on the whole not misleading, example of 'pre-industrial' societies, and is meant to indicate that, in all but a few of the most primitive societies, the social, political and economic structure has been subject to almost incessant change, through migration, cultural or trading contacts, or conquests. This has been true of Africa, through internal movement and war; through the influence of Islam, stretching southward; and, from the sixteenth century onward, through that of the West. It is obviously true of the Middle East, the land route between Europe and Asia; and true of India. And, at least since the sixteenth century, it has been true of South America.

Thus the essentially temporal and historical processes of

culture-contact and diffusion not only affect now, but have affected for many centuries, most of the regions of the world. The nature of the contacts has varied, and the effects have been selective, and as a consequence an extremely complex social pattern emerges. The student of social institutions is thus confronted not only with problems of synchronic likeness and variability, but also with those of diachronic stability and change.

VII

But if this is so, it raises the question, how far any general models can explain either synchronic variation or diachronic change. The validity or fruitfulness of model-building varies inversely as the range of instances which it seeks to explain. Thus the ideal types of development adumbrated by, for example, Smelser[33] have, and are admitted to have, only a tenuous relation with the reality which they are supposed to illuminate. The purpose of model-building is to show, or to remind ourselves, that, *other things being equal*, certain social factors will probably induce certain consequences, and certain social states are likely to be associated with certain social environments. But, as Smelser says, the sources of variation in the reality 'render it virtually impossible to establish hard and fast empirical generalizations concerning the evolution of social structures during economic and social development' and therefore, of course, concerning also the states of society which are the result of development.

Does this mean that comparative sociology must be limited to 'close' comparison within *either* industrial *or* simple societies, for instance? It must surely be clear that this would be a most stultifying restriction. As Goody[34] says, 'It seems doubtful whether the study of man can make much general progress without taking into account the totality of human social organizations'. Indeed, it seems a good deal more than doubtful. A study, for instance, of religion which limited its scope to industrialized societies would really tell one little about human capabilities in this important field. And though the contrast is less striking in some other fields, to ignore the economics of non-industrialized, or the government of non-centralized societies, would significantly restrict our understanding of economic or political institutions.

The answer clearly is to treat as wide a range as possible, as well as one can. Systematic classification and comparison are necessary to explanation. But on the other hand, from a broader standpoint, one of the chief services a comparative study of social institutions can perform is to emphasize the complexity of data. Neat classifications are generally naïve.

The exposition attempted in the following chapters takes the following lines:

1. First, an attempt is made to define the content of the major institutional areas, in such a way as to group fruitfully under one head forms of activity occurring in different societies. In doing so, it is not *assumed* that terms like 'economic activity' or 'law' can be applied with the same meaning to the affairs of all known societies. The assumption is rather that such terms have a definable meaning, or range of meanings, when applied to certain societies (in this case 'modern' societies) and that with such a meaning, the terms can be extended over a certain further range of societies. The question is then of the extent of the range, or alternatively, the degree to which the term is applicable. How far is it possible to generalize the incidence of 'legal' or 'economic' or 'political' institutions?
2. From the empirical data, it seems possible to formulate types of role, or group, or programme, which are associated with each of the major institutions. (Such a typology will be far from complete or precise, however.) These may be taken as the *dependent variables* in a process of comparison.
3. Broadly speaking, the comparison of major sociological interest is between societies which possess, and those which lack, a highly-developed technology. An attempt will be made to test the hypothesis that technologically developed societies are marked by:
   (a) a greater degree of role-differentiation;
   (b) a greater degree of specialization in the functions of groups;
   (c) a greater differentiation between the instrumental and the expressive purposes of programmes; a greater degree

of rational organization of instrumental programmes, and a greater degree of informality and simplicity of expressive ones.

But any such correlations are rendered difficult by the complexity of the data. It is not merely that intermediate stages between (or of) industrial and non-industrial societies can be inserted; rather, that while it is possible to show[35] a broad statistical correlation between the factors normally held to indicate 'development', nevertheless failures in correlation also occur, and these are often important to the sociologist.

REFERENCES

1. Firth, Raymond, *Elements of Social Organisation* (1951), especially Chapter One
2. Radcliffe-Brown, A. R., *Structure and Function in Primitive Society* (1952), Chapter Ten
3. Firth, Raymond, 'Some Principles of Social Organisation' (*Journal of the Royal Anthropological Institute*, Vol. 85, 1955, pp. 1ff)
4. Ginsberg, Morris, *Sociology* (1934)
5. Parsons, Talcott, *Essays in Sociological Theory, Pure and Applied* (Revised Edition, 1954), p. 231
6. Blau, Peter, *Exchange and Power in Social Life* (1964), p. 273
7. Southall, Aidan, 'An Operational Theory of Role' (*Human Relations*, Vol. XII, 1959, pp. 17ff)
8. Southall, *op. cit.*, p. 21
9. Homans, George, *The Human Group* (1951)
10. Those interested in the sociology of football may see Ian Taylor's article, 'Soccer Hooligans' (*New Society*, 7th August 1969)
11. Gough, Kathleen, 'The Nayars and the Definition of Marriage (*Journal of the Royal Anthropological Institute*, Vol. 89 Pt. 1, 1959, pp. 23ff)
12. Leach, E. R., *Rethinking Anthropology* (1961), Chapter IV
13. Hoebel, E. A., *The Law of Primitive Man* (1952), Chapter V
14. Radcliffe-Brown, A. R., Introduction to *African Systems of Kinship and Marriage*, ed. Radcliffe-Brown and Forde (1950)
15. Mill, John Stuart, *A System of Logic* (1843). Especially Book III Chapter 8, and Book VI
16. Naroll, R., 'Some Thoughts on Comparative Method in Anthropology' (*in Methodology in Social Research*, ed. Blalock, H. M. Jnr., and Blalock, A. B., 1968)

17. Murdock, Peter, 'World Ethnographic Sample' (*American Anthropologist*, Vol. 59, 1957)
18. Radcliffe-Brown and Forde (eds), *African Systems of Kinship and Marriage* (1950)
19. Fortes, M. and Evans-Pritchard, E. E (eds), *African Political Systems* (1940)
20. Bohannan P. and Dalton, G. (eds), *Markets in Africa* (1965)
21. Firth, R. and Yamey, B. S. (eds), *Capital, Saving and Credit in Peasant Societies* (1964)
22. Tylor, E. B., *Primitive Culture* (1873), Vol. I, p. 21
23. Durkheim, Emile, *The Division of Labour in Society*, trans. Simpson (1933), Book I, Chapter 1
24. Radcliffe-Brown, A. R., Intro. to *African Systems of Kinship and Marriage*, ed. Radcliffe-Brown and Forde (1950)
25. Stinchcombe, A. L., *Constructing Social Theories* (1968), Chapter III, Section 2
26. Malinowski, B., *The Argonauts of the Western Pacific* (1922)
27. Parsons, Talcott, *The Social System* (1951), especially pp. 26–36. Aberle, D. F. *et. al.*, 'Functional Prerequisites of a Society' (*Ethics*, Vol. 60, 1949–50, pp. 100ff)
28. Radcliffe-Brown, A. R., 'On Joking Relationships' (*Structure and Function in Primitive Society*, Chapters IV and V)
29. Merton, R. K., 'Manifest and Latent Functions' (*Social Theory and Social Structure* (1957), Chapter I)
30. Gluckman, Max, *Order and Rebellion in Tribal Africa* (1963), Chapter III
31. Radcliffe-Brown, A. R., *Structure and Function in Primitive Society* (1952), Chapter IX
32. Evans-Pritchard, E. E., *Anthropology and History* (1961)
33. Smelser, N. J., *Essays in Sociological Explanation* (1968)
34. Goody, Jack, *Comparative Studies in Kinship* (1969), Chapter I
35. For example, by Cutright, P., 'National Political Development: Measurement and Analysis' (*American Sociological Review*, April 1963)

2.

Economic Institutions

I

WHAT KIND of activity, and what kind of institutions, are 'economic'?

A leading textbook[1] defines the field of economics as follows:

> the study of how men and society choose, with or without the use of money, to employ scarce productive resources to produce various commodities over time and distribute them for consumption, now and in the future, among people and groups in society.

Economics is a study of *choices* between *alternative* uses of *scarce* resources to produce commodities ('things of use or advantage to mankind' says the *Shorter Oxford Dictionary*) and to distribute them: decision-making in regard to the production and distribution of commodities.

It is important first to consider the scope of this definition: what does it include, and what doesn't it?

The managing body of an opera company employs scarce productive resources (the skills of conductors, bassoonists and drummers) to produce commodities (performances of *Così fan tutte*, which are certainly 'things of use or advantage to mankind') and to distribute them (by means of live performances, and T.V. showings). Clearly, neither the resources nor the product need be 'material': bread, beef, gold or private yachts. But choice comes in. The governing body, if it is to stay in business, will have to consider the implications of choosing Madame X rather than Madame Y as prima donna—either the short-term effects on box office takings, or the longer-term effects on the prestige or morale of the company: its continuing value as a capital asset. And the zeal of the bassoonists to follow their art, irrespective of pay, is curbed by their acknowledged duty to their wives and families (as well as by the Musicians' Union). The organization of Western society today ensures that artistic activity has its economic side.

But let us now consider another case. The governing body, whatever its name, of a church, also employs scarce productive resources (the zeal of people with training and vocation for the priesthood) to provide the sustained activities of spiritual guidance, teaching, consolation and the like. But are spiritual guidance, teaching and consolation 'commodities'? Clearly, even today, they are desired by many people, who may—or may not—make donations, in the offertory-box, or otherwise. Or taking another, obviously similar, case: a mother may be regarded as in some respects like a skilled craftsman 'servicing' a baby, just as a priest 'services' his flock. The baby desires its mother's attentions (at least, acts as if it does). The attentions, therefore, are 'things of use or advantage to mankind'. Instead of looking after a baby, the mother might have gone into a factory; thus, instead of producing baby-service, she might have produced, say, soap. Are the forgone wages of soap-making the 'opportunity-cost' of baby-servicing, which should be charged to the baby (or to its father, as head of the household)?

In principle this would be a perfectly valid operation on the mother's part; and as of today, in some Western countries, that last question would be a little hard to answer. Let us then put the clock back to the mid-nineteenth century, and see.

The Victorian middle-class woman, having decided to be a wife rather than Florence Nightingale—a fairly easy decision—entered a sphere where, by convention, there was no scale of prices for her services. Her husband, in business, could choose to sell his goods to Mr A rather than Mr B; but she could not choose to sell her services to Mr A, or his baby, rather than to her own family. Such a decision would have had the form, so to speak, of a perfectly valid economic decision; (and indeed she might have felt 'in her heart of hearts' she would get a better return from Mr A and his baby) but social norms (which include, in this case, the Law) refused to allow economic choices to be made in this sphere.

The implication of these norms might perhaps be expressed by saying that maternal and wifely affection (and, in principle, husbandly affection) were to be regarded as part of a diffuse collection of social duties appertaining to everyone as a condition of his or her having a social existence. Therefore no *quid pro quo* was involved: the receipts were indistinguishable from the expenditure.

Today, in the West, the wife's situation is not perhaps quite so clear. There is a certain range of socially permissible alternatives. Increased public facilities—welfare and education services—make it not only possible but socially acceptable to give more of her energy to other jobs, and less to baby-servicing. It is even within the socially-permissible sphere for her to make her husband do the baby-minding, if she can earn more at another job than he can: though this is a rather marginal case. The point is that the sphere of economic choice has expanded, and the sphere of 'diffuse social activities' has contracted, though it still exists. This trend is evidently associated with what it is customary to call 'development' or 'modernization'.

To return to the topic of spiritual teaching, guidance and consolation. This too is a sphere of activity where social mores have not, traditionally, permitted economic choice. A priest does not purvey heavenly grace at so much the litre, but 'full, pressed-down and running over' (to quote the well-known prospectus) irrespective of whether the other party can 'pay' —whatever 'pay' means. He must not hold up supplies, in anticipation of a rise in price. And (as a rule) he must not shift to the purveyance of Buddhism should he find that Catholicism is not selling. It is not that such behaviour is inconceivable; it is just not countenanced by contemporary social mores. And note that what isn't countenanced is not so much that the priest gets paid—normally he has to live—as that his services should be *priced*; that there should, even in principle, be an equation between what he supplies and what he gets. The priest's services, like the Victorian middle-class wife's, could not form part of a bookkeeping transaction. (In fact, it seems that social mores, here also, are changing a little; but that does not affect the present issue.)

This discussion allows us to make a contrast between the priest's and the mother's activities, on the one hand, and economic activity on the other; and we may therefore expand the definition quoted at the beginning of this chapter, and say that economics is the study of how balances are struck between outputs and inputs: while the sociology of economics centres upon a study of the degree to which a society permits or enables the striking of balances. Economic activity revolves about the exchange of Quids for Quos; but for some Quos we are permitted to trade no Quids.

This clearly leads us to consider the question of exchange. Exchange is implicit in economic choices. But it must be remembered that exchange, in one form or another, is a characteristic of a wide range of social behaviour, and not merely of economic behaviour, as this was defined above. How far is it possible to distinguish between economic forms and other forms?

1. We have seen that services and gifts rendered by the mother to her infant, and by the priest to his flock, are made absolutely without expectation of return, even delayed return, and even diffuse return such as gratitude. The deed is its own justification and reward.

   Many gifts are, however, as has often been pointed out, made in order to ensure some return, though this may not be anything which can be brought into an accounting relationship with the gift itself.

2. Distributions made by a chief, or a patron, to his followers or clients, are an example. Typically any notion of a specific return, or any idea of a ratio between gift and return, would be repudiated as inconsistent with the status of the giver. This lack of an accounting relation removes this class of transaction from the sphere of economic action. But what is (at least very often) expected in return is an acknowledgement of dependence, together with continued support. What we may have here is an exchange of wealth for power: a political, rather than an economic transaction.

3. It is also commonly recognized that 'gifts' are usually given with an expectation of some form of return. But the exchange is of a different character from a trading exchange. Gifts made between members of a family on festivals such as Christmas, or on birthdays, are 'family rituals' (to use Bossard and Boll's terms): the gift is a ritual affirmation of the ties uniting the family members; return gifts are expected, as confirmatory affirmations on the part of other

members. The value of each gift is not measured in relation to return gifts, but in relation to the resources (in money, time, ingenuity, etc) of the giver. In general, gifts establish, and mark, friendly relations; and the *friendly* relations could not exist without the countergift. The gift is adjusted to the nature and quality of the relationship; and the adjustment between gift and countergift is not one in terms of marginal utilities to the recipients; its significance is chiefly as a sign that each party has correctly interpreted the nature and quality of the relationship. The gift is not made in order to call out the countergift.

4. Other forms of 'gift', however, expect, or rather require, countergift. The much discussed potlatch of the Kwakiutl and other American tribes appears to have been of this kind. The gift, usually in the shape of blankets or 'coppers', could not be refused, and had to be reciprocated with interest. But though the gift was meant to call out a countergift, and though a clear idea of ratios between the one and the other was apparently entertained, the purpose was rather a competitive bidding for status, one party trying to outbid the other. This, and the lack of *choice* available to recipient, suggest that such exchange is outside the scope of economic action.

It will be appreciated that the sociologist's task is thus one of studying, in varied societies and periods, the differentiation of economic activities, as defined, out of the diffuse body of social activities. His task is also to relate the *nature* of the economic activities of each society to what may be called the social context.

Let us take for a moment these tasks. Consider first the idea of choice. It is evident that if, in any given society, a person chooses to employ his money, time or wits in one line rather than in another, these choices are made in the context of certain characteristics of that society. For instance, in most Western societies the context includes these conditions: the existence of a monetary system, such that the value of almost everything can be measured on a uniform scale, thus facilitating exchange and common standards of valuation. The context also includes a pervading market system, facilitating the meeting of buyer and seller. It includes also a highly organized capital market, so that those needing capital for development can easily find it. These three conditions may be summarised as meaning the existence of a high degree of economic 'communication'.

Furthermore, it is usually held that Western society is characterized by what are known as 'overlapping' rather than 'multiple' role-relationships. That is to say, people tend to play *different* roles to *different* persons, rather than play several roles to the same person, as is likely in a closed rural community. So-called overlapping role relationships would tend to reduce role-conflict, that might otherwise inhibit economic behaviour. (In fact, the antithesis is not so clear-cut as this wording may suggest.)

Such social conditions as these will influence the sort of choice a person will make: they will widen the range of opportunities, and of rewards, for some kinds of 'economic' actions, and restrict those for others. In another society, say a non-monetary, largely subsistence economy, with strongly emphasized obligations to kin and local group, the choices which present themselves will be different. (But, *given the circumstances*, the choices actually made *may* be equally reasonable.) This social environment forms the rules, regulations and usages within which economic choice in any society tends to operate—the 'economic institutions'.

It must be emphasized here, because of a rather widely held misconception, that the economist is not interested *merely* in activities that make for the maximization of money profits. According to Stigler[2] the assumptions underlying contemporary economic theory are these:

Firstly: that individuals (or more generally, units of economic activity) have complete information about what it is they desire.

Secondly: that they have complete information about the technical means to attain these ends. [That is to say, if we may add something to Stigler, that they are able to bring means and ends into an accounting relationship.]

Thirdly: that, in any given situation, they will always choose the technically most efficient means to maximize their satisfactions, whatever these may be. ('It does not affect the formal theory in the least,' says Stigler, 'whether the individual maximizes wealth, religious piety, the annihilation of crooners or his waistline.' But it does interest the *sociologist* to know what his social environment influences him to desire.)

These three assumptions together form what used to be called the concept of the Economic Man.

It need hardly be said that this was a 'model man'; in other words, it was a sort of shorthand way of saying: 'let us suppose that men act "rationally", like this. Then if, in such and such a situation, they did so, what would be the result, in terms of volume of production, changes in demand, and so forth?' The economist in fact made a simplified picture or model of the situation, so as to clarify some of the factors involved. This obviously is done in order to bring clarity of a sort into the often excessively complex situations of real life.

But whether or not the economist is interested, it is necessary for the sociologist to know more about the social factors which influence the scales of preference in different societies. What is held to be, in any given community, a satisfaction?

The notion of economic rationality, though now, it seems, held by many economists not to be a necessary assumption in economic analysis, is, however, a useful guide in formulating a sociological argument. 'Economically rational action' may be defined as the deliberate choice of the technically most efficient *means* to achieve *given ends*. But:

(a) Availability of means is limited
and
(b) Efficiency of means is affected
} by the environment, and by the social structure of the society;

and

(c) Different systems of valuation in different societies may affect the probability of choice of different *ends*.

The comparative sociological study of economic institutions is therefore a comparative study of the relations between social environment and the types of choice made, the latter being 'embodied' in roles, rules, groups, or programmes. It studies how the economic aspect of activities is related to the other aspects in the social matrix. Or, to put it in another fashion, sociology studies the way in which men's decisions as to the methods of producing, distributing, and consuming are related to the character of family relationships, class relationships, religion, culture and the like.

II

Sociological studies of the economic organization of industrial society are as old as industrial society. Similar study of pre-industrial civilizations might be said to have had its origin in Aristotle. But Economic Anthropology—the study of primitive and peasant economies—hardly existed in any serious form before the nineteen-twenties. Before this, such discussion as existed turned largely upon tools, artifacts and technical processes, rather than upon social relations.

One of the causes of this relative tardiness was of course the fact that careful and systematic studies of any aspect of primitive, or of peasant, societies had scarcely begun to appear by the end of the nineteenth century. When they did, they tended to centre upon those kinds of social relationship which had not already been pre-empted by established disciplines. Thus the anthropologist fought shy of writing about economics, even primitive economics, and tended to feel that the exposition of economic issues should be left to economists. Now by the end of the nineteenth century economists were beginning, with considerable success, to build up a formal system, based, naturally, upon the data provided by their own advanced industrial societies. It is not surprising that they were disinclined to pursue the obscure relations of savages. To have done so would have involved making modifications of economic principles which the discipline was at that time presumably unripe to make.

The first step in Economic Anthropology was made by Malinowski in the early nineteen-twenties, by his study of the *Kula* transactions in the Trobriand Islands. Though Malinowski did not regard the *Kula* as an example of economic activity, he nevertheless set forth the fundamental approach of economic anthropology or economic sociology: that what we agree to distinguish as 'economic' activity is in fact part of the totality of social life; and while it is necessary, for purposes of understanding, to dissect it out of that totality, it is equally necessary to put it back: that is, to view it in all its functional relationships to the rest of the society. This has in fact set the tone of later writing. As Firth wrote:

The choice, the behaviour, the values of any one person are conditioned by other people. . . . The less any individual acts in isolation, the more he must be responsive to choices, or the expectation of choices, by others. Economic organisation is set in a social framework.[3]

The outsider, looking at the development of attitudes revealed in anthropological writings, must be struck by one thing in particular: the progressive tendency to regard the inhabitants of simpler societies as human beings essentially like the anthropologist himself. It is rumoured that once when Sir James Frazer, the author of *The Golden Bough*, was asked if he had ever done fieldwork, he replied in horror 'God forbid!' On the other hand, the influence of Malinowski, as a field worker, was probably greater than that of any other anthropologist. But nevertheless, Malinowski referred to his subjects as 'savages', and a tone of condescension is very apparent in his treatises, while his posthumously published diary betrays an unambiguous loathing. In contrast, one of the most prominent of the next wave of field workers, Firth, depicts the Tikopians as his friends and colleagues.

It is plausible to associate this general trend with an increasing willingness to see the economic arrangements of simpler peoples as being, while certainly different from ours and from each other's, rational attempts to understand and cope with their environments, and therefore explicable by means of the same general economic principles.

The position taken up in the foregoing discussion is that, firstly, economics is the study of (accountable or account-controlled) *choice* in the allocation of resources between different productive ends; and secondly, that this definition can be applied in all societies, though the social factors influencing choice, and the degree to which choice is permitted, vary from place to place and from time to time.

However, G. Dalton and Karl Polanyi, in writings which have aroused wide interest, hold a substantially different view.

For Polanyi[4]:

the term economic is a compound of two meanings that have independent roots. We will call them the substantive and the formal meaning.

The substantive meaning of economic derives from man's

> dependence for his living upon nature and his fellows. It refers to the interchange with his natural and social environment, in so far as this results in supplying him with the means of material want satisfaction.
>
> The formal meaning of economic derives from the logical character of the means-end relationship, as apparent in such words as 'economical' or 'economizing'. It refers to a definite situation of choice, namely, that between the different uses of means induced by an insufficiency of those means. If we call the rules governing choice of means the logic of rational action, then we may denote this variant of logic, with an improvised term, as formal economics.
>
> The two root meanings of economic, the substantive and the formal, have nothing in common.

Polanyi thinks that 'formal' economics has relevance only to the industrial West; only here, he believes, is there to be found what Dalton[5] calls the 'market principle', that is to say a pervading market system, such that potential sellers and buyers are in virtually perfect contact, and are able to command virtually complete relevant information, and where the various sectors of the market are integrated, so that prices made therein determine the supply of factors of production. According to Polanyi and his followers, it is only in such a context that 'formal economics', as an explanation of observed events, can make sense.

In 'primitive and archaic' societies, on the other hand, Polanyi asserts that different 'patterns of integration' of the economic system are to be seen. These he calls reciprocity and redistribution. Reciprocity occurs where there are movements of goods between social units (tribes, households or the like) which are on the same structural level, that is, are not subordinated to one another. It refers (using our terminology) to programmes of exchange. Redistribution refers to movements of goods into a structurally superior centre (capital city, ruler's court) and the corresponding diffusion of goods from such a centre into structurally subordinate parts of the society: programmes of tribute-gathering and of distribution of doles or rations.

These relationships are not merely relations between individuals, but are institutionalized, that is, are a set of relations which are normal and are considered proper. And this means that the economic organization must have some structural correspondence with the political, and with other aspects of the social system: redistribution requires some degree of centralization, either in the society as a whole or in areas of it (for instance the feudal manor). This clearly illustrates the idea of an institution, that is, a system of practices and ideas which is both statistically and ethically normative, is functionally related, to a significant extent, with other elements of the society, and whose infraction is likely to be regarded as 'deviance'.

These are interesting ideas, and have produced a considerable amount of useful empirical and descriptive work. Two main criticisms have been made of them. The first relates to Polanyi's definition of (substantive) economics in terms of the production of *material* want satisfactions. This is an unduly restrictive definition, for which no good reason is offered.

The more important criticism, however, is of Polanyi's sharp distinction between industrial and non-industrial, or between 'market centred' and 'primitive and archaic' societies. There are two parts to this criticism. In the first place, reciprocity and redistribution, as principles explaining economic activity, do not exclude the operation of choice, as Polanyi thinks they do. Assuming that alternative means of satisfying needs exist, in reciprocal or redistributive systems (and they are surely likely to do so in some degree) people will choose between them in the same general fashion as in market economies. The difference is likely to be merely that there are fewer alternatives, and less sophisticated means of comparing them. In the second place, Polanyi's distinction is too sharp to fit the observed facts. For one thing, capitalist and market-oriented societies are, as we shall see, by no means unknown outside the West. For another, Western economic and social ideas and practices are rapidly spreading. This does not mean that there are no differences between the two: as we shall see, the differences are very considerable. But what is frequently found is that, within underdeveloped societies, introduced Western ideas and practices occupy a perhaps small but probably growing area, side by side with peasant economic systems. For both practical and theoretical reasons, therefore, Polanyi's ideas lack cogency.

III

But they raise the general question of what criteria are appropriate to distinguish types, or rather stages, of economic organization. Of course the old distinction between 'civilized' and 'savage' or 'primitive' is valueless, indeed is pernicious because confused. For we must note that, in this sort of comparison, two variables are usually involved.

1. Differences in size of the 'National' Product; in the accumulation of capital, including technological experience.
2. The degree to which the social system permits specifically 'economic' activity.

Now these two criteria are distinct. While societies who rank high on 1 probably also rank high on 2, the converse is not necessarily the case.

It used to be supposed that simpler societies were characterized by a collectivist ethos, so that the individual's freedom of action was subordinated to the claims of kin and community, and that therefore his opportunities for individualistic trading and accumulation were very limited. It may even have been supposed that this was the main factor inhibiting development. Recent studies have shown that this is by no means wholly the case: that social values permitting the existence of money, cash sales, trading, interest, credit and even rudimentary banking operations may occur in societies whose capital equipment and gross 'national' product are very meagre—and occurred prior to any known or likely influence from complex societies.

If we were to combine the two variables in some sort of scale, the result would be confusing. And indeed for the sociologist, one of the more interesting features of the comparative study of economics is the relation between the level of technological development and what may be called the economic ethos (that is, for instance, the degree to which the norms of a society permit its members, or some of its members, to regard the fruits of their daily activities as if they were items in a balance sheet). Unfortunately, such a comparison can only be adumbrated in the sections that follow: even if space were sufficient for a full-scale study, hardly sufficient data have so far been collected and analysed.

Furthermore, there would be considerable methodological difficulties. In the first place, how do we measure technological development? First we require to define this concept in terms of characteristics which can be adequately measured, which are equally applicable throughout the range of societies, and are capable of sorting these societies without having bunching or gaps at any points in the range.

Such a measure is not easy to find. Marsh, following Spencer, Durkheim and others, has suggested[6] that a suitable criterion is what he calls 'social differentiation'. He has attempted to develop an index of social differentiation, by scoring each society in Murdock's *World Ethnographic Sample* according to its degree of political integration, and its degree of social stratification; and for national societies additionally according, first, to the percentage of males in the society who are in non-agricultural occupations, and second, to the gross energy consumption of that nation in megawatt hours per capita for one year. This complicated index is at least an attempt at an answer; but the actual figures given by Marsh suggest that the index is somewhat insensitive in the lower range, and somewhat arbitrary in the higher. (Marsh makes no excessive claims for it.)

What does the choice of characteristics such as these purport to indicate about the nature of the modern economy?

Speaking of 'the peculiar Western form of capitalism', Max Weber, in *The Protestant Ethic*, says that:

> its rationality today is essentially dependent on the calculability of the most important technical factors. But this means fundamentally that it is dependent on the peculiarities of modern science, especially on the natural sciences based on mathematics and exact and rational experiment [and upon a] calculable legal system and . . . administration in terms of formal rules.[7]

'Industrial society', as a sociological type, is a complex of elements which are functionally related to one another, and are, at least in broad terms, designed to be so related. This complex has of course been analysed by many authors.[8] Very briefly put, the main features of it are the following:

1. There is a high degree of differentiation. Division of labour

has been widely recognized as an integral part of industrialism, ever since, at least, Adam Smith. But functional specialization now affects most fields of instrumental activity (and some which used not to be thought instrumental): businessmen, the professions, scientists, musicians. It is also seen in other characteristics of industrial society, such as the separation of the industrial unit from the family unit; the greater importance of achievement rather than ascription in filling posts; etc.

2. Functional specialization makes possible the extreme development of what we have called organization: the rational articulation of many elements into complex, designed, purpose-built systems. In what we have called Programmes—procedures for accomplishing specific ends or tasks—the most significant tendency is one towards greater organization. Weber foresaw this in the passage quoted above. The predominant influence of Science today is seen as much in questions of methodology as elsewhere: in the rational arrangement of successive and simultaneous steps of a complex programme, according to what may be described as a scientific method. In this field there are widespread borrowings and lendings, presumably because 'organization' involves a standardized complexity. Thus the discipline called Operational Research is a confluence of Engineering and Administration, and is now used in a wide variety of fields. Thus the pattern of the world is one more and more set by that of the disciplines of science and management.

3. This involves and extends the concept of Bureaucracy. It is interesting that while, in work subsequent to Weber's,[9] Simon,[10] Gouldner,[11] Crozier[12] have qualified his account, and have pointed to irrational elements in bureaucratic systems, at the same time the extent of bureaucratic organization has increased. Not only is Science 'organized' (books are written on Laboratory Administration, including the principles which should underlie the promotion and demotion of scientists), but the pursuit of knowledge itself is bureaucratized, through organized processes of Data Storage and Retrieval. This, of course, has been brought about by the needs, and the resources, of industrial technology: it is a necessary part of the modern industrial world.

4. The application of organization to human life, and in particular to labour-relations, has produced movements of revolt. These have included a variety of forms, from the earlier, more rigid and specific form of trade unions to the more diffuse and complexly organized one of street-demonstrations. Some discussion of this will come in the chapter on Political Institutions.
5. Industrial society is 'universalistic'. The tendency for industrialism is to penetrate all regions; and one of the important findings of recent anthropology is the readiness of most primitive or peasant societies to embrace the ways of the modern economy—when they are persuaded of their effectiveness.
6. Industrialism results in a *universal* rise in wealth. This seems paradoxical, but the gap between richer and poorer nations is of course largely the consequence of population-pressure, itself the result of improved health standards.
7. It results in a tendency towards technological uniformity. Productive processes, based on standardized technological and organizational procedures, tend to result in general uniformity of products, and hence in a growing uniformity of material culture throughout the world.
8. Its development has caused, and itself depends on, an almost total flow of ideas in every direction across human society—limited only in certain areas for political reasons. To some extent the content of communication is standardized by the technical and marketing requirements of the medium; but this should not be exaggerated: the fact is that there is now a medium and a market for almost anything, including the most complex aesthetic and philosophical productions.

Numerous definitional 'models' of Industrial Society could be constructed, differing among themselves according to the characteristics which different sociologists thought it proper to emphasize. But all these are attempts, not merely to label, but to explain the nature of 'industrial society' through exhibiting it as a functional complex.

The characteristic features of societies which are not industrial can also be shown to be interrelated. To a certain extent, if we adopt the standpoint of developed societies, we could speak of those of the 'simpler' ones as 'dysfunctionally related':

the characteristics work together to impede modernization. We can illustrate this by taking the group of South-East Asian countries which were discussed in the previous chapter: Vietnam, Thailand, Malaya, Burma, Indonesia, and the Philippines. While it would be false to say that this, or any other single region is 'representative' in a strict sense, it nevertheless presents typical, and important, features of underdevelopment.

Firstly, while the countries of the region are formally organized as nation states, the effective social unit is, in contrast with the case of industrial societies, more often a local, ethnic, language or religious community which does not coincide with the political one.

Secondly, their economy is basically rural. (There may also be a considerable amount of small-scale trading, or even small manufacture. This is often in the hands of minority groups, such as the Chinese. It may thus be an effect of migration, culture-contact, or diffusion.) But by and large industrial development is rudimentary. Agriculture is small-scale, subsistence, and under-capitalized.

Productivity of the agricultural organization is on the whole relatively low. It is impeded by certain natural factors, including the heat and the rainfall, with their combined effect upon the soil. The fact that the soil is typically overworked and lacks fertilizers also affects productivity. The small size of the holdings helps to reduce unit productivity. There are, of course, variations in this pattern but, on the whole, this is a typical one.

Consequently the per capita income of these societies is relatively low. For example, the United Nations National Income Statistics for the year 1958 gave the per capita income of Burma as less than one-fortieth of that of the United States. Some care is needed in the interpretation of these statistics; nevertheless, the contrast is too great to be overlooked.

From this again it follows that the nutritional levels are also low. Typically, the calorie intake of underdeveloped societies is of the order of one-half to two-thirds that of advanced countries.

Standards of health also are low. Apart from the effects of poor nutrition, there is the fact that the tropical climate is favourable to flies and to mosquitoes—bearers of disease both to man and to cattle. Malaria, dengue, hookworm and other diseases tend to be endemic. These factors are aggravated by bad housing conditions, themselves the effect of low per capita income.

Allied to all these factors is a rapid rate of population increase. For example, the birthrate of Malaya in 1958 was 48 per thousand, which compares with a rate of 19 per thousand for Scotland. In the same country the death rate in the same year was 8·7 per thousand, compared with a death rate for England and Wales in the same year of 12 per thousand. (The death rate was lower, not because Malaya was healthier, but because its population was younger.) We have the condition known as a population explosion. This situation arises from the fact that as a consequence of somewhat improved sanitary and medical services introduced into these societies by Western medicine in recent years the death rate has fallen, while the relative ineffectiveness of contraceptive propaganda, partly because of religious and traditional attitudes, has failed to reduce the birth rate.

The high rate of population growth, and the precarious nature of rural life, have stimulated a drift to the cities (sometimes a kind of cyclical movement of male members of the family from village to city and back) and as a consequence a rapid growth in the Primate City. The existence of large cities has never been peculiar to the 'developed' areas of the world, and the growth of towns such as Jakarta, Bangkok, Singapore, Rangoon and Saigon has been noteworthy. There is however a typical difference between the urban pattern of these countries and that of industrialized ones; it is that in the latter not only are there many towns, but the products and ways of life of the town dominate the countryside. In the former, not infrequently, there is one large city (the 'Primate City') which dwarfs all the others, and this, often having been built as a court and government centre in pre-colonial days, or as a trading entrepôt of colonial merchants, is far more loosely linked with the rest of the country than is the Western city.

These traits are certainly characteristic of 'underdevelopment'. But we must be careful not to give too simplified a picture. The study of these peasant societies generally shows that, within one political unit, there is a wide diversity of 'layers', and a wide range of levels of economic development.

Peasant agriculture may exist side by side with indigenous trading groups of a high degree of sophistication, and on the other hand with enclaves of truly primitive societies. Thus, simple attempts to categorize the structure and outlook of 'underdeveloped' areas are likely to be somewhat misleading, even when represented as only 'typical'. The Parsonian 'pattern-variables', used by Hoselitz[13], for instance, must be employed with the reservation that some attitudes in underdeveloped societies are achievement-oriented, universalistic, and specific.

For, besides our awareness of functional linkage, we should be equally aware of two other elements. One is the element of chance, or of unknown factors. No one knows, for instance, why the Tolai, of New Guinea, have a quite sophisticated monetary, trading economy, and no one ever will. The other is the fact, which was discussed in the previous chapter, that, in all societies above the most primitive, culture-contact and diffusion of traits has enormously complicated the search for functional relationships. There are very few societies indeed today that are really isolated; and, in these cases, isolation is today less a geographical than a social fact. One example is the Negrito, described by Williams-Hunt[14], who inhabit the jungles of Malaya, and are amongst the most primitive of human societies. They consist of a number of small roaming bands, each comprising some twenty to thirty persons. Any one such band has little encounter with others outside a limited range. Each has a simple social organization, with no typical form, and inhabits its particular territory, to which it recognizes some sort of traditional claim. Property rights in the territory inhere in the group, not in individuals; but an individual has rights to certain fruit, and these rights can be handed down to his children. On the other hand, dwellings are usually family property, rather than group or individual. Since the potentialities of the jungle for raising of crops and the like are extremely limited, the band does not reside on any particular place, but roams slowly about within its territory, perhaps at the rate of some five to six miles a day, rarely staying more than three days in the same location, so as not to exhaust the soil. The Negritos raise no crops, nor do they domesticate animals. Hunting is confined to small game which are killed by the use of blowpipes or bows with poisoned arrows; but their economy is based mainly upon the gathering of berries, nuts, pith of plants, leaves, shoots, roots and the tubers of the wild yam. Since they can store little of this, it has to be done daily: the economic cycle is a short one.

In such societies as these, with only the most rudimentary command over the environment, specifically 'economic' roles can hardly be said to exist at all: and economic programmes are at the simplest kind of organizational level. Economic choice and planning are strictly minimal.

Compare them with another primitive society: the Eskimo. Though living in regions still less hospitable, these peoples show appreciably more complexity. Their residence pattern changes with the seasons: in winter they inhabit compact villages, while in summer the family-groups scatter over the the territory in order to pursue their economic activities. Since the supply of food is restricted, the groups are small and are migratory.

The nature of the environment prohibits the growing of crops, and domestic animals, save for dogs, are not kept. Food production means the hunting of fish, and of seal and caribou. The nature of the prey and the environment dictate the social organization of this production. In winter and spring, seals are hunted: this is chiefly done by individuals operating by themselves. In the summer caribou are hunted, and this is best done not by isolated individuals, but by groups or families. Thus a marked seasonal rhythm characterizes productive activities as well as residence pattern.

There is a higher degree of material culture, in the shape of houses, sleds, boats and harpoons, which may be either individual or family property. Communication technologies are much more developed than is the case with the Negritos; the Eskimos are accomplished sled operators and drawers of maps. Furthermore, there is much contact and cultural diffusion within Eskimo society, and, in Greenland and Alaska, between Eskimos and whites. Economic choice and planning, though still very restricted, have a wider range than with the Negrito.

What one would like to know here is, why is there a higher level of material culture and of technical expertise in the second case than in the first? Rather speculatively, we may suggest the following conditions:

1. Foreign (white) culture-traits were forced upon the attention of the Eskimos to a much greater extent than with the Negritos; the Arctic was economically important to the whites, the jungle not very important to anyone.
2. This by itself would not have been sufficient, as other examples show. We may also note that *change*—seasonal change, in social structure or in hunting organization, was already a recognized component of Eskimo society, but not of the Negrito.
3. Thirdly, the Eskimo groups had coped with their environment to the extent of developing a technology of travel and communication, so that *the reception of new ideas from other groups* was something with which their culture was already familiar.

We may suggest that their social organization had endowed them with the capacity to take up and assimilate influences from without, whereas the Negritos' had not. Admittedly the evidence to test this idea is slight: but it is certainly desirable to bear in mind the hypothesis that diffusion and communication depend, not merely on the presentation of new cultural elements from outside, but also on predisposition and capacity to take them up and use them.

IV

The regularized or normative ways of carrying on economic activity—that is, the economic institutions—of a society are thus affected by the social environment, including men's ideas as to what is *not* economic activity. They are affected, too, by diffusion: but diffusion is only effective where the receiving society possesses institutional facilities enabling it to make use of the diffused trait. It is not possible, in the limits of this chapter, to give anything like a full discussion of this topic. We shall take certain important aspects or components of economic institutions, and attempt to relate typical forms of them to the environments in which they occur.

We shall consider the following components of economic activity:

Trading Procedures:
The use of money.
The use of markets.
Organization of the trading unit.

Some Economic Roles:
Middleman
Entrepreneur
Operative
Professional

The Use of Money

In Western societies, it is the rule that most commodities are freely exchangeable one for another at ratios which are known or can be easily ascertained. Not all commodities: there is no range of market prices for wives in Western society (though there is in some other societies) nor of maternal care or the consolations of religion; but, in general, finding a price for a commodity encounters neither moral obstacles nor technical difficulties.

It is important to notice the distinction. In Western society, the hindrances to wife-purchase (or to husband-purchase) are moral and social: the Christian tradition refuses to see a human being as the property of another, whether of her husband (or of his wife), or of the head of her maternal kin-group (partly because of this, the kin-group itself is disappearing). Were this not so, the Western world would have to hand quite adequate techniques for such transactions: Mayfair boutiques; supermarkets for husbands; hire-purchase; cut-price stores; or, in rare cases, Sotheby's: all these are able to cope with the finest discriminations of species, quality and convenience.

In other societies, obstacles and difficulties also confront the exchange of any commodity for another. These may be moral (though the particular moral precepts and prohibitions may well differ from one society to another); but the immediate cause may also be technical.

To appreciate this point, let us consider an entirely hypothetical society where there is no money, and the only means of effecting transactions is by barter: the exchange of one commodity *directly* for another. In such a society, any man who possessed a donkey and wanted a pig would have to find a man who not only had a pig, but also wanted a donkey. If he had a pig, but wanted, not a donkey but a hundred coconuts, then both men would have to go and find a third man, who had coconuts and wanted a donkey. The first man could then barter his donkey for coconuts with the third man, and then barter the coconuts for the second man's pig. But if the third man did not want a donkey but wanted bananas, then they would all have to go off and find a fourth man. . . . Worse still if the donkey were not the exact equivalent of the pig. Perhaps the best that could then be done would be for its owner to throw in one stringy goat as a make-weight. One of the men might well then be getting a bad bargain. . . . In such a society, people would soon learn not to want anything that they didn't have (or couldn't steal) and this would inhibit development.

The example is a hypothetical one, intended to remind the reader of the functions of money.

Money is the name given to the medium of exchange current in any society. Put in the simplest terms, its effect is that, if a man has a donkey (and wants a pig) he can exchange the donkey for whatever amount of money it is currently exchangeable for, and use this money to exchange with the other man for that man's pig. The second man is just as willing to have the money as to have the hundred coconuts, because he knows he in his turn can buy coconuts with it. Furthermore, he knows he is more likely to get the precise current value of his pig.

Primarily, therefore, money obviates the frustrations inherent in a system of pure barter: it facilitates exchange. To do this perfectly, it should have certain characteristics. It should be easily identifiable and unmistakable. The operations of addition and subtraction should be able to be performed on the units. If there is more than one denomination, the value of each should be expressible in terms of the others. There should be an adequate supply of it for the needs of the community. Its exchange value should remain fairly stable.

Because it is a medium of exchange, money may also become a store of wealth. A man may badly need one donkey, but a hundred donkeys would be less than no use to him. Money is the best all-purpose, all-time store, because it can be freely exchangeable at any time and for any other commodity he may want: or almost freely. And it needs less looking after than donkeys (or houses, or works of art, or even stocks and shares). But if it is to have this function, money must again possess certain characteristics: it must be durable, and not much subject to changes in value.

It is quite obvious that the complex financial and marketing systems of industrial societies could not exist without a monetary system which is relatively efficient (though no doubt capable of further improvement). It is also true that the majority of non-industrial societies are today at least partly monetised. Sometimes we know that these monetary systems were introduced (Spain introduced coinage into South America); sometimes they were, so far as we know, independently invented (but this is only a guess). But though now there are few societies which are limited to pure barter, there are considerable differences in the inclusiveness or effectiveness of monetary systems.

Sometimes they may be 'limited in purpose' and 'of limited translatability'. During the nineteen-twenties, in a book and some articles, Armstrong[15] described a monetary system then current in Rossel Island, in the South Pacific. There were two kinds of money, called respectively Dap and Kö. Dap money consisted of polished pieces of shell: one piece of shell was one unit. A unit of Kö money consisted of ten bits of a different sort of shell, threaded on a short string. There were twenty-two main denominations of Dap money, and sixteen of Kö.

This money had characteristics which strike us as odd. In the first place, the supply of money was very limited, and apparently, when Armstrong wrote, had not been increased for some time. Thus the eight highest denominations of Dap consisted of only 81 coins in all, each highly prized and known by its own individual name. In the second place, values expressed in Dap money could not be translated into values expressed in Kö. This seems to have been partly because the spheres of operation of the two currencies did not completely coincide: thus, only one certain denomination of Dap money could be used for transaction in wives, concubines and pigs. In the third place, Armstrong tells us[16] that the only way it was possible to express a relation between two denominations of Dap was that 'the value of a coin x in terms of a coin y is expressed by the length of time y would have to be let out on loan in order that x be repayable': a concept very much like that of our interest on loans. These peculiar characteristics were—perhaps had to be—associated with a great prevalence of borrowing and lending of coins, such that a special profession of 'brokers' existed, who made their living by borrowing at a lower rate of interest and discounting at a higher. They also practised a magic by means of which they claimed to be able to make their debtors pay up quickly and their creditors not want to be repaid.

It would be reasonable to call this system a monetary one. The Kö and Dap act, within their spheres, as media of exchange. It is however hard to believe that it could ever support an elaborate economic system, had the Rossel Islanders had the other facilities to organize one. Its defect lay of course chiefly in its lack of rational organization for a *monetary* purpose. Values expressed in one set of coins could not be translated into values expressed in the other; values of one denomination could not be easily expressed in the values of another. The rules of operation were obscure and intricate. Now as a general principle, the greater complexity of organization an economic system (or any other) is to have, the more simple and general its fundamental rules of operation must be. In this case, rational organization demands simplicity; and it also demands a clear differentiation between the instrumental use of these objects (as media of exchange) and their expressive use (as things of beauty or wonder in themselves). To achieve 'development' this appears to be necessary. We are not concerned with the question whether the differentiation is good in itself, or whether 'development' is good in itself.

Mantoux[17] says that in the early stages of modern economic society the development of financial organizations preceded the development of industrial. The development of the former was necessary for the development of the latter, but, just as clearly was not *enough*. Raw material, technology and other factors were also needed, industrial development being a highly complex function. An illustration from another primitive society may be taken.

The Tolai of New Guinea [18] at some time and in some manner now unknown (but certainly before the arrival of Europeans), lighted upon the idea of using as currency a certain species of small shell. This is functionally linked with a highly commercialized economy, where a considerable variety of commodities enter into exchange. The existence, and the particular nature, of the currency made for the existence, at a rudimentary level it is true, of other financial institutions. The shells, which were called *tambu*, were threaded on rattan strings, and were measured in fathoms or fractions of fathoms. Thus they could be very easily counted or reckoned, and the value of any one commodity, stated in *tambu*, could be easily related to the value of any other. So far so good. The strings were wound in coils of up to 500 fathoms, for storage. In earlier times, each Tolai was compelled to store his coils of *tambu* with his matrilineage elder: this was both the consequence and the cause of prestige and power for the latter, since all who had stored their *tambu* at his house would wish to protect this against enemies. The monetary system was thus associated with characteristic forms of political power and stratification. Further, these elders acted like bankers, not only in the storage of their kinsmen's money, but also because the elder would use some of it to finance productive activities such as the planting of food-gardens. If these financial adventures were too speculative, the depositors might find that all their money had been lost.

Those who were possessed of *tambu* coils were generally reluctant to break into them. Thus if they lacked small change, they would pledge a coil with their elder, and later redeem it, sometimes paying interest. The elders thus acted not only as bankers but as pawnbrokers too.

The Tolai had, it is clear, adaptable financial techniques. Exchange seems to have been highly generalized: in pre-colonial days, human flesh was bought and sold for shell-money. Indeed, their attitudes were in some ways more capitalistic than those of the West, for they believed that you *could* take it with you: believed, in fact, that it was only the well-to-do who went to Heaven.

What their system did not give them were the means of organizing long-term productive assets. A man's accumulated stock was disbursed on his death, and indeed was accumulated largely for the purpose of funeral disbursal, in order to enhance his prestige. But this custom was itself no doubt linked with the fact that plant and machinery for the creation of further wealth were unknown—certainly unprocurable—until the Europeans made available such things as trucks and copra-dryers after World War II. It was a sort of Capitalism without Industry, by itself incapable of promoting economic growth, but associated with an attitude of mind highly receptive to the idea of industrial capitalism when the technological means to this end were available.

This last society is one among several studied in recent years,[19] which illustrate the existence, in 'primitive' or 'tribal' societies with a low level of material wealth, of quite sophisticated financial machinery and highly capitalistic attitudes. It is thus not universally true (though it is true sometimes) that primitive societies remain primitive because the individual pursuit of wealth is foreign to them, or because they have not the idea of suitable financial machinery. In fact both the practice of trade and the concept of money are not only very widespread but very ancient too. Both have been shown to have existed, even in England, in the second millennium B.C. 'Development' or 'modernization' does not depend on the presence or absence of one factor alone, but on the conjunction of a large number of factors.

The Use of Markets

The market plays an important part, not only in modern industrial societies, but in peasant societies as well. But it has been asserted that, in these two kinds of society, the 'market' is a fundamentally different thing. Bohannan and Dalton, in their book *Markets in Africa*,[20] have made an important distinction between what they call the 'market principle' and the 'market place'. Industrial societies are characterized by the presence of the market principle. Peasant societies have market places, but not the market principle. Others again are without markets at all.

'Market places', in Bohannan and Dalton's terminology, are physical locations, actual areas where buyers and sellers meet in person. But the 'market principle' refers, not to places, but to systems of organization and communication whereby information about conditions of demand and supply pervade the whole economy in such a way that production decisions of all kinds are guided by the market cost of factors of production, or by the sale price of products, incomes are derived from the market price of the output, and thus market prices integrate the various sectors of the economy.

It would seem that, for Bohannan and Dalton, these two forms are not so much independent as, to some extent, mutually exclusive. In particular, in economies which are served by market places, but not by the market principle (in their term, where markets are 'peripheral') the basis of the economy is subsistence production: market sales are not the dominant source of material livelihood for the majority of the population. The common indicator of a peripheral market is the minute quantities which are conducted through markets. Participants are sometimes what are known as target marketeers, that is those who engage in market selling sporadically to acquire a specific amount of cash income for a specific expenditure and then stop. Selling is not for them a way of life but an exceptional expedient.

With regard to price formation, supply and demand forces are operative, but are affected by a variety of social factors which impinge on price making. These include the traditional norms of the just price; the obligations of kinship or of clanship; the eagerness of market women not to sell out quickly because the market is a place of entertainment, and so forth. Prices made in the market place do not, as they do in societies marked by the market principle, perform the function of allocating factor resources among alternative lines of production. Although those products which enter the market are apportioned by prices determined by supply and demand, there is absent that feedback effect on resource allocation which makes the market system so important in western economy.

As a formal distinction, this is useful. There appears however to be some reason to think that Bohannan and Dalton are overdoing the sharpness of the contrast between markets in simpler, and the market in industrial, societies. Dalton, speaking of markets in what he calls 'primitive economy' says 'mutual dependence is not structured through the market mechanism: . . . the bulk of material income is not derived from, and therefore does not depend upon, market sales of output'. It depends what 'the bulk' means; but it is certainly possible to read into Dalton's words the implication that the market is either all-important (as with us) or not important at all. In fact, there are mid-way cases. For instance, Foster,[21] speaking of a peasant society in Mexico, shows that the role of the *market-system* there is to promote a form of inter-regional trade: the existence of a number of local markets, spread over a wide area, enables the specialisms (either in handicrafts or in crops, and whether due to special skills or special climates) to find buyers sufficient to enable them to maintain their existence. In a region having in close proximity different climates or other conditions promoting *specialization*, markets have an important structural role.

In their discussion of the broader social functions of markets, however, Bohannan and Dalton have some valuable things to say. They point out that 'market places' can be utilized for almost every conceivable purpose that requires a large number of people to be brought together in a controlled situation. They are, like many other institutions of simple societies, multi-functional. Division of labour and specialization are here, as elsewhere, the attributes of developed, rather than of simpler societies.

In the first place, markets serve as networks of communication. They are one of the most important points for the dissemination of information. Announcements may be made at markets. Where societies are virilocal, markets give a necessary opportunity for women to meet their kinsfolk.

Markets also provide a gathered audience. Hence their role as places of entertainment. Bohannan and Dalton assert that usually 'the market day falls off into a beer drink'. The market place can also be, and often is, used for the recruitment of sexual partners.

The control of market places is in the hands of the political authorities in simpler societies today, as in medieval Europe. Either, as in West Africa, they are in the hands of indigenous authorities, or as was the case in East Africa until recently, in those of the colonial power. This is so, because it is politically advantageous to control produce which goes through the market. This was the origin of what Polanyi called 'ports of trade' on the Guinea coast, where the locally most powerful ruler controlled the export and import trade in pre-colonial times.[22] (With this might be compared the pre-colonial Malaysian phenomenon of chiefly control of river courses and mouths, for the purpose of revenue raising.) In return for these advantages, the political authorities provide a market peace.

Markets were often used as centres of judicial activities. Judges might set up courts there, or at least be present so that cases could be brought to them. Bohannan and Dalton tell us that no African chief could refuse to hear a case brought to his attention at market. Lastly, they may serve religious purposes.

Organization of the Trading Unit

Analytically, one may distinguish several *sets* of types.

(a) Degrees of Differentiation:

1. *Multipurpose.* Membership of trading unit identical with membership of a family, and economic production is part of the normal life of the family as a whole.
2. *Partial Differentiation.* Some, but typically not all, adult members of the family are members of the same firm; the family depends for its support mainly on this firm; but the day-to-day running of the firm is separate from that of the household.
3. *Differentiation.* No special connection between any firm and any family.

(b) Complexity of Organization:

1. *Sole trading* without fixed, permanent location. (Peddler; *Pasar*-type.)
2. Sole trading, but with *permanent business location.*
3. *Partnership.*
4. *Corporation.*

Type (a) 1. The Amatenango of Mexico may serve as an example of Type (a) 1.

Manning Nash in his article, 'The Social Context of Economic Choice in a Small Society',[23] gives a description of the economy of this group of peasant Indians in Mexico, in which there is only a low degree of specialization of the unit of production.

In this society agriculture is practised, but it is insufficient to provide what is deemed to be an adequate living, and it is supplemented by a form of industry which centres upon the making and selling of pottery. Pottery making (by hand) is spread widely through the community; there are no 'specialists in pottery'. The unit of production is the household, and the women are in the main the operatives. The pottery is made for the local market, and therefore the artifacts are limited by the size and by the cyclical character of local demand, which is greatest just before seasonal festivals.

Level of production is determined, in the first place, by factors which are common to the whole society (the seasonal cycle of demand). Secondly however, it is affected by differences in family-structure: in particular it seems to be a function of the ratio of women (producers) to young children (competitors with pottery making for women's time and attention). That is to say that the energies of the family-unit are diffused over a number of activities which compete with production for the time and energies of the household. Wealth also inhibits pottery-production: the richer the household, the more children it can keep alive, and so the more competition for women's energies. Here is an instance of role-conflict, arising because of a low level of differentiation. The family, though it is the unit of production, cannot be a purely 'economic' concern. And, while the economic efficiency of an industrial society is, in general, maintained because inefficient firms tend to be liquidated, families can only be liquidated at the risk of destroying the society itself. In the early part of this chapter, a distinction was made between on the one hand 'economic' activity, that is, activity involving 'accountable choice' in the field of production or distribution, and on the other the diffuse collection of non-accountable social activities which occur in all societies. Among the Amatenango, the organization of society makes for little separation between the two in day-to-day living. This seems to be true in the wider society, just as within the family.

For it is important to notice that this particular form of the productive unit exists in a social system which appears to *inhibit* individual initiative and advancement. What Nash calls 'levelling mechanisms' include firstly restraints on inheritance.

Amongst the Amatenango, inheritance is bi-lateral, with equal shares for all the offspring. This, given that the choice of mate is fairly wide within the society, makes for a sort of scrambling of property between generations. The large landowners change from generation to generation. These are factors making against successive transmission of wealth. But further, there exists the obligation to disperse wealth in the interests of social duties. In Amatenango society there is a series of offices in which a man, as representative of a family, must serve. These use up time, and in some cases may involve large disbursals of money in hospitality. The acceptance of such an office is virtually obligatory: thus, it is not regarded as a means of increasing prestige or any similar 'good'. Hence wealth is levelled down, and few families with exceptional resources exist in the society. There is a democracy of poverty, which is the result of a different scale of values from those which have emerged in the west. The composition of the production units restricts the urge to maximize either returns or profit. The level and rhythm of output are consequences of the ceremonial cycle. Notions of witchcraft and the supernatural combine to keep wealth from being used for economic ends. All these, says Nash, contribute to the steady state of small reduplicative productive units with little interest in, or incentive for, technological or social motivation.

It is important to see that this institutional pattern, as it presents itself to us, is the fruit of an interaction between institutions and the social (and natural) environment. If we may adapt a somewhat overworked word, it is a 'social rationalization' of the situation. It offers a code for action in circumstances for which the Amatenango (and similar peasantry) can conceive of no better answer. Foster[24] proposes what he calls the concept of the 'limited good' as a principle to explain attitudes and programmes in peasant society. Briefly this principle states that, in these societies, the awareness by the people themselves of the meagreness of return for effort, and of their irremediable, chronic poverty, engenders an attitude which depreciates any unusual energy or initiative as futile and foolish, and at the same time is envious and hostile towards inequalities, because of a belief that the more A has, the less remains for everyone else—a sort of 'wealth-fund' notion, analogous to the 'wages-fund' theory of nineteenth-century England.

Possibly one might, in such a case, speak, in a metaphorical way, of 'society having chosen' such a constellation of attitudes and values. But the important point is that such a social climate restricts the sphere in which *individuals may exercise* economic choice. There is little differentiation of economic roles; and economic programmes show little differentiation or organisation.

Type (*a*) 2. A curious and interesting example of this type is offered by Chinese firms in Malaya. Data are taken from the writer's own studies. The contemporary stage of development of these firms seems to be the result of three sorts of influences, pulling in different directions: the traditional ideals of filial and family piety; Western individualism; and the actual situation of the Chinese who immigrated into nineteenth-century Malaya.

Chinese immigration into Malaya took place mainly in the nineteenth and early twentieth centuries, when the opportunities offered for and by the development of mining and of commerce attracted large numbers of young single men from South China. Predominantly these came as individuals, not as families; either they came with the intention of settling, or they commuted back and forth for a while, as traders, and settled afterwards.

The sense of family obligation, which was so prominent a part of Chinese culture, appeared to have existed with these immigrants; but their families of orientation were no longer a part of their social environment. Hence, those who set up as traders or in primary production or processing did so as individuals; sometimes brothers joined them later, but the concern was the creation of an individual, not a family.

This sole trader would often, in due course of time, bring his sons into his business. Yet, although the family firm would appear to be the culturally preferred type, it is not so commonly found as this would lead one to expect. In a random sample of small or medium partnerships, drawn from the files of the Singapore Register of Business Names in 1960, those in which the partners were kin comprised about 36 per cent.

Furthermore, justifications of the family firm are often made locally on the grounds, not of cultural ideals, but of its efficiency. It is, for instance, asserted that the obligations of honesty, loyalty and good-feeling between Chinese kin-members offer some substitute for the absence there until recently of qualified accountants: if you trust your partners, you need not check your books. (In fact, good-feeling and honesty among Chinese families have been far from complete.) Or it may be justified by the argument that family members' savings are the cheapest and most convenient source of capital for the firm.

In a competitive trading economy the structure of a firm cannot for long be such as to prevent its profitability. The number of partners, and therefore of family, in a firm must depend on the size of its market. Even in a Chinese firm which is all of one family, not all the family will be members; some of the males are likely to hive off on their own.

Furthermore, while in some cases there was an identity between firm and family, such as obtained among the Amatenango, this seems to have been mainly among smaller firms (and among market-gardeners) and more in past than present. There was a custom whereby the members of the family (or at least the male members) had the right to walk into the family shop and help themselves out of the till; but this seems to have died out.

Members of the family, other than those specifically acknowledged as partners, have no right to a say in the control of the firm; and no right to a share in profits or in assets. While there is some feeling that the partners of a family firm ought to find jobs therein for needy relatives, these ought not to be important or responsible jobs; such posts should be open only to merit.

However, the advantages of a family partnership were sometimes quite real, at least to the senior partner. In old-fashioned businesses, the head of the family had complete control, and the sons, even if partners, might not know the extent of capital or of liabilities. The sons' drawings from the firm were at the father's discretion, and the father had power to dispose of its assets without their knowledge.

In general, the Chinese firm seems to be a transitional type, a result of contrary influences: the need for individual initiative versus the feeling of family loyalty; and the pull of tradition against innovation. It is an instance of somewhat complex culture-contrasts.

It was said above that the justification of the family firm is often given on grounds of rationality. It appears to be the case that Chinese clans act as trade-protection organizations. In her article 'Trade and Social Control in Java'[25] Dewey asks why it is that the Chinese are more successful at inter-regional trade than are the Javanese. She answers that this is not because of personal ability; the Chinese is not more intelligent or more apt than the Javanese; rather it is because of the tight community bonds which link the overseas Chinese together. They are minority communities, but also they are communities with strong family, clan and language-group ties. These operate so that a Chinese trader can get credit and business help, not only from his own family, but from his own language community, or his own clan, wherever in the South Seas members of these groups might live. On the other hand, he can only get it while he is honest in the eyes of the Chinese business community. A defaulter risks complete ostracism. Thus there are important sanctions, which go to make for the business efficiency of the firms of this community. There is no doubt of the existence of such links; but some doubt as to whether they are not now deliberate insurance-machinery, rather than the diffuse links of kinship typical of simpler societies.

Khalaf and Schwayri, in an article upon family firms in the Lebanon,[25a] give similar arguments, in support of their functional efficiency, to those noted above. They point out that, in a country where shortage of professional skills is widespread, there is no real reason to think that a relative of the head would be less efficient at the job than a non-relative; also that in the Lebanon the scale of economic activity is not large enough to make it necessary to employ either many people, or people with specialist knowledge; and thirdly, that here, too, the belief exists that 'the environment is hostile', and therefore the relief from anxiety, which comes from being able to trust one's kin, is an economic asset.

Type (*a*) *2*, the 'family firm', is of course a type of unit which has been very common in the industrialized countries of the West. Evidence suggests that here too it could be justified rationally in the early period of industrial development on grounds similar to those noted above. The contrast of 'traditional' and 'rational' action, given us by Weber, must be used with care; to regard them as antithetical may sometimes be mistaken. Traditional action may well be rational, in periods and places where change is proceeding slowly; and may even be rational, in the short run, in periods of change when the actors are unable to control the forces of change.

The trend towards complexity of organization means also a trend to *Type (a) 3*, where a firm ceases to be identified with any family group. The growth of the large public corporation involves an almost irresistible movement to dispersal not only of ownership but of control.

Organization of Unit

The typical 'organization' is both a *complex*, and a *deliberately designed*, system. The definition thus excludes diffuse, non-specific bodies such as the family; while (in the economic field) the stages of peddler, partnership, and corporation are stages of increasing organization.

Type (b) 1. The sole trader, though a single individual, represents a more complex economic stage than does Amatenango.

The divorce of the trading unit from the family is to be seen in West Africa. Bauer, in his book *West African Trade*[26] reported that in general wives and children were independent economic agents as much as dependent relatives. They almost invariably took part in trade and participated to some extent in the economic life of the country. The wife was expected to make some contribution to the family income. In parts of Nigeria and the Gold Coast (now Ghana) a man expected his wife to trade, and was likely to regard the bride-price partly as an investment in a trading concern. In parts of the Gold Coast a husband could divorce his wife if she failed more than twice as a trader. On the other hand, women often traded in order to save enough money to return the bride-price and thus be able to divorce their husbands. The children also generally traded, as there were few adequate schools and, according to Bauer, little else to occupy them. The fluidity of activity extended to personal relations where they bore closely on the economic life.

Bauer says that a prominent African trader in Lagos, whose children were being educated at expensive residential schools and universities in Britain, asserted that his wife was one of his principal customers, and that she bought goods from him both on cash and on credit terms. This was apparently not unusual; nor was it unusual for wives to sue their husbands for commercial debts.

Geertz[27] distinguishes the *Pasar* type, that is to say the peddler or haggling trader in a market, which he contrasts with the more 'organized' *Toko* (shop or firm) type. Although Geertz is writing specifically of Javanese traders, his ideas can be generalized. The characteristics of the *Pasar*, or peddling, trader are, firstly, that he works on a small fixed capital; he has a short forward view; his organization is flexible; he operates with a sliding price scale (haggling). The sliding price scale, says Geertz, provides the flexibility needed where economic conditions are unstable, market information poor, and trading hyper-individuated; but it does so 'at the cost of stimulating an essentially speculative, *carpe diem* attitude towards commerce'.

Here we may see emerge something which is implied in the concept of organization: what may be called time-scale. The *Pasar* type, the sole-trader, flexible and operating with negligible fixed capital, can and does take a short view; the characteristic of the *firm* is to plan ahead, to plan for self-perpetuation.

The sliding price scale, too, is an indication that with the *Pasar* trader the competition is between buyer and seller as to who can get the best bargain; while with the shop or firm type of trader, the competition is not against the buyer but rather between sellers, because the fixed price system stimulates competition between retailers in the offering of other inducements to the buyer for his patronage.

But, in Java, the *Pasar* trading system has some of the characteristics of a highly developed economy. In the first place trading as a vocation, is among the chief goals of the *Pasar* trader's existence. Further, he has been regarded by the ordinary Javanese as someone to be despised, someone who stands outside the ethical order of Javanese society, rather in the same way as the Jewish trader stood outside the society of medieval Christendom. The absence of any guild organization means also the absence of permanent groups with regulative powers over the members, and possessing therefore the ability to maintain within such groups standards acceptable to the wider society, and thus the standing of the groups in the eyes of outsiders. Lastly, the relations among traders, and those between traders and customers, are highly specific. They are insulated from general social ties. Geertz believes that all four of the attributes commonly believed to be distinctive of highly developed economic structures—that is those of specificity, universalism, achievement, and neutrality—are parts of the characteristic *Pasar* pattern.

This typical status and attitude of the trader was implied in Weber's use of the term 'pariah'. The word should not, of course, lead one to minimize their actual importance. The function of the trader, whether peddler or shopkeeper, in societies in the early or middle stages of development, is to draw the peasant producer into the orbit of a developing money economy, by forming a system which effects a more or less regular economic communication over a relatively wide area. Indeed, the classic explanation of international trade forms the pattern to explain the role of the trader in these societies.

Van Leur[28] some time ago pointed out the importance which for many centuries the peddling trader had had in the economy of the South Seas. It appears also be the case that many founders of moderate-sized Chinese firms in, for instance, Singapore, were originated by what were known to the Chinese as *Shoei Keh* ('visitors from over the water'); that is to say, people who had begun by trading on a very small scale, between China and the South Seas, and personally commuting between the two regions, gradually building up a clientele, reputation and capital until they could settle down to make a stable firm. The importance of the *Pasar* or peddling trade is undoubtedly considerable, economically as well as socially, in many regions.

Type (*a*) *2*. With the 'firm' type, that is, the business which has a fixed location, a different sort of organization emerges. The *Pasar* trader's job involves him, on Geertz's evidence, in a marvellously intricate pattern of manoeuvres, but is, in Geertz's words, 'overcomplicated' and 'underorganized', as well as over-traditional. It appears to be the case that innovation in business is the outcome of rational planning and that this is promoted by the 'firm' type of concern: the fixed capital, in the form of an office or shop, carrying a larger amount of stock, requires more integrated planning, and planning further ahead, so as to use capital to the best advantage.

The position seems to be consistent with the celebrated thesis of Max Weber on the relation between Capitalism and Protestantism.[29] Weber held that the Capitalism which has appeared in modern Europe was a new form of activity: what was new in it was not the search for gain, which had been widespread in all ages, but rather the relentless, *systematic* labour in the world at one's vocation. It was essentially a system based on accounting, in which 'a calculation of capital in terms of money is always made. . . . Everything is done in terms of balances: at the beginning of the enterprise an initial balance, before every individual decision a calculation to ascertain its probable profitableness, and at the end a final balance to ascertain how much profit has been made.' It involved also the separation of personal from corporate property. Further, Weber held that modern capitalistic activity differed from pre-capitalistic, in that the latter 'consisted essentially in a series of individual undertakings' (and this certainly brings to mind the characteristic activity of the *Pasar* trader). But some of Weber's other distinctions should perhaps be received with a certain degree of caution. As will be mentioned later, Yamey questions whether the book-keeping actually used by merchants until early in the nineteenth century (as contrasted with the book-keeping set out in the textbooks) was commonly anything more than a series of memoranda, from which it would be impossible to strike a balance. In other words, this particular sign of the capitalist spirit was often lacking among earlier capitalists. Perhaps we may say that (as Weber himself emphasized) the development of capitalism was the outcome of numerous factors; and what was necessary at one conjuncture may have been, at another, less necessary, and an impediment to other qualities (enterprise, imagination, a genius for pulling off scoops).

Types (*b*) *3* and (*b*) *4* are, naturally, stages of greater organization. A partnership is a concern which is both owned and managed by more than one person, whose relations to one another are fixed by mercantile custom or, in modern societies, by the law. One of the main legal—and socio-economic—questions here relates to the liabilities of the several partners to one another and to outsiders. In English law each and every partner is individually liable for the debts of the firm to the extent of his whole estate. Other systems mitigated this liability to some extent.

The corporation, unlike the partnership, is in law an entity separate from the individuals who compose it. Its own assets are distinct from their assets: thus it exemplifies Weber's separation of corporate from personal property. It is again curious that Britain, the leading industrial nation for most of the nineteenth century, here lagged behind other European countries, and did not introduce general limited liability until around the middle of that century, despite the frequently appalling results of delay.[30]

But in the modern economy organizations such as unlimited partnerships, where each partner is liable for the debts of his firm to the full extent of his own personal property, are untypical, except in concerns such as lawyers' firms in which a special degree of probity is necessary on grounds of public interest; or in concerns so small that the costs of joint stock organization would be unwarranted.

In the modern corporation, the legal principles of joint stock and limited liability operate to reduce the risks to those putting up capital, and thus to widen the field from which capital may be drawn. In this system, the capital of an organization is divisible into small units, which may be separately vended, so that ownership may be minutely divided. A person holding any such shares is only liable for the company's debts to the extent of his holding. The effect of this, so far as concerns the present argument, is to tap wider areas for capital, because small savings can be agglomerated. And small savers can be attracted, because of the limitation of their own liability. Thus sources of capital are spread; the risks are spread; there is greater ease of getting capital, and of transferring ownership. (At the same time, management can be divorced from ownership, and can therefore reside in a specialist professional group.)

The system is, of course, both a consequence and a cause of increased disposable national income.

In mixed economies, that is, those which are basically agrarian, but with an admixture of commerce, and with rudimentary small-scale industry, what takes the place of the modern stock market and other financial institutions?

One source of capital has often been some kind of mutual benefit society. Geertz,[31] Ardener, [32] and many other writers have described the widely-spread 'rotating credit associations'. These are groups, perhaps of neighbours, who undertake to pay regularly, say once a month, a small subscription to a central fund, held by one of them, acting as banker. Each month, too, one member takes the kitty. The order may be based on a simple rotation, or there may be a monthly Dutch auction in which the member able to offer the biggest discount wins; or some other system may be followed; but each member is entitled to one, and only one, draw per cycle. Among the purposes for which these are used is certainly that of providing small-scale capital for businesses. The advantages are clear: it is a simple system, easily understood; premiums and returns move on a regular system; and it is reasonably secure, since the participants, usually being neighbours, are linked in mutual ties, and financial improbity would be unsuccessful: the neighbours' eyes are effective auditors.

A more developed phase occurs when the organizer becomes as it were a quasi-professional, running several associations concurrently. He is here operating for completely commercial motives; a still later stage (reported by Anderson[33]) occurs when the organizer becomes a firm with a permanent, fixed location, a full-time staff, and formal rules and schedules. At this stage, it may be regarded as a rudimentary bank. The social importance of these organizations depends upon the degree to which they can effect a transition to more developed economic stages, through affording training in monetary budgeting and the like. Anderson, Freedman and others discuss this question, but it has not yet, perhaps, been sufficiently studied.

But the potentialities of this system as a source of capital are obviously very limited. Another source is represented by groups with which the firm has a special connection: the most obvious example is the family. As mentioned above, the savings of family members are often looked to as a source of capital. Specific interest might be paid, probably at a lower rate than would otherwise have to be given, but even if it were not directly paid, the more diffuse advantages of family prosperity might be an incentive. Unrelated members of the household, such as servants, might also invest.

Another characteristic of firms of *Type* (*b*) *2* illustrates their transitional character: it might be called the principle of flexibility of costs. Even in fixed-location firms, a high degree of competition leads to small profit-margins and to the desire to reduce costs. In Singapore (to take this example) this is achieved by reducing fixed costs, especially of wages: employees, and even managers, are given a very small fixed wage, not subject to annual increment, and to this is added a 'bonus', payable at the end of the year. This is supposed to be related to profits; and it will vary according to the worker's length of service and capabilities, and also according to how much the boss favours him. It is in fact an arbitrary amount, save to the extent that firms in the same line of business have to keep more or less in step. Apart from the fact that fixed costs are minimized, the system benefits employers in that, having to pay it away only annually, they have the use of their money longer. For the employee it is preferable to his firm's bankruptcy; but the more important reason is the existence of chronic under-employment, and the consequent weakness of trade unions.

Economic Roles

Middlemen. The middleman is an example of a role or a variety of roles, whose more specifically economic functions are similar in character to its more general social functions.

Middlemen play an important part in the economies of under-developed societies.

Bauer, in his survey of West African trade,[34] shows that small cash reserves, which are a feature of such economies, mean small-scale production. This gives rise to the need for bulking of output among a considerable number of producers, in order that the distributive process shall be carried on economically. This again requires the intervention of numerous middlemen at different stages and numerous markets at different levels.

The distributive processes tend to be broken up among a succession of middlemen. And it is rational activity for the middleman, despite its petty and laborious character, because, in such economies, labour and time are the factors in best supply. A similar role in Java is discussed by Alice Dewey.[35] Here again there are inbuilt features of such societies which favour it. Advanced industrial economies are characterized by vertical integration, which is made possible by relatively extensive capitalization. It is also made possible by the resources for mass communication. In simpler societies the institutional basis for vertical integration exists to a much smaller degree. In the economic field the units of production, as has been seen, are small and scattered. There is a lack of communications, both in the material sense and in the sense that the producer knows only the needs of his immediate area, and is debarred by linguistic and cultural barriers from a wide acquaintance with the total possible public. Hence the need for middlemen to communicate between separate levels of production and consumption. But the middlemen themselves suffer from lack of capital and from limited communication. Hence the need for second or third or fourth stage middlemen in the total system which exists between the original producer and the ultimate consumer. Dewey shows that the Javanese producer is linked to the local market by what she calls a first-stage carrier. In the local market there are second-stage carriers, who are the intermediaries between the local market and the larger market further away which itself serves a number of local markets, and this again is only one stage in the total chain of communications. The number and the long line of intermediaries in the distribution of produce essentially derive from the economies to be obtained from bulking very large numbers of small parcels. In a society characterized by imperfect communication, this form of organization is a functional one.

Besides being due to particular conditions of economic organization and resources, the intermediary also emerges as a consequence of certain rather analogous forms of cultural organization, in particular to culture contact or breaks in culture contact. The 'banian' in early nineteenth-century India was a Hindu whose business was that of intermediary between English trader and Indian customer, separated by mutually incomprehensible languages and procedures. His function may be said to have been that of selective communication: to pass on to the Indian information about the Englishman's goods and prices, and to the latter the Indian's offers, while concealing from each the other's sharp practices. For this he received commission from both sides. This instance perhaps illustrates the ambiguities latent in the term 'function': but, more important, it indicates the real nature of the intermediary: he is the link between two economic and cultural spheres. The same is true of the 'compradore' who flourished in the trading relations between China and the West in the nineteenth and early twentieth centuries. The Western merchants required interpreters, not only of language but also of ways and customs; even if they had possessed this knowledge, the Chinese Government would not have permitted them to use it. For the obstacles to communication also included social distinctions: the disdain felt for the Chinese merchant by the Chinese official, and also the contempt felt by all Chinese for all Barbarians. It is in fact an instance of the intermediary coming in as a remedy for social inequality between the parties to a transaction. The intermediary serves in the double role of 'conductor' and of 'lubricant' to prevent socially undesirable embarrassments. This interpretation is borne out by other examples of the role, in different places and times. For instance, Gernet, in his article 'Sale in China in the Ninth and Tenth Centuries'[36] shows that a sale in ancient China was regarded as inherently an affair between unequal parties, the person desiring to sell being in a position of economic or social inferiority to the one prepared to buy, much in the same relation as that of a borrower to a lender. This inequality between the parties leads to the introduction of intermediaries, in order to relieve tension and the danger of losing face.

In fact the middleman, intermediary or broker is a sociological type of great importance, his importance, however, tending to vary inversely as the degree of development of the society. In industrial societies the role of course exists but it is a much more specialized one. The role of broker resembles those found in patronage relationships, which will be discussed in the chapter on politics. Patronage-clientage is associated with a political system characterized by wide social distance and inadequate channels of formal communication between levels; and patronage (which includes the activities of intermediate patronage) essentially involves finding one's own advantage in bridging these institutional gaps.

Communication is clearly, in a sense, innovation: somebody, or some group, is being introduced to something new to them. The middleman, as such, becomes in certain circumstances an entrepreneur.

The Entrepreneur. A great deal of discussion has gone on over the meaning and content of the entrepreneurial role, and over the question, when and where have entrepreneurs been found. Disputes over the answer to the first question have naturally led to disputes about the second.

The significance of the debate has been due to a fairly general agreement that the something called entrepreneurship has played a very important part in economic growth.

Summarizing, one may say that the main questions at issue seem to be: What activities, or what functions, does 'the entrepreneur' perform? Are these typically performed by the same individual? And is it proper to speak of 'the entrepreneur', meaning by this an individual man, or should one rather talk about 'entrepreneurship' meaning by this some specified kind of activity which may however be exercised by a committee or a team? Finally, is entrepreneurship or the entrepreneur found in all types of society, or only in some?

The literal translation of entrepreneur is of course 'undertaker'; but the business or trade which this translation immediately suggests represents practically everything that an 'entrepreneur' is not. For it is agreed by pretty well all writers that the entrepreneur performs at any rate *some* of these functions:

1. He initiates *new* lines of business;
2. He takes economic risks;
3. He brings together new combinations of the factors of production;
4. He organizes complex concerns.

The disputes about the nature of entrepreneurship are largely concerned with the relative importance, or the relative 'typicality', of these functions.

It may be suggested that the answer to this question varies according to the natures of different societies. Some give little scope at all. It is clearly true that, as Jenks[37] says, 'Societies with rigid definitions of the claims of kinship, for instance, which definitely sanction for concrete individuals the bulk of their conduct, present almost insuperable obstacles to the effective working out of entrepreneurial roles.' There are some societies which have no place for the entrepreneurial role (the Negritos, perhaps); in other societies some functions are practicable, but not all.

On a previous page, mention was made of the Shoei Keh, or international peddling-trader, initiating one-man trading expeditions across the South China Sea. This was certainly risk-taking, both of person and of capital. It was also the inception of new lines of business: not new absolutely, as would be the first promotion of a technological invention, but bringing something into an area where it had not been previously known.

Geertz[38] describes Balinese businessmen (both individuals and groups) who pioneered the organization of business for various specific objects in that island. The point here is that, not only were the specific purposes novel in Bali (as well as economically fruitful) but the idea of *business organization* itself was novel in that area. They also qualify for the title, given the definition above.

The great potter Josiah Wedgwood was, amongst other things: (a) the builder of a large and complex manufacturing concern; (b) the founder of a tradition of pottery-making which combined high quality with mass production; (c) one of the first to use deliberate scientific investigation for the purpose of industrial innovation; (d) a pioneer of what is now called 'industrial design'; (e) a pioneer of planned aggressive marketing (an aspect of his work interestingly described by McKendrick[38a]).

The case of Wedgwood points one or two morals. This combination of initiatives could not have been carried on by one individual either much after his time (it would have been too large a task for one person), or much before it (for example, he owed a lot to the atmosphere of scientific cultured curiosity associated with Priestley and Erasmus Darwin, and described by Schofield).[39] Easterbrook[40] has suggested the idea of 'entrepreneurial climates'. He suggests that the entrepreneur has thrived only in a highly selected environment: one which gives him certain securities. These are, says Easterbrook: (a) 'entrepreneurial security'—that is to say, the mores of the society must approve, or at least permit, freedom of competition; (b) 'social or "want" security'—'security against want for that part of the population which matters politically', so that they shall be able to adopt a hospitable attitude towards experimentation; (c) 'ethical security', which, Easterbrook tells us, rests on the presence of social sanctions sufficiently strong to ensure acceptance of entrepreneurial activities as 'good'. People should 'have faith in enterprise'; (d) 'political security'—that is, there should be a sufficient degree of external and internal security.

These conditions may be fairly obvious. What is perhaps more interesting is the question of the structure of entrepreneurial roles. To begin with, the social origins of entrepreneurs tend to vary in different societies. The factors involved here are complex, and can only briefly be touched on. In the first place, and paradoxically, entrepreneurship itself may be deliberately 'instituted' by government, as part of a national plan. This appears to have been the case in Meiji Japan.[41] In other cases, entrepreneurial leadership may follow from the possession of status in other fields, as Geertz[42] shows from Bali: or from threats to an established status, which may provoke the threatened to move into new fields of activity, as a reaction. On the other hand, the Shoei Keh of nineteenth-century China came almost exclusively from the poor agrarian class: they experienced the 'push' from holdings which were barely sufficient to support a family, and were therefore susceptible to the 'pull' of business exploration. They were also helped in that their capital equipment needed only to be modest.

British entrepreneurs in the eighteenth century came from a wide range of social classes; but dissenting religion played a disproportionately large part in their backgrounds. The chief factor here, thinks Hagen[42a], was not dogmatic difference, but intellectual independence. Thus, at this period, enthusiasm for technology was not the outcome of formal education, but mostly of self-teaching. This is linked with the fact that the size of concerns in the early Industrial Revolution was in the main small. The spirit of enterprise was promoted by small-scale and flexible concerns,[43] with a simple level of organization. Yamey, for example,[44] tells us that 'the vast majority of [English business] enterprises used a simple form of record-keeping (which may conveniently be called "single entry") until well into the nineteenth century' and goes on to ask 'whether the constraint resulting from over-scrupulous attention to accounts may be in conflict with a spirit of risk-taking and enterprise?'

Today, 'attention to accounts' is certainly an integral part of business enterprise. So is dependance upon a highly bureaucratic organization of science and technology. Here, if anywhere, is an example of the elaborate organization of economic programmes: perhaps the rational organization of entrepreneurship.

Economic Roles in Industrial Society

It is a commonplace that the coming of industrial systems, wherever this has occurred, has made profound changes in social relations. Adam Smith, in *The Wealth of Nations*,[45] drew attention to the economic importance of the division of labour for increasing productivity. Alexis de Tocqueville, in *Democracy in America*[46] drew attention to the equally important political consequences: it brought to the worker's task a stultifying monotony which deadened his intelligence and increased the power of the master over him. And Marx, writing a few years later, asserted that the effect of industrialism was to polarize society into two great classes, the bourgeoisie, wielding power through their control of the means of production, and the proletariat, who possessed nothing save their labour-power. And, like Tocqueville, he drew attention to the effect of his conditions of work upon the proletarian, adapting Hegel's term 'alienation' to describe this effect.

There has been a good deal of controversy about the meaning, and the applicability, of this term. Tocqueville, without using the word, described clearly one aspect of the condition: 'a man who has spent twenty years of his life making heads for pins . . . no longer belongs to himself, but to the calling he has chosen'.[47] But it was left to later workers to analyse the concept. To Blauner[48] it contains four meanings: (a) 'powerlessness': the inability to control management decisions and work conditions; (b) 'meaninglessness': the inability to see the relationship of his job to the total production process; (c) 'isolation': lack of a feeling of community or of 'belonging' in the industrial situation; (d) 'self-estrangement': the inability to find in the work a means of self-expression. Any given worker, at any given time, may not be influenced by all these kinds of 'alienation'; furthermore, some forms of job are, even at the present day, much less likely to produce it than are others: skilled crafts, carried out in small shops, are less productive of it than is assembly-line work.

It is presumably the case that alienation, in all its meanings, is a consequence of the worker's forming part of a 'socio-technical' system: that is to say, a complex organization of men and machines. Since the beginnings of the present century, the disciplines of Industrial Psychology and Industrial Sociology have arisen partly in order to study the factors which may produce alienation, and to devise measures to reduce their effect. Earlier studies took account mainly of such objective factors as lighting, lay-out of benches and so on; later, with the celebrated Hawthorne studies[49] attention shifted to such factors as the worker's desire to be treated as a human being, and not as a hand, and to his propensity to form small but powerful informal groupings within the factory, often hostile in some degree to the formal organization.

Although the term alienation certainly indicates something of high social importance, the concept is difficult to use empirically: difficult to measure, and also to impute with confidence to the specific work-situation, rather than to the more general effects of mass-society.

The manager or executive is also a role, and one which, if not peculiar to modern society, is at least characteristic of it. But the role of executive is a role not only in, but of, an *organization*, and the concept of organization is an instance of the way in which modern society makes not only for greater differentiation, but also for greater generality. The organizational form is one which is common to a number of fields of activity—military, medical, ecclesiastical and so on. What we have to say about it will go in the chapter on Political Institutions.

Lastly follows some discussion of the role, or group of roles, of the professional persons. These, it is true, are not peculiar to industrial societies. Doctors are an ancient profession—said not to be the oldest. Something will be said, in the appropriate places, about artistic and religious professionals in non-industrial societies. But in modern society the professional appears to occupy a distinctive place.

For this reason it is possible to speak of 'the professional role' —in the singular. Though doctors differ from lawyers, and these from architects or accountants, all have something in common.

What they have in common, as Talcott Parsons asserts,[50] is a certain peculiar relation to society. While the 'desire for profit' is supposed to characterize the businessman, the professional is said to be characterized by the 'ideal of service': these, says Parsons, are two different institutionally directed means of achieving success. The second is socially necessary, since the organization of our society requires that some occupational roles should be mediating and fiduciary; therefore the ideals of service insisted on by professions are means of achieving their goals. Thus the professional person (such as doctor, lawyer, architect) typically has the following characteristics. He is in command of a high degree of specialized skill: not merely knowledge, but skill and also judgement: the ability to make the right decisions in complex situations. This command of knowledge, skill and judgement has to be publicly warranted—usually by the possession of a diploma from a body of high standing, granted after passing a course; and often by the entering of the person's name on a statutory list. Furthermore, he is a member of a professional society or institution (Royal College of Physicians, Institute of Civil Engineers, Institute of Actuaries) which may maintain standards of conduct, or the level of learning, or act as a status-symbol.

These requirements are designed to secure the prestige and the authority of the professional, both in his relations with his client and with the community in general. This is necessary for the effective playing of the role, since, as Parsons says, the professional stands between his client and the community. With his client, he is in a position of authority and of trust (and this is quite evidently so with doctors or lawyers). The patient is unable to fill a normal place in society, and unable to cure himself. And thus the doctor or lawyer has a duty to treat his patient, or take up his client's case, and give his best service. But at the same time, he has the duty to deal with his client in a way approved by the community. He represents his client before the community, but he represents the community to his client. Thus he is, according to Parsons, at the same time an 'institutionally legitimate means of tension release' and a 'mechanism of social control'. These norms are typically embodied in codes of practice, recognized by the law of the land.

Professional education is an important sociological topic. As Merton[51] shows in regard to doctors, it is not merely training in knowledge and skill, but also 'training for uncertainty': the fact that his profession requires the doctor, when qualified, to be able to act on his own responsibility in situations of crisis makes it all the more necessary that there should be a strong and trustworthy institutional tradition of learning and practice to support him directly while he is training, and to validate his work afterwards. Professionalism, however, offers in addition a number of significant sociological issues.

For one thing, modern society is as much a 'professional' as an 'industrial' one. The complexity of modern life requires a greater and greater degree of technical skill and training. In one sense, professionalism is the antithesis of the worker's alienation: planning and administration are shared among a larger and larger number of executive and technical levels and positions. This has several consequences of sociological interest. One of them is the increasing number of occupations which, as time goes on, become generally recognized as 'professions'. There is, in Britain, no statutory definition of a profession; but if the possession of a 'professional association' is a reliable sign, Millerson[52] writing in 1964, mentions 158 of these in Britain, of which more than half were founded since 1919. This growth, it must be said, is partly the result of the increased prestige of the concept 'profession'. Also of the need felt by present-day individuals to unionize. But the emergence of numerous sub-species of engineers, for instance, is largely the result of the specialization of technical operations: as in living organisms, growth leads to division.

At the same time—and this is true throughout all modern societies—the professional role has changed since, say, the nineteenth century. The nineteenth-century doctor worked as an individual, and so did the lawyer; even if he worked in a small, loose, partnership, it was not questioned that he was individually responsible. Today both doctor and lawyer may more and more be salaried employees, with the possibility of serious conflicts between the role of employee, a subordinate and also a link in a bureaucratic system, and the professional role.

The organized complexity of modern society creates problems of another sort. There is a danger of functions, as well as of skills, becoming obsolescent. Architects have discovered this, if we may believe a recent President of the Architectural Association. St Peter's could be built by an *architect*, because it was not merely a 'machine for living in'. But in such machines, technological adequacy is the prime requirement, and if it is not quite true that the architect now does little more than fit together the productions of heating, lighting, ventilating and sanitary engineers, at any rate it seems rarely to be practicable to achieve aesthetic interest at the same time. W. A. Allan, referred to a few lines earlier, expresses this by saying that architects have not yet discovered for themselves 'a specific major responsibility to society which society itself sees and shares'. Michelangelo, Wren and even Robert Adam would have been surprised by this remark, which certainly emphasizes the mutability of social roles under industrialism.

REFERENCES

1. Samuelson, Paul, *Economics: An Introductory Analysis* (6th Edition 1964)
2. Stigler, G. J., *The Theory of Price* (1946).
3. Firth, Raymond, *Elements of Social Organisation* (1951), Chapter IV
4. See Polanyi, K., Arensberg, C. and Pearson, H. W., *Trade and Market in the Early Empires* (1957), Chapter 13; also, for discussion, Le Clair, E. E. and Schneider, H. K., *Economic Anthropology, Readings in Theory and Analysis* (1968), Sections IV and V

5. Bohannan, P. and Dalton, G. (eds), *Markets in Africa* (1965), Chapter I
6. Marsh, Robert M., *Comparative Sociology: a codification of cross-societal analysis* (1967).
7. Weber, Max, *The Protestant Ethic and the Spirit of Capitalism*, trans. T. Parsons (1930)
8. See for example Aron, R., *Eighteen Lectures on Industrial Society*, trans. Bottomore (1967)
9. Weber, Max, *The Theory of Social and Economic Organisation*, trans. Henderson and Parsons (1947)
10. Simon, H. A., *Administrative Behaviour* (1954)
11. Gouldner, A., *Patterns of Industrial Bureaucracy* (1954)
12. Crozier, M., *The Bureaucratic Phenomenon* (1964)
13. Hoselitz, B., *Sociological Aspects of Economic Growth* (1962)
14. Williams-Hunt, P. D. R., *An Introduction to the Malayan Aborigines* (1952)
15. Armstrong, W. E., 'Rossel Island Money' (*Economic Journal*, Vol. 34, 1924)
16. Armstrong, W. E., *op. cit.*
17. Mantoux, Paul, *The Industrial Revolution in the Eighteenth Century* (1928), Part I, Chapter 2
18. Epstein, T. Scarlett, *Capitalism, Primitive and Modern: Some Aspects of Tolai Economic Growth* (1968)
19. For another, see Pospisil, L., *Kapauku Papuan Economy* (1963)
20. Bohannan, P. and Dalton, G., *Markets in Africa* (1965)
21. Foster, G., 'The Folk Economy of Rural Mexico with Special Reference to Marketing' (*Journal of Marketing*, Vol. 13, 1948–9)
22. Polanyi, Arensberg and Pearson, *op. cit.*
23. Nash, Manning, 'The Social Context of Economic Choice in a Small Society' (*Man*, Vol. LXI, November 1961)
24. Foster, G., 'Peasant Society and the Image of the Limited Good' (*American Anthropologist*, Vol. 67, 1965. But see also criticism by Kaplan and Benson in *American Anthropologist*, Vol. 68, 1966)
25. Dewey, Alice, 'Trade and Social Control in Java' (*Journal of the Royal Anthropological Institute*, Vol. 92, Part 2, 1962)
25a. Khalaf, S. and Schwayri, E., 'Family Firms and Industrial Development: the Lebanese Case' (*Economic Development and Cultural Change*, Vol. 15, 1966)
26. Bauer, P. T., *West African Trade* (1963)
27. Geertz, C., *Peddlers and Princes* (1963), Chapter 3.
28. Van Leur, J. C., *Indonesian Trade and Society* (1955)

29. Weber, Max, *The Protestant Ethic and the Spirit of Capitalism* (1930)
30. Shannon, H. A., 'The Coming of General Limited Liability' (*Essays in Economic History*, ed. E. M. Carus Wilson, Vol. I)
31. Geertz, C., 'The Rotating Credit Association: a "Middle Rung" in Development' (*Economic Development and Cultural Change*, Vol. II, 1962)
32. Ardener, Shirley, 'The Comparative Study of Rotating Credit Associations' (*Journal of the Royal Anthropological Institute*, Vol. 94, Part 2, 1964)
33. Anderson, Robert T., 'Rotating Credit Associations in India' (*Economic Development and Cultural Change*, Vol. 14, 1966)
34. Bauer., *op. cit.*
35. Dewey, Alice, *Peasant Marketing in Java* (1962)
36. Gernet, J., 'La Vente en Chine d'après les contracts de Touen Houang (IXe–Xe siecles) (*T'oung Pao*, Vol. 45, 1957)
37. Jenks, L. H., 'Entrepreneurial Personality' (*Explorations in Enterprise*, ed. Aitken, H. G. J., 1965)
38. Geertz, C., *Peddlers and Princes* (1963)
38a. McKendrick, N., 'Josiah Wedgwood: an Eighteenth Century Entrepreneur in Salesmanship and Marketing Techniques' (*Studies in Economic History*, ed. Carus-Wilson, Vol. III)
39. Schofield, R. S., *The Lunar Society of Birmingham* (1963)
40. Easterbrook, W., 'Possibilities for a Realistic Theory of Entrepreneurship' (*American Economic Review*, 1949, reprinted in Aitken, *op. cit.*)
41. Hirschmeier, J., *The Origins of Entrepreneurship in Meiji Japan* (1964)
42. Geertz, C., *Peddlers and Princes*
42a. Hagen, E., *The Theory of Social Change* (1964)
43. Mantoux, P., *op. cit.*, Part III, Chapter 2
44. Yamey, B. S., 'Scientific Bookkeeping and the Rise of Capitalism' (*Economic History Review*, June 1949).
45. Smith, Adam, *The Wealth of Nations* (1776), Chapter 1
46. Tocqueville, Alexis de, *Democracy in America*, trans. Reeve (1960)
47. Tocqueville, A. de, *op. cit.* (Vol. II, Book II, Chapter 20)
48. Blauner, R., *Alienation and Freedom: the Manual Worker in Industry* (1963)
49. Roethlisberger, F. J. and Dickson, W. J., *Management and the Worker* (1939)
50. Parsons, Talcott, 'The Professions and Social Structure' (*Essays in Sociological Theory, Pure and Applied*, 1954, Chapter II)
51. Merton, R. K., Reader, G. and Kendall, P. (eds), *The Student Physician* (1957), Part III
52. Millerson, G., *The Qualifying Associations* (1964)

3.

Legal Institutions

I

IT MAY safely be said that there is no instance known of a human society without some sort of regulating principles to guide its life. They may be quite simple ones; they may be implicit, rather than formulated; they may be nothing more than those of the Fox Indian as reported by Miller[1]: 'I do things the same as I did them last year'. The existence of some kind of norm is inherent in the nature of society. But what sort of norms are we talking about when we speak of 'law'?

Even if we ask this question about the law-systems of the West, the answer to it is by no means fully agreed. Indeed, the act of comparing less familiar ones with these may, in this topic as in others, help to clarify, rather than complicate, the issues. However, two definitions from the West, each combining the virtues of neatness and dogmatism, will serve to start our discussion.

In the early nineteenth century, John Austin, the famous legal philosopher and follower of Bentham, defined law as 'a command which obliges a person or persons to a course of conduct'.[2] This command, said Austin, issues from a determinate superior with the threat of sanctions if the rule be not obeyed. These sanctions distinguish a law from a rule of morality. Law is thus laid down by the sovereign, either mediately or immediately—it is a rule laid down by a political superior for a political inferior.

If we consider how this definition applies to Western societies, we find that it immediately raises what is perhaps the central question: what really is the relation between Law and Government?

Characteristically, the laws of Western societies emanate from the same source—a monarch, a dictator or junta, a Parliamentary government—as that which controls the administration. While not all laws are expressly in the form of commands (some laws *permit* things to be done, or give people discretion to do things) nevertheless in such cases there is at least an implied command that others shall not hinder people in doing what the law permits. Thirdly, the general objectives of law and of government appear to be similar: to restrain 'deviance', and to promote approved change.

Nevertheless, Austin's definition leaves several important issues out of account.

In the first place, a sociologist can hardly ignore what has up till now been a widespread tendency among men to distinguish between, indeed to contrast, Law and Power. Law, it was widely held, was something laid down by God, or was, as it were, the Rule or Pattern of the Universe: was eternal, immutable, not arbitrary, as were the whims of a ruler. The Law was therefore above the Ruler—ideally, even if it did not work out that way in practice. To illustrate the existence of such a view in the major civilizations, one need only mention the immensely influential doctrines of Natural Law, in Greece, Rome, the European Middle Ages, besides, for example, China.[3, 4]

Even now (or, at least, up till now) it would seem to be true to say that while many modern legislative enactments take the form of commands, a *mere* command (for example, an order from a gangster to a member of the public) would not normally be regarded as a law (though it might well be obeyed, if the gangster were armed). At the least something additional to mere force, or the threat of force, is necessary to the definition. Writers have described this additional something by saying that law has a normative element: that it sets a standard, and that people feel that it is *right* to obey it. In practice things are, of course, not quite so simple. Most people obey less from reasoned approbation than from habit. The moral basis of some legal systems, those of police-states, for example, may be denied by the majority of their subjects. Also, general acceptance may well go with particular evasion: some 'law-abiding' people are quite prepared to travel on a bus without paying a fare, if they can manage it. Nevertheless there is an element of acceptance, which does not depend *merely* on sanctions. At the least, the average man feels that the law in general (if not every particular law) ought to be obeyed by people in general (if not always by himself).

The second criticism of the Austinian definition is that much law cannot be traced to the acts of a 'determinate superior'. Even modern systems, such as the English and the American, to an appreciable extent are customary, rather than enacted. 'Many of our most ancient legal rules were never explicitly created by a legislature or a court. When they made their first appearance in legal opinions and texts, they were treated as already being part of the law, because they represented the customary practice of the community.'[5] It is true, of course, that any of these rules could at any time be made the subject of a mandatory enactment by the superior, if the legislature thought it worth taking the trouble to do so. They are, if the phrase may be coined, latent commands.

But now take the case of modern Public International Law. Here the law is a body of rules designed to guide the conduct of sovereign states in their relations with one another. But, at least in the present state of international society, there is, above these states, no ultimate superior, nothing which can have over them either sovereignty or duly approved powers of effective sanction. Does this mean, therefore, that International Law is not something to which the term law can properly be applied? If we were to say this, nevertheless we should have to admit that International Law is meant to obtain the allegiance of the states of the world, individually, in that it appeals to a consensus—either a moral consensus or one which is founded upon the perception of common interests. This appeal to a consensus, as we shall see, is itself a characteristic of juristic systems. Furthermore in many important, though 'non-political' fields, such as sanitary regulations, International Law in fact works, precisely because of the existence of a lively sense of common interests felt by the Governments of different nation-states, who in turn enforce these regulations upon their subjects.

This point is a significant one; it suggests the possibility that other institutionalized processes may exist, which do not involve the Austinian 'determinate superior', with his threats of displeasure, yet which those involved may find it right, prudent or convenient to accept and obey.

At almost the other extreme are the definitions propounded

by the 'legal realist' school of jurists. For these writers, law is defined not in terms of rules, but in terms of what people actually do. Law is what is done in law-courts. Law is the decision of a court, the action which the judge in fact takes, and until the court has passed judgement on any given case, no law on that subject yet exists. In the words of Mr Justice Holmes, '. . . the prophesies of what the courts will say, and nothing more pretentious, are what I mean by law'.[6]

One might be tempted to say that, in this view, the law is a Happening. But of course the judge is not merely an individual, but the occupant of a role; and though he may be influenced, during the course of any hearing, by political prejudice or indigestion, he is also influenced by a great body of traditions, codes and expectations, which effectively control his actions.

One very important effect of this definition is to emphasize that Law as a social institution comprises not merely statutes, decrees or commands, but also a complex organization of roles, positions, groups and what not, to interpret, apply and indeed enforce these decrees.

The explanation of the emergence of this view is that in the Anglo-American tradition, the law consists not only of statutes, but also, and largely, of case-law, that is of the interpretation of those decrees by judges who are deciding on cases in court. The statutes which are one of the ultimate sources of law are often expressed by the legislature in general terms, and it is the function of judges on the bench to apply them to particular issues. And in applying them they shape the nature of law, sometimes according to what they conclude that reason or public policy requires. This is notably so in judicial cases which involve questions of politics or of morals. It seems likely that during the nineteenth century in Britain such questions as that of the legality of trade unions, of strikes, and of picketing tended to be decided in accordance with the judges' assessment of the political situation.

In this system, therefore, law develops in part through the judgements given by judges, passing upon actual cases in court. It is not only a body of statutes, but also the application of them to cases.

Nevertheless, even granted these phenomena, study of 'what the judges say' shows that the law is not merely a Happening.

Past cases bind the judges; it is only where no precedent exists which can be applied clearly to the case in hand that the judges are enabled to interpret in accordance with what they consider to be morally or prudentially proper. And where they do interpret the law, this interpretation must be in the light of what is, in their view, in general accordance with justice and right reason. Thirdly, where change takes place through the judge's interpretations, it is generally because of, or as a reaction against, changes which are taking place in society at the time. In other words, law is not arbitrary. Hence we may feel that, while the tenor of Justice Holmes' dictum is at least partly justifiable, the wording, as quoted above, is not.

Both these influential definitions, taken together, suggest the following provisional conclusions: that a legal system involves, not only rules, but also their interpretation; not only decrees, but also the machinery for giving them effect, and not only norms, but also the social context from which these norms emerge: the customs, and what might rather loosely be termed the 'moral climate' of the community.

All this would be true, at any rate of a Western system such as England's. This, as all Englishmen are aware, is exceedingly complex, so much so that in fact very few of them know more than a small part of it; and yet, by a sociologically interesting paradox, all of them are deemed to know it all: acceptance of the law is a part of citizenship. We find, comprising what is normally known as the legal system, a variety of different elements. In the first place there is a legislature whose task is to produce laws in the name of, and therefore acceptable to, the community. We have departments of state, whose duty is to execute these statutes, and as a part of this duty to issue regulations under them, which in turn have also the force of law. We have, thirdly, local authorities also issuing their own subsidiary legislation. Fourthly, we have a considerable variety of tribunals—law courts, arbitration tribunals, juvenile courts, and so forth—whose job is, in one sphere or another, or at one level of authority or another, to settle disputes or punish offences by the interpretation and the application of the rules produced by the legislating organs. Fifthly, we have conciliating bodies, such as Marriage Guidance Councils, which, although they do not authoritatively interpret or apply the law, do suggest courses of conduct in the light of legal provisions, as well as of morals or custom. Sixthly, there are the professions, of barrister, or of solicitor, whose job is to act as intermediaries between courts and police, on the one hand, and the general public on the other. And lastly, there are bodies like Universities or the Inns of Court to teach and to maintain standards of jurisprudential learning.

All this, in a country such as England, is included in the 'legal system'. Also, there is a less clearly defined body of customs and of moral and religious norms, in some sort of relation to this legal system. These are not usually regarded as part of the law properly speaking, except insofar as the law protects them, and save insofar as the law is, in some way or another, based upon them.

This example of a legal system is evidently a complex one. For our present purposes, it may be analysed into three sectors:

1. Substantive law: that is to say, those rules which attach particular rights and duties to particular categories of people in particular situations.
2. The processes for ascertainment and declaration of rules of substantive law.
3. The processes for application and enforcement of those rules.

Systems of law such as those of the Western world thus combine both substantive and procedural rules. It is significant that, for authorities such as Hart,[7] the existence of *both* classes of rule is an essential feature of law. The reasons why the existence of substantive law (what he calls 'primary rules') alone would be insufficient are given by Hart as follows: first, primary rules by themselves would merely set separate standards of conduct and not form a connected system. Secondly, there would be no means of settling trouble-cases, of ascertaining facts or deciding upon issues. Lastly, the absence of 'secondary rules' (by which Hart means those regulations, whatever they may be, which set up the machinery for making, interpreting and carrying out the primary rules) would have the result that no opportunity was provided for change, adaptation and growth.

In Hart's terminology, these necessary secondary rules form three classes. In the first place there must be 'rules of recognition', laying down the means of declaring and identifying primary rules. (In Britain, they would indicate recorded statutes and case law, originating in Parliament and the courts respectively.) Secondly, there must be 'rules of change': rules which empower an individual or a body to introduce new primary rules to effect changes in the legal system where these changes are demanded by differing pressures or differing needs. In our society this power is held primarily by the legislature, secondly by the courts. Thirdly, there must be 'rules of adjudication': that is to say, rules empowering individuals or bodies to make authoritative determinations of the question whether, on any particular occasion, a primary rule has been broken. This duty in our society is of course fulfilled mainly by the various courts of law.

An analysis of British or other Western systems suggests that this definition meets the facts. Both primary and secondary rules exist; the latter without the former would be meaningless; the former without the latter would lack the application and enforcement which seem an integral part of Western concepts of law. But the question is, does the definition apply to other societies? Are both sorts of rule identifiable, and if they are, do we discern variations in their character and importance?

The first difficulty we encounter is that the sort of regulations which can, without much argument, be described as law—at any rate, law as understood in Western societies and in those systems derived from them—is something which is only clearly discerned in societies at a relatively complex stage of development. If we consider only the sphere of what Hart calls 'secondary rules' we will see characteristic differences: in Western societies, for example, the law is recorded in an enduring form: and the machinery for ascertainment, decision and enforcement is highly complex and sophisticated. These organizational characteristics could only appear, and indeed would only be needed, in societies which possessed not merely chiefs, but also complex economic and political organizations.

If we decided to give the name 'law' only to what was found in societies showing centralized political organization, however, we should come up against the second difficulty: we should be unable to cope with the many societies without written codes or specialized police but in which there is something other than mere custom, or mere religious precept: societies in which some recognized arrangements exist to settle disputes about social rights and obligations, and to penalise offenders against social norms. In fact we find—what should not be very surprising—a sort of continuum, showing fairly fine gradations of differentiation and of rational organization.

In the main, for reasons of space, this chapter will be concerned with the processes of ascertainment and declaration. But comparisons of substantive rules and principles would also reveal significant trends. Diachronic comparison within the English legal system, for instance, shows trends towards differentiation and rational organization, which can be associated with the development of a financially and industrially complex society. Two simple examples, from social security law and from that relating to theft, will illustrate.

The nineteenth-century law on social security was simple in the extreme. There was a rudimentary Poor Law, and a minimum of regulations to safeguard the contractual rights of an individual member of a voluntary insurance society: this was virtually all. The development of the social security legislation of today arose, in the first place, from a realization that a high level of industrial output depends upon a healthy working population. But it was also made possible by concurrent developments in communication, education and bureaucratic organization, without which a comprehensive administrative system of the sort designed would be unworkable. These developments were themselves associated in a complex fashion with industrialization. Lastly, national insurance was made possible by advances in techniques of life and sickness expectancy calculation which were the outcome of earlier, more rudimentary voluntary insurance schemes. Social security legislation—the development of elaborate codes embodying, in detail, organized provision for a complex range of situations—is a simple illustration of the fact of interrelationship between law and both the demands, and the opportunities, of the socio-economic system.

A second illustration can be taken from the law relating to theft. Jerome Hall's work *Theft, Law and Society*[8] shows in a most interesting way how the development of legislation relating to the appropriation of goods which are the property of others has followed the development of economic and political change.

Hall starts by discussing the Carrier's Case, an English law case of the late fifteenth century. The facts were that a merchant had given a number of bales of wool to a carrier of goods for transport from London to the port of Southampton. But the carrier broke open the bales of wool while they were in his possession, took out the wool and appropriated it to his own use. He was arrested and came up for trial. The question was whether he could properly be convicted of the crime of theft. By the law as it then stood, however, only those could be charged with theft who had *seized goods from out of the possession of another person*. The carrier of course had not done so: he had been given the bales, and only misappropriated them when they were already physically in his possession. Apparently he was not guilty. This seemed to the judges a profoundly unsatisfactory state of affairs. They therefore, after consideration, in effect made an interpretation of the law which brought it into line with what were in their view the requirements of society. They pointed out that the carrier had in fact *opened* the bales, taken out the wool and made away with it. He had been given possession only of the bales, not of the wool; and therefore he had in effect taken the wool out of the possession of another; by so doing, therefore, he had brought himself within the ambit of the crime of theft. The carrier, therefore, was convicted. Here, indeed, was creative interpretation. But why was the possibility of letting the carrier go unconvicted profoundly unsatisfactory to the judges *at that time*? It was so, says Hall, because the law was felt to be out of step with the economic requirements of a period when trade was increasing, especially the wool trade. The judges' purpose here was to extend the application of statutes or rules to cope with the problems of a time of change.

We are concerned here with an alteration in substantive law, primary rules. But we also see, without surprise, that changes in Hart's 'primary rules' come about by way of the action of bodies whose existence is called for by his 'secondary rules'. Discussion of the one involves discussion of the other.

Hall further shows that similar needs and similar determinations account for legal change later in the development of England. In the seventeenth century, a clerk or a cashier or a servant could not be charged with theft if he made away with money belonging to his employer or to a third party, if this money had come into the servant's hands properly in the way of employment: if he had been given possession of it in his capacity of cashier in a financial office. If the money had come into the servant's hands in the way of employment he was not guilty of theft, because theft meant seizing property out of the possession of another. But the end of the seventeenth century and the early eighteenth century was a period of the rise of banking and financial institutions in which cashiers and clerks received money from customers, and the growth of such institutions would clearly be gravely prejudiced if this legal position continued. This period therefore is that of the creation of new forms of legal offence such as that of embezzlement, the misappropriation of funds for which one is in a position of trust. The first embezzlement statutes had application to particular institutions such as the Bank of England and the South Sea Company. Later there was passed in 1799 a general embezzlement statute applying to all forms of financial or banking institution.

The pattern of socio-economic conditions, says Hall, helps to account for these law changes. The period saw, firstly, the expansion of mercantile and banking credit and the use of credit mechanisms. Secondly, as a result of the above development, clerks were employed in important positions and received valuables from third persons. Moreover, the interests of commercial classes increased in importance and as a consequence of this they had greater representation in the legislature. Fourthly, and again as a result of these first three factors, there came about a growing change in attitude regarding the significance to the public in general of actions which previously could plausibly be regarded as merely private breaches of trust. Here, then, is an example of the interrelated development of law and of the economy and political society.

We may infer that the process of legal change works something after the following manner. First, at any moment of time, for example, the beginning of the fifteenth century or the end of the nineteenth, we have the legal machinery at a certain stage of its development, the consequence of past economic, political, and other possibilities and demands. We have also a flow of potentially causal events: clerks making away with money entrusted to them; workers suffering hardships through industrial injuries, and being inadequately protected; in other words a series of 'trouble-cases'. The attempt to cope with such trouble-cases tests both the substantive and the procedural law. The question then arises, are the remedies provided by the law, as it then is, such as to satisfy the sense of fitness entertained by society, or to satisfy the interests of important groups in it? If not, pressures arise either to re-interpret or to alter the law. Thus what happens is the result of a complex of social structure and mores, political pressures, and the initial state of the legal apparatus.

The particular set of legal provisions—embezzlement statutes, the precedents established under them, and the like—act as rules or guides for the conduct of judges and other legal officers, in the appropriate situations. In other words, they are one of the 'programmes' composing the institution of Law in England. They also, it should be clear, exhibit a growth in 'instrumental organization': as means towards certain ends, they become, not just more elaborate, but more *rationally* elaborate, in terms of the logical relation of complex means to complex ends. This trend would appear to be general in Western law systems.

The relationships between law on the one hand, and economic activity, political activity, moral or prudential values and other elements of society on the other hand, are clearly not simple ones. Law is not simply the reflection of moral standards, which in a developed society necessarily conflict one with another. But to say that law is simply the reflection of political or economic power would again be too naïve: in fact, one of the problems to be considered in a sociological study of law is the relation between law and the pressures put on members by their social environment.

We have noted two definitions of law: one that of Austin, the other that of the Legal Realists. Let us now consider a third.

Hoebel[9] tells us that 'for working purposes a law may be defined in these terms: a social norm is legal if its neglect or infraction is regularly met, in threat or in fact, by the application of physical force by an individual or group possessing the socially recognized privilege of so acting'.

With this may be compared the formulation given by Simpson and Field[10]: they tell us that law is the aspect of a culture 'which employs the force of organized society to regulate individual and group conduct and to prevent, redress, and punish deviations from prescribed social norms'.

These formulations resemble Austin's in that he also regarded enforceability ('sanctions') as the thing which differentiated law from other norms. But these two definitions make clear, indeed they emphasize, that, in law, force is backed by, or rather depends upon, social approval.

They resemble the 'Legal Realist' definition in that they emphasize the essential part played by machinery of application. But they invite a wide comparative view, by not specifying any particular machinery. For them, law could exist without professional judges, or full-time police. In fact, they invite us to ask the question: If no formal legislature, no specialized judiciary, or 'bar', no full-time police-force, exist in Societies X, Y and Z, then what (if anything) takes their place: fulfils their functions?

All these three types of definition reveal important aspects of Law, but none by itself is complete. To summarize, and conclude this discussion, the following more compendious one is proposed.

Law is found where there can be distinguished:

1. A *body of substantive rules* relating to the rights and duties of persons in a society, and to the behaviour appropriate to these.
2. A *body of procedural rules* providing the methods to interpret, apply or change the substantive rules.
   1. and 2. (a) These bodies of rules have *authority*
   1. and 2. (b) And are *enforcible* with social approval.
   1. and 2. (c) From these emerge the 'programmes' applicable in given situations.
3. Social *groups* and social *roles*, concerned with the interpretation and application of these rules.

But not only the nature of these rules, roles and groups, but the degree of differentiation within them and of rational organization of them, may vary widely from society to society.

II

Bearing in mind these various notions of the law, we may accordingly turn to a comparative study of different cultures. What variations does such a study show in principles and procedures: in 'programmes'? What variables are associated with such differences? With different social conditions, does one find different law systems? Or does one find nothing to which the term law can usefully be applied? Is 'law' the fruit only of a politically or industrially advanced society such as our own? These are problems to which we will now turn.

We need, first, criteria to use for comparison. It was suggested above that the development of English law proceeded by way of differentiation of roles and instrumental organization of programmes. Using these criteria, we can set up the following four variables:

1. English law, and indeed the law of Western societies, have evolved *specialized* procedures and specialized organizations. Is it true that all law systems have such, specialized, formal procedures?
2. Western law is enforcible by such means as the courts, the police, prisons and the like. Is this so in all law systems, or are there some which do not have machinery for enforcement?
3. In Western systems, *ethical principles* only to a small and a diminishing extent determine legal issues. Are there systems in which these have a wider function than is found in the Western systems?
4. In Western systems, all law is related to the acts of an *ultimate law-making body*. Are there law systems in which this is not so?

Using these guides, we will sample a small number of illustrative cases.

1. *No formal procedures.* Let us consider in this connection a society which has been discussed by Hoebel in his book *The Law of Primitive Man.*[9] The society is that of the Eskimos.

The Eskimos are a primitive society, characterized by small and scattered social groups and by the absence of any preeminent or fixed centre of authority. Leadership is exercised by some individuals, who do so by virtue of their own personality rather than by any formal authority structure.

Amongst the Eskimos, according to the observers whom Hoebel cites, wrongs such as personal injuries are purely a matter for personal, or for family, redress. This redress generally takes the form of a counter-injury, either to the body, or to the social status, of the offender. In such cases there appears to be no form of community enforcement: nevertheless, it seems that the community at least puts up with, at best fully recognizes, this means of disposal.

But Hoebel, following Boas, notes a distinction between cases of single, isolated crime, and those of recidivism. In the latter case the question is no longer of private wrong, but of a public offence. A homicidal recividist is regarded as a social menace, a public enemy: and a certain rudimentary form of social or collective action against this public offender is to be seen. A single murder is a private wrong, redressed by the kinsmen of the victim. Repeated murder becomes a public crime punishable by death at the hands of an agent of the community.

Hoebel cites the case of an Eskimo who induced the wife of a native of Cumberland Sound to desert her husband. This was no crime, merely a private offence. The husband in his turn planned to take revenge upon the offender; but the offender, getting in first, shot the husband. Still this was merely a case of private wrong. However, he went on to shoot the husband's brother, and for good measure shot a neighbour as well. At this point, public opinion began to feel that the social order itself was in danger. As a consequence the headman of the society asked every man in the village whether he thought that the offender ought to be punished. Everyone agreed. So the headman went with the offender upon a deer hunting expedition, and in the course of it shot him in the back, and killed him. Here we note firstly that approval of the community was sought in advance by the headman for his action. Secondly, we note that the killing of the offender was done surreptitiously: there was no combat, no deed of heroism. What we have was rather the carrying out of a socially approved penalty through institutionalized force. There appears in this instance to be discerned a certain rudimentary feeling that society has the right and the duty to remedy situations likely to undermine its stability and security.

It is clear that both substantive and procedural rules are of a very rough and ready sort. All the same, we can hardly say that they do not exist. And the ones just cited are not the only 'secondary rules'. Regulated combat also plays an important part in the settlement of disputes. This may consist of wrestling, buffeting, or song-duels. A wronged husband may wish to lower his wrongdoer's social status by exhibiting his own mastery of the arts of wit and abuse. The wrongdoer, to the like end, will seek to display his. These song-duels may be accompanied by head-butting: 'the singer, if so inclined, butts his opponent with his forehead while delivering his excoriation. The opponent moves his head forward to meet the blow. He who is upset is derided by the onlookers and comes out badly in the singing.'[9]

Two comments may usefully be made here. Firstly, it is well known that various forms of such 'wager by battle' played an important part in the earlier stages of Western law-systems, and indeed were to be found until relatively recent times. If these are to be called judicial procedures, it becomes more difficult to refuse that term to the Eskimo system. Secondly, it is clear that these procedures are not methods of discovering the facts of the case. In a small community, with a rudimentary administrative system, the facts either are likely to be already well known, or if not that are likely to be beyond discovery. The procedures are rather means to obtain clear, and publicly accepted, *settlements*. If your opponent's butt knocks you over, you have lost—whether in fact you seduced his wife, or not. Order, rather than justice, is the aim of primitive 'law': or rather, it would be better to say that it is preferable to seek an orderly settlement, which can be attained, rather than a scientific demonstration of the truth, which in the circumstances is often unattainable. The ascertainment of relevant evidence is in Western law based upon some two centuries of forensic science; the ascertainment of what is just, upon more than two millennia of concentrated ethical, political and economic thought.

Procedural rules here are rudimentary, and still more so are substantive ones: nevertheless it seems fair to say that some such, which are both approved and enforced, are discernible;

there are no specialized legal roles, and no specialized legal groups: but still, diffuse though they are, some such roles and groups exist. In this primitive economy and society we find a system which is admittedly borderline; nevertheless, because of the existence of these characteristics, one which it would be sociologically fruitful to regard as law.

2. *Enforcibility*. As a second example, let us take the society recently studied by Gulliver, the Arusha of Northern Tanganyika.[11]

The social environment of this juristic system can be described briefly as follows. The Arusha are an agricultural people whose population was, at the time when Gulliver studied them, some 62,000. They were an acephalous society, having no central authority. In these circumstances, cohesion was obtained by the intermeshing of several principles of social structure. In the first place, the whole society was divided geographically into a number of local sub-divisions, which Gulliver calls parishes. In the second place, throughout the society there was a patrilineal descent system, which linked groups of people within the same parish in lineages, perhaps two-generational, or perhaps including descendants of a common grandfather or great-grandfather.

In the third place, there was an age-group system. Young men of the same age in the same parish, who were initiated at the same time, formed an age-group with strong bonds, which endured as that particular cohort advanced in seniority. Throughout all the parishes the set of concurrent age-groups, which Gulliver calls the age-set, also had certain links of loyalty, though less strong than those within each age-group in a given parish. Thus there existed a series of layers, as it were, of increasing seniority, each with specific public duties. Furthermore, between each age-group and the next-but-one group there were ties such that the senior one would act as a sort of patron or protector of the junior in such things as litigation.

Out of each system there emerged leaders. These were people selected for this status, rather than stepping into it through ascription. They were selected as having qualities of character and intelligence. The qualities which such a leader (called by Gulliver a 'spokesman' or 'councillor') ought to show were those of intelligence, patience, skill in debate, a diplomatic and persuasive manner, and the ability to assess individuals and opinions. These qualities, Gulliver tells us, contrast with the approved characteristics of an ordinary Arusha man. The ideal Arusha was quick to take offence, quick in action, and violent in behaviour. The ideal councillor or spokesman was, we have seen, of an opposite type of personality. Gulliver explains this by saying that the councillors were the consciences of the Arusha society. Their duty was, while supporting an individual of their lineage, age-group or parish, in his disputes with others, to consider nevertheless the wider interests of the society also, and the way in which such disputes could best be settled peacefully. Thus they had the duty of caring at the same time for the interests of the individual and for those of the community.

These three systems provided a set of corporate groups, established categories of people, which largely determined both the kind and the strength of support and constraint to which men were subject when disputes occurred and when a settlement of them was attempted.

Each sub-system provided regularized means of dealing with overt conflict between individuals. In the first place, Gulliver distinguishes the public meeting of members of a parish. This was intended to deal with disputes between members of the same parish, but of different age-groups and of different lineages. It was the smallest group which contained both parties to the dispute. Because it contained both parties, decisions arrived at in the parish assembly were enforced by diffused ties of loyalty to the group. On the other hand, since the authority of corporate age-groups and the influence of age-group leaders were restricted to a single parish, they were unwilling to consider the complaint of a member of another parish; while no one would, as a rule, trust his fortunes to the assembly of a parish other than his own.

The second form of meeting was that of members of the same age-group. These meetings were concerned with the settlement of disputes between members of the same age-group. The same principle applied here as applied with the parish meeting. The conclave of the age-group was the smallest group which contained members of both parties to the dispute. Affairs between age-mates were no concern of other age-groups. Further, a solution to the dispute was thought more likely to be found through the friendly conciliation of fellow age-mates rather than through a more public disputation between members of the same age-group in the presence of members of different age-groups. However, if such a dispute was not readily resolvable in the conclave of the age-mates, then it could be removed to the wider group of the parish assembly.

Thirdly, disputes between kinsfolk, members of the same lineage, were to be dealt with by a meeting of the lineage itself.

The principle of informality appears to have governed the judicial procedure of the Arusha. The preference was always for the smaller and the more informal group, as a court for the settlement of disputes. What Gulliver calls the conclave, comprising members of a basic nuclear group and operating in informal conditions was always it would seem the preferred arrangement, particularly where the dispute was of a minor kind. Only where settlement was impossible in the smaller, more informal group was a larger one used. Informality, it was felt, brings agreement. Here we see a contrast with the principles of juristic procedure in the West, where the belief is that formality of procedure, through the elimination of personal bias, brings justice.

Gulliver points out several basic juristic principles. In the first place there was the principle of the illegitimacy of self-help or recourse to violence. If a thief is caught, the aggrieved person must not beat him, but must take him before the appropriate court. If he does take the law into his own hands, he may well lose his cause when the matter comes up for settlement. Self-help was regarded as inefficient; furthermore it was a negation of the principle of group cooperation.

Secondly, a plaintiff had to seek to convene an assembly, or a conclave, through the agency of a recognized man of influence in his group. This was important, because the plaintiff needed to secure the sympathy, advice and support of the notables of his own group. The point here is that in Arusha juristic procedure a meeting or a conclave was not an arbitration, and not a judgement assembly, but a negotiation, or a dispute between partisans.

Gulliver says that there was an accepted procedure which governed all these assemblies. The parties were segregated one from the other in the place of assembly. Each disputant was surrounded by a cluster of his own closer associates. Each disputant had the right of a full opportunity to argue his case, and this right was always respected. A speaker had the right to speak without interruption. These opening addresses were followed by witnesses for either side. Then the discussion was opened more widely, and supporters of either side could take the floor. As the discussion became more general, a phase of suggestion and counter-suggestion began. It would become apparent that one side or the other was making some proposal for the settlement of the quarrel. This proposal would be taken up by the other side, rejected, modified, counter proposals made. And so, through the back and forth of debate, at length some arrangement which was either explicitly or implicitly agreed to by both sides became formulated and accepted. There was a pragmatic flexibility in the procedure, accompanied nevertheless by an orderly attempt at reaching a settlement.

Further, most spokesmen and notables took their responsibilities seriously, and though they were avowedly on opposite sides in the dispute, they were generally ready to come together against the unruly behaviour of others. It was only by their willingness to work together to maintain orderly discussion that an assembly could carry on its work adequately. The system was workable despite its extreme informality and its lack of any force to support its decisions, because of deference to wider issues of social cohesion on the part of the leaders.

In the absence of centralized authority and roles of specialist coercion to which both disputants were subject, and failing the recourse to self help, how were disputes brought to a successful conclusion? The answer which the Arusha give is: 'We discuss and discuss the matter in dispute, and then we agree. When we agree, that is the end. What else is there to do?' That is to say, discussion went on until, in the normal case, an agreement satisfactory to all parties was arrived at. And because of mutual agreement, there was no need, or only marginal need, for enforcement through specific penalties. What chiefly made for settlement of litigation was the general desire that every dispute should end in concord. And the Arusha were critical of courts such as have in recent years been introduced by the colonial or the metropolitan power, because the acceptance of a decision by the courts is enforced upon the parties. In the indigenous system, acquiescence in decisions was enforced by the over-riding need to keep in with one's group, and this need itself arose because of the need, in a small, simple, face-to-face community, of continuing support by one's own lineage or age-group members.

While, however, amongst the Arusha there existed commonly accepted norms of behaviour, such as that property should be respected and theft is wrong; that one should abide by the terms of a contract (bride-wealth when agreed upon should be duly paid); and that one must not take the law into one's own hands when redressing a grievance; nevertheless between these norms and the details of the settlement finally agreed upon in a particular case there was, Gulliver says, not uncommonly a gap. It might, for instance, have been agreed by both parties that a particular marriage-settlement involved the payment of bride-wealth of a given amount. It might also have been agreed that, of the amount contracted for, some had not yet been paid. Nevertheless a settlement might well substitute a much smaller amount of bride-wealth to be paid than what was agreed to be outstanding. In other words, the Arusha recognized that in this world ideals cannot always be achieved, and that it is better to have a settlement which both sides will acquiesce in, so that it brings peace to the society, than to seek unsuccessfully for a settlement which is more in line with ideal justice.

Here we begin to notice a weakness in the Arusha system. How far did the processes of litigation result in 'justice'? Without analysing the meaning of that difficult concept, we may at least say that justice is not likely to be found where a court lacks the means to enforce its decisions, and where a party possessing greater power or influence may be better treated than one possessing less. Gulliver brings forward evidence to show that this may at least sometimes have been the case. So far as the question of inequality is concerned, it appears that the basic principles of group loyalty themselves might lead to what Western lawyers would regard as injustice. Suppose A and B, the two parties to a case, were only distantly related by age or lineage, and lived in different parishes. Then if the case were heard by an assembly of A's fellows, the loyalty of the majority would be on A's side, and the strength of B's case be ignored. Again, if the dispute were between a member of an older, and one of a younger, age-group, the weight of general social influence which the older man could muster behind him might well prejudice the younger man's case. It was only when the parties were near in age or closely related by lineage or residence that they approached equality of 'bargaining-power', and the system therefore worked best in such cases.

No doubt too much should not be made of this. It is not likely that the society would have remained stable at all—as it appears to have done—if its methods of litigation had not given at least fairly general satisfaction to the majority. Nevertheless cases of partiality, or of overdue influence, did arise.

'The law,' says Hoebel, 'has teeth, and can bite.' Did this system of the Arusha have teeth, or was it equipped only, so to say, with the lips and tongue of persuasion? The answer would seem to be, chiefly the latter, though their use could at times be fairly vigorous. Physical force, as a means of securing obedience, was disapproved of, and rarely used: then only by a notable against a *younger* person *of his own party*. These rare cases were, firstly, cases of clear obduracy, which had, as it were, to be expiated in sight of the whole society; and secondly they were cases where the use of force (within one's own group) was both regarded as legitimate, and was practicable.

Arusha society as a whole had no centre of power. Consequently, certain procedures were characteristic of its litigation. These included negotiation between the two sides, rather than a taking of the cause to the judgement of a neutral third party. This negotiation went on until both sides were satisfied, or at least the stronger. The acceptance of a solution came because of the satisfaction which it gave. There was an overriding desire to settle: Order, that is, had priority over Justice. Amongst the Arusha, therefore, there was pressure on the parties to accept the result of negotiations; but the sanction was the very diffuse one that the party who refused to accept would be at odds with his neighbours, his lineage, and his age-mates; and this, in a small face-to-face community, would impose considerable hardship upon him. Besides, each party needed to muster supporters to strengthen his case, so the principal on each side had to acquiesce to a large extent in the settlement arrived at by his spokesmen: this was because of the general need to keep in with his more important supporters. On the other hand, settlement only came through general acceptance of a proposal by the spokesmen, councillors and supporters of both sides. The law therefore, ultimately depended upon acceptance of it by the society in general, and this came through a perception that, on the whole, it worked. The dispute procedure furthermore could only give reasonable justice where the dispute was between members of 'in-groups', for instance, of the same parish; groups having a common loyalty. Where this was not so, recourse was often had in recent times to the courts of the colonial power: here we can see a limitation to the effectiveness of the Arusha system.

Clearly, these practices show considerable differences from the law-systems of the Western world. The former, like those of the Eskimo, are not a recorded system: neither 'primary' nor 'secondary' rules are written down. Hart explicitly asserts that the rule of recognition always involves the existence of written sources of law. Clearly, this would exclude all pre-literate societies from the class to which the possession of a juristic system can be attributed.

It is true that if neither substantive nor procedural law is written, it is liable to undergo the sort of unintended change that is the result of lapses in the collective memory of members of the society. Paradoxically, bodies of traditional law are probably more subject to change than are the laws of modern societies. Furthermore, an unwritten system is hardly a vehicle for the sophisticated analysis of juridical concepts. In this respect, as in others, Arusha law has the characteristics of a simple stage of development: the procedures, the 'programmes' are simple, unevolved, and only apt, it seems, for a limited range of situations. Completely to deny it the name of law seems, however, to be a rather extreme position. If, for instance, some principle governing rights and obligations can be enunciated publicly by some prominent person and with general approval, this would seem to be 'recognition' enough. Such would appear to be the case with the Arusha.

Lastly, it differs, as we have seen, in that there are no specific or formal means to enforce decisions. In Britain, the popular symbol of the law is still the policeman: a sort of 'neutral enforcibility' is the mark of law. It is the more diffuse influences of public opinion which ensure that the consensus arrived at in Arusha assemblies and conclave are honoured.

Law, among the Arusha, is not the *command of a determinate superior*—because, of course, there is no determinate superior to command. The source of law—that is of those decisions about the nature of rights and obligations, and about the behaviour appropriate to them—lies in the group itself, under the informal guidance of men of influence. In the field of law, role-differentiation among the Arusha is slight. Both legal authority and political power are widely diffused, but, so far as they inhere in anything other than the whole group, inhere in the same informal, unorganized collection of men of influence.

Paradoxically, it is the absence of a political superior which leads Gulliver to suggest that the Arusha process is 'political' rather than legal. It is a bargaining struggle between parties structurally equal, which the party with the most influence is liable to win, rather than the submission of a case to a neutral and superior third party.

Nevertheless, as Gulliver shows, litigation is not a mere power-struggle between out-and-out hostile parties. In their conduct of cases, the spokesmen, it seems, recognize an obligation towards the underlying values of the society which is normally as strong as that towards their own party. They behave, that is, rather like counsel and judge in an English or American law-court. Given that there is a close enough relationship between the parties for a case to be conducted at all—and this is certainly a limiting condition of Arusha justice—its conduct must not depart too far from fundamental principles.

But this limiting condition is of great importance. As we have seen, no single indigenous judicial assembly exists, before which *any* two parties will stand on an equal footing. Before any assembly, *some* people will be at an advantage by reason of lineage, residence or age. Justice may usually be even-handed as between the litigants who decide to come before it; but it is not manifestly even-handed as between all potential litigants. In order that this can be so, at least there should be *either* a lively sense of common interests throughout the *whole* community, or an administrator of justice with ultimate political power over the whole.

We must at this point consider more fully the relation between political power ('sovereignty') and law. We saw that Austin's definition of a law as the command of a determinate superior was inadequate. Some laws are not of this sort. Nevertheless, the characteristic which distinguishes a *system of law* from any other collection of approved precepts is that the former contains provisions for applying and enforcing them. Now in societies like the Eskimo, the Arusha and many others, application and enforcement offer both fewer problems and fewer opportunities. There is less social differentiation; less social change: therefore the pattern of rights and duties is simpler and is widely understood, so that more consensus exists about what is proper conduct. On the other hand, because there is little social differentiation, no one exists with the power to enforce decisions upon others.

Where power becomes centralized, then one begins to see a difference in the legal system. But the difference is more that the ruler seeks to get into his hands the *administration* of the law, rather than law-*making*. Thus one of the characteristics of Western European society during the early Middle Ages was the struggle between king and feudal nobility for the right, or power, to administer justice, to maintain their own court and judges, and times of hearing cases. In England the struggle was quickly won by the king; less quickly elsewhere. One significant aspect of this development is that the ruler who administers law can help to increase uniformity in the law throughout his territory, and this helps to promote central control. But perhaps more important is the fact that, whatever the substantive law may be, the *administration* of it is a sign of political power.

In perhaps the majority of centralized political societies, therefore, the ruler is regarded more as the guardian than as the creator of law. This did not necessarily mean that in such societies law was static: it showed plenty of movement both in mediaeval Europe and in the Byzantine Empire under Justinian and his immediate successors, to take two examples. But the movement was regarded as a process of discovery of what the true law was, and not one of inventing law. Thus even in the

Byzantine Empire, whose government was among the most autocratic, the Emperor was subject to the law, which he might perhaps at times evade, but could not legitimately overthrow. The reason of this paradox is clearly this, that power is arbitrary, but authority must have such elements of stability as will make it acceptable—'believed-in'; and in societies where change cannot be controlled, law must all the more be regarded as something beyond the reach of human interference; laid down from the beginning. Thus the very frequent attribution of divine origin to laws; the view that the antiquity of a law is the sign of its goodness; and the principle that an older law voids a newer one, instead of the reverse, as with modern states. The notion of systematic programmes of law-creation, in order to fulfil ends of social policy, is new, and is itself a clear example of instrumental organization.

3. *Law and morals.* This leads us to the third ground of distinction, which is concerned with the relation of law and morals. It is in general true that Western judicial procedure seeks to dissect out delimited issues in order to pronounce a clear and distinct judgement. What is assessed and pronounced on is a particular act, perhaps a linked series of acts, but not the totality of a man's conduct. What are asserted in the judgement are his rights or obligations in regard to this particular issue. If I trespass on my neighbour's garden, the court will pronounce on my duty in this instance to this neighbour, and not drag in my conduct to other parties not concerned in the particular case. Other systems exist, however, in which the issues are deliberately thrown widely open. One such system is that of the Barotse.[12]

In general, Barotse society was far more complex than either the Eskimo or the Arusha. It was much larger, in terms of population. It was based on a much more complex economic system. Also it was based on a more complex polity, with a centralized Kingship, and with inequalities of political status: it contained a politically paramount group, the Lozi. There was a considerable degree of role-differentiation.

In some respects the Barotse judicial process resembled those of the West to a striking degree. In the first place, there were well-defined courts with established judicial procedures. The judges were specialists. The court had a fixed location. There was a well-defined procedure: the parties appeared, witnesses were heard, and a formal judgement was pronounced. The judgement was given in the name of the king, and it was enforced by a police force. Furthermore, what Gluckman calls their 'true genius in law' showed itself in considerable subtlety in the analysis of juridical ideas. All these attributes are recognizable by us as familiar attributes of a legal system: the Barotse system showed a greater degree of instrumental organization (was more differentiated, more rationally elaborated) than the other two.

Nevertheless, the differences are equally apparent. According to Gluckman, the court saw its law-giving function as involving the support of general ethico-social principles. The issues before the court tended to be widened by it so as to form the occasion for sermons on the general moral obligation of the parties. The judges saw their duty as one of reconciling the parties before them.

> Though in relationships between kin there is no formal system of equal exchanges, people in practice balance what is done to them against what they do. When a major quarrel occurs, their sense of being stinted or not recompensed, together with feelings of envy and dislike comes to the surface . . . the case therefore became a general venting of grievances, into which the judges patiently inquired, ruling out nothing as irrelevant. That is, to achieve their purpose of reconciliation, the judges' concept of relevance had to be very wide.

Here there is an evident contrast with the British system where the general venting of grievances takes place, informally, outside the court, whereas within the court the issues are carefully circumscribed.

Law among the Barotse was regarded as the maintainer of general social duties. Gluckman tells us that

> large parts of the judgements [made by the judges in court] read like sermons, for they all lecture on the theme, 'your station and its duties'. The standards publicly stated for the parties are the norms involved in their social positions and relationships: members of a village must be loving and forbearing accepting mischances in a spirit of give and take . . . the headman must be impartial in settling disputes among his followers; children must

> love and help their parents, and brothers one another. These are statements of [Barotse] law and morals in which the ultimate values are that children should love one another to strengthen their father and their village that the country may be well built. The essence of the judicial process is to state these norms to the world and to assess against them the behaviour of the parties in a specific series of situations.

The aim of the judicial process was that when the parties had had their right doings and wrong doings indicated to them they would be reconciled and live together harmoniously in the future.

Here again there appears to be a contrast between Barotse and, let us say, British judicial behaviour. Of course, it is open to a British judge to moralize on the Bench: but the judge who habitually does so will in most cases be looked upon by his colleagues as a tedious old windbag. The aims of the procedure are in the two cases by no means identical.

The one exception which Gluckman gives to this general principle of procedure itself proves the rule. The exception is that of marital cases. Marital cases, he says, were not always approached by the courts with an eye to reconciliation. Marriage amongst the Barotse was a far from stable relationship. The divorce rate was very high. A woman remained, after marriage, primarily related to her own kin groups, and her children acquired legal rights in these through her. The law did not defend the permanent maintenance of any particular marriage, if either spouse had broken the rules of marriage. Marital ties were not like blood ties, which were virtually unbreakable. Therefore, although the judicial process of reconciliation, as it is described above, was present, it was less marked in divorce suits once the woman had shown that there were good grounds for her claims to freedom.

These general juristic principles are exemplified by Gluckman in what he calls 'the case of the quarrelsome teacher'. Here the court had before it two suits: in the first, the teacher claimed damages for the spoiling of his garden by the goats of the defendant, and the defendant in turn admitted liability. In the second suit, the defendant himself counter-claimed because of the teacher's threat to drive him, the defendant, out of the country. It was on this latter issue that the court seized its opportunity to cross-examine and to upbraid the teacher upon his general behaviour. It did this as overseer of the work of all public functionaries in the country. But it did so as well because in Barotseland relationships are multiplex, and these have to be protected in their entirety. The suit over the goats raised the whole problem of the school's position in the community, and that had to be safeguarded. The civil suit over the goats included a criminal trial of the teacher. In criticizing his handling of the school, and his relationships with the people the judges lectured on a teacher's station and its duties.

There would appear to be a significant contrast in this between Barotse and, say, Anglo-American juristic principles. Partly it is that the latter system delimits the issues before the court; but also it looks today less towards intent, and more towards objective consequences, whether involving moral fault or not. This distinction does not hold entirely: in certain issues *mens rea* determines the criminal quality of an act. But, to a growing degree, intent is irrelevant to the question of guilt. And one may cite in this connection the doctrine of strict liability, in British and other Western systems: that is, the principle that offences against certain sorts of regulations (for example laws regulating the purity of food; some traffic regulations; or currency offences), may be penalized though the parties are innocent of any intent to offend, or even unaware that they have done so. The doctrine of strict liability, according to Friedmann,[13] seems to arise in the general idea that, in a society which is technologically highly complex, the connection between an individual's intentions and the objective consequences of his actions tends to become remote. Furthermore, many persons who commit such offences are in fact corporations rather than individuals, and therefore the question of guilty mind is hard to establish. Thirdly, in such a society, certain sorts of events are likely to be so dangerous to a society in a complex stage of organization that the person doing them, whether wickedly or negligently or whether purely accidentally without moral blame, must be penalized. Individual morality, on this view, is an issue unrelated to the administrative efficiency of political systems. This again suggests a significant relation between economic or social development and the development of legal systems.

4. *Law not the act of a Sovereign.* We proceed now to discuss the fourth and last basis of our comparison of law systems.

In British, as in most Western systems, all forms of law are systematically connected. Not all rules or principles of, for instance, British law originated in known acts of a political superior; but all today exist by the sufferance of the political sovereign (the Crown in Parliament) which has thus the final decision on what the law shall be. So all forms of legal rule, whether statutes, administrative regulations, or by-laws, are issued under the authority of the law of the land, and must be consistent with it. But in other societies there are instances of the co-existence of several unconnected systems of law. Co-existing with the law system issued in the name of the sovereign, there may be systems of, for instance, customary law, which in practice do not depend upon the central law system.

This situation arises not because, as with the Arusha, there is no central authority. It occurs in peasant societies, where monarchs exist or have existed. It arises where the sovereign's communication with certain groups (for instance, rural peasantry) is intermittent, and where the royal law is inappropriate to the issues of their daily life.

In such conditions, a situation is found similar to what Jenks[14] tells us operated in medieval Europe: the King applied his own law to those immediately subject to him; groups such as merchants and traders had their own codes of commercial practice; and in the villages up and down the country there were bodies of custom, probably differing somewhat from village to village, and, though unwritten, well understood by the older villagers. According to this 'customary law' disputes between villagers were arbitrated and settled.

In Europe, village customary law, together with mercantile custom, became swallowed up in the general law of the land: mercantile custom because the sovereigns were alive to the importance of trade; and both this and local customs because many European monarchs succeeded in achieving a fairly high degree of administrative centralization. Elsewhere, for instance in China, India, or Indonesia, customary law may co-exist with that emanating from the sovereign power because the latter is ineffective in certain geographical areas, or in certain fields of social relations. It may be the sign of a failure of communication between various parts of the society.

An example can be taken from pre-Communist China.[15] In the Manchu period, particularly, the Imperial law was merely a penal law. It punished crimes, whether against the emperor or against social morals; whether of neglecting the duty of respect to one's parents, or the duty of proper conduct of ceremonies; but there were large areas of social relations (for example commercial transactions) with which the law of the land was unconcerned.

Secondly, the procedure under the Imperial law was rigorous. The unavoidable consequence of a legal case, once started, was punishment for at least one person. If the plaintiff proved his case, the defendant was punished, but if the plaintiff failed to prove it, he himself was punished for the crime of bringing false accusations. Punishment was often corporal. Consequently there was a general disinclination to approach the official courts, and this was increased by the fact that judicial procedure was often corrupt. These three characteristics of Imperial law gave rise to forms of judicial procedure which were quite distinct from the Imperial law.

One example of such customary judical procedures were those administered by commercial guilds over their members. The commercial guilds in China were of long standing, and grew to great importance in the Manchu period, owing their existence partly to the Chinese talent for trading, and the immense importance of its inland trade, but partly to the low estimation in which trade was held by the official and governmental classes. These commercial guilds and their activities spread, during the nineteenth century, to the Chinese settlements overseas, where they still continue to be important. Their purpose was, and is, to protect the trading interests of their members. This protection would clearly include provision for the quick, cheap and safe settlement of commercial disputes.

In settlement of disputes between its members, the guild proceeded in the following manner.[16] In the first place, it prohibited members from having recourse to the ordinary Imperial courts, except where permission was given by the guilds themselves—probably a rather unnecessary precaution. The guild's own procedure was by arbitration. A member with a grievance against another member would go to the head of the guild, and would state his case. The guild would get hold of the other party, and find out if he agreed to arbitration. If so, the names of arbitrators were proposed to both parties, who were each asked whether they consented to those persons. The arbitrators would go into all the facts of the case, hear both sides, try to get each side to see the right in the other's case, and appeal to their good feelings. The procedure was not one of negotiation, as with the Arusha: the arbitrators pronounced an award. But, nevertheless, the award was not the application of abstract legal principles to the case, as is with the British juristic procedure. It was rather an attempt to secure harmony through agreement.

Where a dispute involved the members of two different guilds, the officials of a third guild might be asked to arbitrate.

The principles involved can be exemplified by a discussion which the writer once had with a prominent Chinese businessman in Singapore. A court case, settled in the colonial courts under English law, had recently been reported in the papers. This was a case where an old father and his three daughters-in-law were contending for the estate of the rich son of the father. (All the daughters involved were polygamous widows of the son.) The court had awarded the estate to the father, on a point of law. The businessman was asked what he felt should have been done. He replied, divide it between all four parties; Chinese arbitration would have given, he said, a decision which would have satisfied all parties by dividing the estate between them, rather than letting it all go to one—and particularly to the father, who was not a dependant. The principle of giving the greatest satisfaction to the greatest number is thus exemplified.

Hearing, conciliating, and arbitrating form part of the duties of the leaders of commercial Chinese guilds. But this arbitration or conciliation is also characteristic of the procedure for settling disputes in many peasant communities: those of India, Indonesia, or West Africa for instance. Here again, there is a customary law which goes side by side with the king's law, or the colonial government law. The characteristics of such systems are: firstly, that the arbitrator is himself part of the face-to-face community of which the parties also form members. He is not exalted like the British judge. Furthermore, the disputes in which he acts as conciliator are an integral part of the social living of the community. They are social events and also dramatic entertainments. There is in the community a strong appreciation of rhetoric and its part in the juristic procedure. Furthermore, disputes, as Srinivas points out,[17] are cathartic events in that they provide for the members of the community a renewed insight into the nature of their social relations. Therefore, the arbitrator is expected to have, and does have, a large previous knowledge of the issues involved and of the parties to them. He knows the personal veracity of the parties, and he knows how things came to be as they are. In order to fulfil his role, that is to say, the arbitrator is required to bring to the case a wide general knowledge of it, in contrast to the judicial ignorance of the English judge.

Because of this background knowledge, the arbitrator can himself assess the value of evidence, without the formal procedure which is necessary in a Western court. While in Western law there are numerous procedural rules as to what may be received in evidence, and of how the evidence may be tested, in these simpler societies such rules are not necessary. Thus, proceedings are less formal, less bare, and less narrow.

But also, finally, the arbitrator has got to live with the result of his settlements. Therefore he must, in order to live peaceably, get a settlement which satisfies either both the parties to the dispute or at least the stronger of the two. The danger here is that the cases may be decided upon political grounds, that is to say on terms of the strengths of the different parties, rather than in accordance with principles of justice. Colonial powers, like the British, have tended to suppose that even-handed Justice will, when provided, be recognized by all as preferable.

On the whole, indeed, the development of legal systems has been in the direction of certitude, impartiality and enforcibility, and this involves central administration and enforcement. Close contact between societies of different stages of development—such as comes, for instance, through the immensely important social influence of colonialism—is likely to result in the conquering power's law 'overlaying' the indigenous law-systems, which may take on a contingent, or even suspect, existence.

The laws of any society, like its other social institutions, are subject to change and development. We have seen earlier in this chapter that in some cases the changes are due to development of contradictions, or of new needs, political or economic, within the society itself. This has been the case with English law. But in other cases, and indeed in the modern world many other cases, the change is due to influences coming from without the society. They may be due to conquest, or to the influence of more powerful societies contiguous to the one in question. The effects of such conquests, military or economic, are of great importance, since they have affected the development of many modern law-systems. It will be useful here to give one example, and that one of the most significant: the reception in India of English law.[18, 19]

In India, as in most colonial societies, the Imperial power, when it took over the control of the country, found in it already existing systems of law, of various degrees of sophistication. As in other colonial territories, it was found necessary in practice to apply, so far as it could be ascertained, the native law in certain matters, but to ignore or disallow it in others. Thus in family relations, inheritance, or questions of caste and religion, the British attempted to apply Hindu or Mohammedan law; whereas in criminal cases or in commercial matters those systems were deemed inappropriate, mainly because they clashed with British moral or economic principles. The British had therefore to consider how such systems might be supplemented or supplanted.

Before the coming of the British, Indian law was, compared with English law, of a rudimentary character. There was in the first place the king's own court which moved from place to place on circuit to give justice. Secondly, and in practice more important, there were the village courts which went by a variety of traditional customs. These were arbitral in character, following the procedure described previously. It is of course misleading to speak of them as administering a body of traditional law: in fact there were as many different systems by which cases were tried, as there were village courts. It follows that there were a multitude of systems all of which in India vaguely followed Hindu religio-juristic ideas.

The early British traders when they needed to have recourse

to justice worked through the existing laws as they found them, and so far as they were able to understand them. But on the founding of the Presidency towns of Fort St George and Fort William the courts there applied English law. In the first place this was applied in cases between British traders only. But later, necessarily, it had to cover such Indians as became involved in the litigation. Thus by degrees, but inevitably, British judges had to apply what they understood to be Hindu or Mohammedan law in cases which involved persons of these cultures.

Outside the Presidency towns, and before the British conquest of India, the British operated under licence from the Mogul emperors. They governed through local agencies, and these had to take account of local custom. Consequently the British courts had at that time to apply the personal law of Hindus and Mohammedans in cases where English law would be completely inapplicable. Nevertheless, it was a provision of the English system that in all cases the courts had to apply what were known as the principles of justice, equity, and good conscience. To the eighteenth or nineteenth century English mind, this in fact meant that in all doubtful cases what had to be applied were principles familiarized by English jurisprudence.

By the end of the eighteenth century British political thinkers had come to realize the existence of a venerable native religion, philosophy and culture in India. This realization was owed in part to statesmen such as Warren Hastings, and somewhat later to the efforts of orientalists such as Sir William Jones. The effects of this awakening of understanding were seen, rather oddly, in British ideas as to Indian legal organization.

One consequence of this interest in Indian thought was that the British became aware of the existence of Hindu and Mohammedan systems of jurisprudence or legal philosophy. With the discovery by European scholars of the Dharmasastras, it came to be felt that here was a legal system which could be, or indeed ought to be, used in judicial procedures involving Indians because it was held to be the native and proper law to be applied to them.

Consequently, the judges in the high courts under the British system in India were required to apply, where necessary, native law, and, since they of course had not been trained in it, were to be guided in its interpretation by native learned men, or pundits.

But it was soon pointed out that to do this was inconsistent with English judicial procedure, where the judge is the judge both of law and of fact. It was therefore improper for him to receive instruction in the law from the pundits. There was, in any case, a distrust of the reliability of the pundits, in part perhaps chauvinistic, but arising in part through a misunderstanding of what the pundits supposed themselves to be doing. When they interpreted the law, they were supposed by the British to be doing something which an English lawyer would do when interpreting English statutes. But in fact, and in the view of the pundits themselves, the Sanskrit legal texts were not law in the Western sense, any more than the laws of Deuteronomy are. It would be impossible to derive from them a clear and unambiguous rule or rules, applicable to a specific case of even moderate complexity before the courts. Interpretation was therefore something different from the interpretation of Western statutes, and was less uniform.

However, from the middle of the nineteenth century the British courts in India operated under a different procedure, in which judicial knowledge of Hindu law was assumed. To aid the courts, digests or textbooks of Indian law were prepared, similar to the textbooks on English law which were familiar to the judges: a further instance of the 'overlaying' of the indigenous system.

The effect of this was to make rigid the interpretation of Hindu legal rules. It approximated the Hindu law system to the English one, whereas the essence of simpler law systems is, as we have seen, that they are more flexible than those of developed societies.

It has been held that the values implicit in the procedures employed by the British courts in eighteenth-century and nineteenth-century India were profoundly disruptive of Hindu and Mohammedan society there, partly because of the procedural differences between the two systems, which made for incomprehensibility, and a sort of alienation of the Indians from the courts. Partly however it was due to fundamental ethical and cultural differences. The British view of law was that justice holds all men equal before the law. The Hindu view, on the other hand, was that differences among men in society are central to their legal identity. Village tribunals applying the Hindu view attempted to compromise in issues between the parties from a desire to abate conflict, to promote harmony, and because the need for harmony arises from the lack of enforcibility of their decisions. On the other hand, with the English law, lack of knowledge on the part of the judges of the social background in Indian disputes led to an inability on the judges' part to evaluate the testimony of witnesses. It thus led to the prevalence of false witness, or rather to serious effects arising from lack of veracity on the part of witnesses, and to the judgements and the principles of the judgements being obscure to the parties.

The British brought a court system to India, and this required a written law. It required precedents and principles. Hence arose the codification of the supposed Indian law, in order to bring it on to the same basis as English law. As used such law systems differed from customary local practice.

These differences were early examples of differences and conflicts which have accompanied the introduction of Western law systems into simpler societies. Any question of rightness or wrongness hardly admits of an answer, even were a sociologist prepared to give one. It has been held that the continuance of indigenous traditional law hinders the economic and political development of simpler societies. And it is certain that what appears to be the inevitable political and economic development of societies in Asia, Africa and elsewhere requires fast and fundamental changes in their law. At the same time these should be as far as possible understandable changes, and it seems certain that in the short run the methods by which English law was introduced into India increased confusion and obscurity in the parties about the actions of the courts, and therefore increased the distaste for recourse to law on the part, at least, of the poor.

REFERENCES

1. Miller, W. B., 'Two Concepts of Authority' (*American Anthropologist*, Vol. 57, 1955)
2. Austin, John, *Lectures on Jurisprudence* (1863)

3. Paton, G. W., *Jurisprudence* (2nd Edition 1951), Chapter IV
4. On Natural Law Theories in China, see Needham, J., *Science and Civilisation in China* (1954–), Vol. II
5. See Dworkin, 'Is Law a System of Rules?' (in Summers, *Essays in Legal Philosophy*, 1968, p. 54)
6. Paton, *op. cit.*, p. 68
7. Hart, H. L. A., *The Concept of Law* (1961)
8. Hall, Jerome, *Theft Law and Society* (2nd Edition 1952), Chapters 1 and 2
9. Hoebel, E. A., *The Law of Primitive Man* (1952), Chapter 5
10. Simpson and Field, 'Law and the Social Sciences' (*Virginia Law Review*, Vol. 32, 1946)
11. Gulliver, P. H., *Social Control in an African Society* (1963)
12. Gluckman, Max, *The Judicial Process among the Barotse* (1955)
13. Friedmann, W., *Law in a Changing Society* (1959), Chapter 6
14. Jenks, E., *Law and Politics in the Middle Ages* (1898)
15. Van der Sprenkel, S., *Legal Institutions in Manchu China: a Sociological Analysis* (1966)
16. Jernigan, T. R., *China in Law and Commerce* (1905)
17. Srinivas, M. N., 'The Study of Disputes in an Indian Village' (*Regional Seminar on Techniques of Social Research, UNESCO Research Centre on the Social Implications of Industrialisation in Southern Asia, Calcutta, 1958*)
18. Derrett, D., 'The Administration of Hindu Law by the British' (*Comparative Studies in History and Society*, Vol. 4, 1961–2)
19. Rudolf, L. I. and S. H., 'Barristers and Brahmins in India' (*Comparative Studies in History and Society*, Vol. 8, 1965–6)

4.

Political Institutions

I

Obviously there is a close connection between legal or judicial institutions, on the one hand, and the activities called Politics and Government on the other. Politicians make laws, and bureaucrats administer them. But Law and Politics are not just two names for the same thing. 'When we speak of the political system,' say Almond and Powell, 'we include all the interactions which affect the use of legitimate physical coercion. The political system includes not only governmental institutions, such as legislatures, courts, and administrative agencies, but *all structures in their political aspects*. Among these are traditional structures such as kinship ties and caste groupings.'[1]

'Legitimate physical coercion' implies a right, in some circumstances, of *complete* control over the actions of any person. Such a right could hardly, in any organized society, inhere anywhere save in the sovereign, or the government, or the representative of the community as a whole.

If we accept the view that Politics is that activity which is associated with the use of legitimate physical coercion, it follows that Law is a part of Politics. Nevertheless it is a very special, in some ways distinct, part. The formal characteristics of a law—a juridical rule—may be said to be three: Clarity, Fixity and Finality. By 'Clarity' is meant that the law is enshrined in a unique formula: the text of a statute, for instance; and the meaning of the formula appears from a rational construction of the words which compose it. Naturally this will not apply in preliterate societies; but in those, it is a defining characteristic of a juridical rule that its substance can be enunciated authoritatively, and with general consensus. 'Fixity' implies that the meaning deduced from these words remains the same in different areas of the society, and over time. Naturally this characteristic again is not completely present; even where laws are written or codified, they are subject to some reinterpretation to fit changing circumstances. Nevertheless such changes of meaning are only minor incidents. 'Finality' means that a law, once formulated and passed by a duly constituted authority, cannot be countermanded (save by the passing of a new law by a duly constituted authority) and cannot be defied, save at the risk of destroying either the defier, or the politico-legal system.

These formal characteristics of laws mean that, as well as being norms or directions to citizens or political subjects, they are decisions about trouble-cases—nodal points, as it were, in a series of political activities. They help to summarize the 'state of the game' at a certain point: they are part of the 'score' in political contests. But the game itself is distinct from the score.

This discussion leads us to see that political activity consists in contests for the power to make laws, or, more generally, contests to answer the question, Who governs?—that is, who wields ultimate power (if anyone does), for how long, in what fields, and in what manner? It is the area of conflict, stratagems, bargaining and influence, alliances, agreements and disagreement, and the grounds for them—all in relation to the exercise of legitimate force in a society: the power to use the various engines of government to decide and settle differences. Political 'conflict', we should observe, may have two meanings. In the former, it describes the behaviour of individuals or groups striving against one another for identical ends (for example, two parties striving against one another to attain office). Here the political structure and the roles remain, though the incumbents change. This is better called 'competition'. In the second meaning, it describes the behaviour of individuals or groups striving for different, and incompatible, ends: for instance, of one group attempting to 'preserve' a politico-social system and another attempting to 'smash' it. Here the structure itself is likely to change. Both these programmes are relevant to 'politics' but the distinction between them is important; 'competition' it has been held, tends to make for social stability: the competition between would-be incumbents upholds the legitimacy of the structure. Competition may thus be regarded as an 'equilibrium' concept, conflict as a 'processual' one.

We must now consider another difficulty. Implicit in the foregoing discussions is the idea that political activity has two aspects: one, the operation of legitimate coercion; the other, conflict, bargaining, decisions. In principle, the latter could exist in the absence of the former; and, as we shall see, societies do appear to exist where no relevant inequality is *institutionalized*. In such societies, the range of needs and opportunities for decision making is small, and the societies did not experience significant change in the periods in question. Obviously change is likely to give rise to social conflict; and the existence of social conflict normally gives rise to the exercise, and thus to the institutionalizing, of power.

Most people would think of 'political' activities as essentially concerned with the organization and rule of territories—nation-states, local government areas, colonies, even tribes; but not with the internal relations of families, say, or schools. Is this limitation methodologically fruitful? It has been criticized as being illogically restrictive, and as excluding consideration of situations which are of essentially the same kind, but do not happen to be concerned with territories. Thus, it is said, it fixes attention upon less relevant similarities, and prevents comparison of more essential elements. It has therefore been held that 'political' should be defined rather as referring to certain types of relationship in whatever situation they occur. S. E. Finer, for instance, puts forward the following definition of a 'political predicament'.[2]

> If I insist on red curtains but my wife insists on green—a political predicament exists. If I demand free trade, and others protection—a political predicament exists. If Russia wants a disarmed Germany and the Western Powers wish to rearm her—again, a political predicament exists. In all cases, what *I* wish to do is such as automatically to bind *him* to do something he does not want to do: and what *he* wants to do is such as automatically to bind *me* to do something *I* do not wish to do. The characteristic features of the predicament are identical: in the first place the policies pursued are such as by their nature to eliminate the alternatives (and thus involve their champions' compliance with the victorious policy); and in the second place no unanimity exists as to which policy should be pursued.
>
> (a) A political predicament does not arise unless there are two or more actors. . . .
>
> (b) Nor does a political predicament arise where the policies in question are compatible: for they can be pursued side

by side. An untidy but practical way of solving political predicaments is to modify the original, competing policies until they reach this condition.

(c) Nor, finally, does the political predicament arise unless there are two or more policies; i.e. unless there is a lack of unanimity. . . .

It appears that Finer, while putting forward a view similar in general to the one followed here, wishes to regard 'political' as a quality common to a wide variety of situations, even domestic ones. Such a view has advantages. It facilitates comparative study, helps us to see new aspects of social structure, and breaks down academic ankylosis. It runs, all the same, the danger of diffuseness, resembling the definition of Economics which is sometimes put forward, that 'Economics is the study of choice'. Economics is indeed the study of certain kinds of choice; and one kind of choice has interesting and important resemblances to all other sorts; but in fact economists don't concern themselves with all forms of choice. And political scientists do not regard all forms of conflict situations as their peculiar subject-matter; quarrels of spouses over the colour of curtains, or of schoolchildren over the possession of comics, have not, so far as we know, been the subject of political science monographs. A definition of anything must bring instances together; but also, if it is to be useful, it must *exclude*; what it is to include, and exclude, is a question to be decided by reference to the explanatory fruitfulness of the definition. The definition we have chosen separates an important, and in practice distinctive, kind of behaviour. Political conflicts, according to the definition followed here, are those which centre upon the use of 'legitimate physical coercion'. That is, they are conflicts to control the operation of the judicial and executive systems. Where there is conflict over the policy of a town-council in evicting squatters, in levying a tax or rate, or in refusing to build a local concert-hall, under authority conferred by statute, these are political conflicts: though moral, or economic or aesthetic issues may enter, ultimately the question is of where and how legitimate (legal) force can be brought to bear (through the appropriate executive). Either you force the council, by due process of law, to do *this*; or the council similarly forces you to do *that*; either the People use their powers under electoral laws to throw the council out; or to keep it in. But Smith's dispute with Mrs Smith over the curtains, or Bill's with Johnny over the possession of *Beezer*, are different: economic, moral or aesthetic issues may be involved, but the issue of legitimate force is not (the law may come in to prevent them quarreling; but this rather supports our contention). It may be convenient to use the terms 'Public' and 'Domestic' for these two sorts of conflict or activity: 'Public' where Law and Executive are involved; 'Domestic' where they are not.

Let us compare this argument with Max Weber's definition[3]:

> We wish to understand by politics only the leadership, or the influencing of the leadership, of a political association, hence today, of a state. . . . A state is a human community that (successfully) claims the monopoly of the legitimate use of physical force within a given territory. . . . Hence, 'politics' for us means striving to share power or striving to influence the distribution of power, either among states or among groups within a state.

This definition of Weber's, which sees politics as a characteristic of *states*, had a special and limited purpose: he was defining politics in the context of contemporary European political activity. Nevertheless in his writings generally he chiefly concerns himself either with the political systems of industrial societies or with those others where authority is centralized, or at least oligarchical: where, that is, not only the existence of a territorial 'state' is discernible, but where the state had assumed peculiar importance among other social elements. It is somewhat curious that the anthropologist Radcliffe-Brown[4] appears to take a similar position, and to limit 'political' societies to those which possess *centralized* authority. For one of the questions which a sociologist would like to study is, whether 'interactions affecting the use of legitimate physical coercion' —contests to answer the question, Who governs?—can exist without a 'State', that is a centralized organization. The answer may, perhaps, be No: but he would prefer not to use a definition which excludes the possibility.[5]

This reminds us of the distinction between personality and territoriality as two distinct principles of political allegiance. Sir Henry Maine, the founder of comparative jurisprudence, held that the original bond of common citizenship was one which was based upon kinship, or on the belief that citizens were such because of either a real or a fictitious kinship bond. The transition from the tribe, based upon relations of kinship, to the state, based upon territoriality, was for Maine one of the great revolutionary changes in the development of mankind. And indeed it is an aspect of the contrast between what Parsons calls 'particularism', where a man's rights, obligations and personality are defined in terms of his relations with particular persons or groups (e.g. his kin-group) and 'universalism' where they are determined on impersonal grounds (in this case, the fact of citizenship or nationality).

Politics, we may agree, is about conflict at the 'Public' level: but what are the goals, the purposes, of the kind of conflict behaviour which is specifically 'political'? Let us start by considering the relations of Politics and Government. Easton[6] gives a sort of operational analysis of the process of government in the following terms. It consists in:

1. The expression of interests or demands
2. The making of policy-decisions, laws or orders
3. The putting into effect of these decisions
4. The adjudication of disputes that arise over these decisions
5. The maintenance of public support for the governing body.

It is clear that what Finer calls 'political predicaments' will, or at the least may very probably, arise in all these forms of interaction: the clash of rival interest-groups; the competing claims of different departments or bureaux for public money; the clash between different parties for succession to office: these are examples of the usual types of conflict which go on. They are struggles to attain the following ends: to obtain, to retain and to exercise power; or to limit the exercise of power by others. Power, in the definition propounded by Max Weber 'is the probability that one actor within a social relationship will be in a position to carry out his own will despite resistance'. An alternative definition, in some respects more suitable, is that 'power is the ability to carry through a planned course of operations, in respect of a social system, whether resistance is encountered, or not'. It will be realized that power does not depend wholly upon the use of physical force, but may be achieved, at least initially, through moral force, diplomacy, guile or fraud.

Bringing together the foregoing discussion, the following

definition is put forward. Political activities are those conflicts carried on by and between groups (usually through leaders or representatives) for the attainment, retention, exercise or limitation of 'Public' power. Further, because of the relationship between power in society and law, such conflicts tend to legitimate themselves, either by being carried on with deference to the legal norms, or by the seizure of the lawmaking and administering systems. Political *institutions*, lastly, are the established patterns of political action and relationship—including roles, norms, groups and programmes—found in human societies, each pattern tending to have a certain normative significance in its society.

This suggests a distinction between policy and administration. It is possible to make at least a formal distinction between, on the one hand, policy as a plan, and on the other, administration as the machinery by which it is carried out; and to feel that the contests and bargaining come at the policy-making stage, rather than at that of execution. But of course this is not much more than a formal distinction. Policy and administration transform into each other. What is good policy depends upon the machinery available for giving it effect; and furthermore, administrative decisions upon how a certain policy is implemented may well change that policy itself.

The subject matter of politics used to be the study of formal governmental bodies such as Legislatures and Cabinets. But to understand the nature of 'political' activity in, say, a Western nation, much more than the study of these would be required: political parties, local caucuses, old-school-tie (or other) networks, interest-groups and action-groups are also to be included in the list of political phenomena. In societies other than Western, different groups or roles may be found: chiefs, prophets, caste-groups, and so on. The need has therefore been felt for some general concept which can act as the object of political study: one which can be used comparatively. Almond and Powell[7] propose the concept of the 'political system'. The political system is for them that aspect of the social system—that constellation of roles, norms, activities—which is associated with the use of legitimate physical coercion.

The concept of a system, as used here by Almond and Powell, is derived from the discipline known as General Systems

Theory. It involves the ideas of *inputs*, *conversions* and *outputs*. The first and the last refer to interactions between the system and its environment: inputs would include, for example, the receipt of taxes; but also of demands for specific action (Almond and Powell propose the two terms 'supports' and 'demands'); outputs would include, say, the provision of public services. Conversion processes are internal to the system, and include, for instance, financial administration and control. 'The conversion processes . . . are the ways systems transform inputs into outputs. In the political system this involves the ways in which demands and supports are transformed into authoritative decisions and are implemented.'[8]

Almond and Powell state that the conversion processes of one political system can be compared with those of others according to a sixfold scheme.

> We need to look at the ways in which (1) demands are formulated (interest articulation); (2) demands are combined in the form of alternative courses of action (interest aggregation); (3) authoritative rules are formulated (rule making); (4) these rules are applied and enforced (rule application); (5) these applications of rules are adjudicated in individual cases (rule adjudication) and (6) these various activities are communicated both within the political system, and between the political system and its environment (communication).[9]

These, together with what Almond and Powell call the system's *capabilities*: that is, what function it performs in its environment; and its *system maintenance and adaptation functions*—how it acts to maintain itself, as a going concern, through activities such as education—constitute variables in terms of which comparison between different political systems can be made.

II

In actual comparative studies, the use made by the authors of this somewhat elaborate and interesting scheme is restricted. They point out, it is true, that even the most simple peoples are 'susceptible of being analysed' by the authors' three-level scheme. There are 'conversion functions', 'system maintenance and adaptation functions' and 'capabilities' in societies which lack any specialized political roles, groups or programmes. And indeed it is true that such functions exist in some form or other in any society, since some form of system maintenance, and some form of conversion, are part of the functional prerequisites of any society. No doubt it is useful to point this out; but the analytical use which the concepts can be put to can only be evaluated after more studies directed to these aspects of simpler societies have been made. At present, they are more fruitful in what Duverger calls 'close comparison'—e.g., between societies with complex organizations of government. For wide cross-cultural comparisons, Almond and Powell use criteria similar to those employed in this book: 'structural differentiation' and 'cultural secularization'. By the latter they mean 'the process whereby men become increasingly rational, analytical and empirical in their political action'.

We need not pursue Almond and Powell's discussion any further just now. In fact, the classification most usually proposed by comparative sociologists for political systems is a threefold one. First come *stateless societies*, in which no centre of authority exists, and no established structure of political power. Next, *segmentary societies*, in which political organization comes through the balancing of ties and obligations between counter-balancing groups in the society. Third, we have the type of society in which *centralized government* has emerged.

Political organization is, naturally, related to such things as the nature of the physical environment, population density, and economic organization. An example of a stateless society, one of the politically most rudimentary kind, will illustrate this dependence of political structure upon other social factors. We will take the description of the Australian aborigines which is given by Meggitt.[10]

The aborigines gained their livelihood by hunting for small animals, by fishing, and by gathering of natural products. They had no horticulture or domestication of animals. There was little processing of commodities, nor was there regional specialization. Because of this, there was little barter or trade, and even ceremonial exchange did not play a prominent part in their lives. Because of the inhospitality of their environment they had a need to wander over their territories freely. This in its turn led to a low estimation of material possessions. It led also to extremely low population densities—which varied from three persons per square mile to one person for every thirty to forty square miles.

With this rudimentary material development went, nevertheless, a high degree of complexity of religious ideas and ritual. The people themselves regarded these, rather than material techniques, as being important for ensuring both man's and nature's productiveness. These religious beliefs and ritual were a part of what Meggitt calls the Pan-Australian Totemic philosophy:

> the view of the universe that regarded man, society and nature as interlocking and interacting elements in a larger, functionally integrated totality. According to aboriginal belief, each variable in the system had an eternal, moral commitment to maintain itself unchanged for the benefit of the others, and to contribute to the proper functioning of the system as a whole. . . . Thus it was the duty of every man to ensure, mainly by magico-religious means, that the *status quo* be preserved, an obligation that obviously ruled out most possibilities of cultural innovation.[11]

Every tribe showed a striking range of social groups and categories, each one having some particular function. There were, for example, groups that were based chiefly on local ties —to some shrine, for example; there were also groups which were mainly for the cultivation of obligations of kinship and descent.

The tribe was the maximal unit; but was in fact not an effective organization itself, since the whole of its members very rarely assembled in one place. Tribes generally comprised a number of local groups scattered over the territory. These varied greatly in structure and composition. They might, for example, include patrilineal moieties and patrilineal clans, matrilineal moieties and matrilineal clans, endogamous moieties of grouped generation levels, age grades, and other forms of grouping. Meggitt suggests that the reason for this variety of structure is an historical one: it is probably due to diffusion of cultural elements resulting from movements of people in past times.

The two fundamental variables of kinship and locality together formed the basis of the political system of the aborigines.

The tribe, as was said earlier, was not, because of its diffuseness and the lack of communication between parts of it, an effective political unit. It failed to be so because it was virtually impossible to bring the members of it together to hear and discuss plans and policy. The tribe came together, Meggitt says, usually only at seasonal intervals which could be planned in advance because of their regularity from year to year. So far as there was decision-making, the effective decision-making unit consisted of the local community: more exactly the largest portion of the tribe which exhibited solidarity. Full membership of the local unit depended chiefly upon birth or conception in the appropriate territory, together with some sort of spiritual or residential connection with it. Mere residence, in the case of the aborigines, gave only certain privileges but not rights.

When a situation arose which demanded joint action, the principles of action and of selection of the leaders were, Meggitt says, more or less standardized or rigid. What people ought to do on that occasion was what had been done before, or what the ancestors or the culture-heroes had done on similar occasions in the far past. To follow the precedent of the 'Dream-time' was the correct procedure: the procedure which was socially approved and required. And this clearly meant a high degree of standardization and continuity of group activities over long periods of time.

The aborigines also illustrate another characteristic facet of political activity at this level. There existed in the society interlocking sets of norms which were clearly understood by the people, were publicly accepted by them, and were sanctioned by their religion. These norms covered all sorts of activities which would fall to the lot of the individual in such societies, and therefore they left little need and little room for the decision-making of leaders, chiefs, or headmen.

Consequently a third aspect of political activities in such societies can also be discerned here. Power and authority and leadership were something which did not inhere permanently in any person or any group. They flowed from one person to another in such a manner that no one was above other people except fleetingly and for very specific purposes. The organizing of large-scale activities would be carried out by some individual; but it might be any individual in the group. An expedition for the purposes of revenge, or a betrothal ceremony, might fall to the lot of some person or persons, because of his connection with the victim, or with the bridegroom. But he would be the organizer for that particular occasion, and the fact that he had done so then gave him neither the obligation nor the right to do so on any other occasion. Power was, as it were, mobile, and flowed evenly between different members of the society.

For all these reasons there was no formal apparatus of government, and no lasting authority structure. There were no recognized political leaders; no differentiated *political* roles, or norms, groups or programmes, and the scope of decision-making was very restricted. Such a society is 'political', in our sense, to only a very rudimentary extent.

Environment, sparseness of population, economic organization, and culture thus formed an interlinked social system. The reciprocal action of political and of religious ideas upon one another is something familiar to us from the history of European nations and of Asian kingdoms: it is important to notice that this relationship is found also in very simple societies. We have seen an example of this in the case of the Australian aborigines, where, rather as in medieval Europe, the relationship of man to God is a type of the relationship of man to man. We will also see in another example the way in which beliefs about the supernatural powers of the universe mirror, or are mirrored by, the received ideas about authority-structure. The tribe of American Indians known as the Fox has been discussed by Miller.[12] The cosmology of this society was distinguished by the fact that no hierarchy of priests, wizards, medicine men or the like existed to mediate between the individual and the source of supernatural power. There was a sort of spiritual democracy, in that each individual was directly related to the source of supernatural power, and could enter into direct relations with it by himself. Furthermore, his relation to spirits was not one of inferior to superior, rather it was a relationship characterized by mutual obligations: the spirit was in as great need of the human being as the latter was of the former. It followed from this that power—spiritual or magical power—was available to all universally, and was unlimited in its extent. Each person could become the recipient of power, but this did not mean that he was better placed than anybody else, because every other person in the society was equally able to obtain it. Furthermore the possession of power was temporary and contingent.

This picture of spiritual power relationships, in which contest or competition never resulted in any permanent reordering of relationships, but only in a purely temporary one, was reflected in Fox ideas of social relationships, and in their social structure. In the social world, as in the spiritual world, each person had direct access to the source of social norms. Each person had access directly to the body of 'procedural rules' (as Miller calls them) which governed the working of the Fox society. Each individual therefore felt responsible for knowing and acting in accordance with the regulations of his society. This of course meant that these rules were basically simple: the correct procedure to follow today was the procedure which had been followed last year and the years before. The simplicity, permanence and standardization made possible an internalization of rules of such a character that the individuals or the society collectively could trust themselves to carry out the required procedures of the society so as to cope with the repetitive demands with which it was confronted. Consequently there was an almost entire absence of any specific centres of authority. The village had a village chief, but his functions did not involve any directive authority. He required to be a mild person, without any aptitude for initiating behaviour. He was rather a symbol of peaceful and harmonious relations within the village and of non-aggressive behaviour. He was expected to act as an arbiter and a peacemaker in cases of dissension, but this was as far as his authority extended. The Fox sometimes called him 'the kindly chief'.

The decision-making agency, where concerted action was required, was the village council. But nothing was decided upon there unless every member agreed on the decision, and this meant a virtually complete democracy, since everyone was welcome to attend and take part in the sessions of the council. The principle seems to have been that no decision should be taken which regarded action if it were made by any group which was smaller than the whole village or society.

In certain cases leadership was required. A war expedition was naturally one of these cases. Even here, however, the war-leader had little real decision-making power. He was authorized to size up the situation, and to suggest the best action. Nevertheless, no one was obliged to abide by his suggestions if he did not wish to do so. Furthermore, the war-chief only held his position during the expedition itself; and moreover, at the termination of this expedition, the war-chief who had held this position for a few days was regarded as being so spiritually or magically dangerous that he was not allowed to re-enter the village until he had undergone a ceremony to revoke his temporary authority. Clearly the Fox society was a small one; the range of its likely activities was also small; and the rate of social change was slow. These attributes made it possible, and indeed desirable, that decision-making should be widely diffused. It was possible for each individual in the collectivity to control the plan of action which governed its conduct, because this plan was one well known to all, and to which habitual responses were adequate. This society, as Miller reports it, again can hardly be called a 'political' one: partly because 'legitimate physical coercion' apparently played an insignificant part, and because power here is not, so to say, a scarce good, to be fought for, but also for another reason, which we perceive here: politics depends on change.

The Fox society has exemplified something which was previously seen in aboriginal society: that is, a repetitive stability in the social structure. It was not an example of another characteristic which the former society also exemplified, and which is found as a principle of political organization in many simpler societies, that is the balancing of complementary obligations, or 'interlocking sets of norms'. An instance of such a group is the Korofeigu, living on the southern end of the Bena Bena valley, in New Guinea.[13] The Korofeigu are an agricultural people, who also raise livestock, particularly pigs. They are divided into four exogamous groups, which, according to their own account, are patrilineal as well as local. The ties which make for solidarity within such a group are, in the first place, a 'brother-sister' tie, which is established between a bride (who is brought in from another group) and a male member of the group to which her husband belongs. They include, secondly, ties between age-mates. Thirdly, there is a pattern of communal obligations and cooperation in relation to gardening. And fourthly, there is the tie through the custom of letting someone else raise your pigs on your behalf. It will be seen that these crosscut one another, that is to say each person is involved in obligations or loyalties towards different sections in respect of each different tie.

The fifth tie is, in the ideology of the Korofeigu themselves, the tie of kinship. Each territorial group is supposed to be composed of a number of patrilineal lineages. But in fact, according to Langness, who has studied this society, about one half of the total persons there are not agnatically related, that is related through males, at all. Furthermore, there is no difference in status between those who are agnates, and those who are not. The rights which are conferred on a person by reason of his residence in the territory equal those which are conferred by birth. The ownership of land is based, not on descent principles, but on the question of whether a person is tilling the land. There is in fact plenty of land, and therefore no land-hunger. So far from kinship determining residence, residence in the territory determines whether a person shall be regarded (fictionally if necessary) as a kin member. 'People do not necessarily reside where they do because they are kinsmen; rather they become kinsmen because they reside there.'

The reason for this difference between ideology and fact seems to have been that the pattern of warfare here required much manpower. The warfare of the Korofeigu and their neighbours, says Langness, aimed at complete and total destruction of the enemy, and therefore the best way by which a group could survive was to take into it as large a number of persons as it could.

The aspect of political activity to which we have directed attention here is Allegiance—the norms and programmes designed to minimize public conflict within the group, and to promote loyalty, in order to withstand the threat of 'change' as a consequence of external hostilities. What we have to note here is that, although descent or kinship notionally plays an important part in political allegiance or organization, it may to some extent be a fictional device to demonstrate an allegiance which is in fact secured by other means. In this, and apparently other New Guinea societies, there is a considerable degree of optation in the descent system. That is to say, a person can in a measure choose the descent or lineage to which he shall belong. In this it would appear that New Guinea societies differ from others such as African societies, where little or no optation in the descent system is to be found.

The important fact of the existence of networks of social ties which are based upon different principles, and which therefore make it difficult or impossible for an individual to take action of a hostile character against another member of his society can be illustrated by one more instance. This is of the Tonga, described by Colson.[14]

The Tonga exhibit the following bases for social ties. In the first place, they are divided into groups of matrilineal related kin called Mukowa. The Mukowa constitutes a group in the sense of being a collection of people with habitual contact. Secondly, the Tonga are divided into fourteen matrilineal clans. These clans do not form units. All members of the same Mukowa are members of the same matrilineal clan, but the converse does not hold. Each clan is an exogamous body, and the Mukowa is therefore exogamous too. A person can only make offerings to the spirit of his or her own Mukowa. Therefore, since the society is matrilineal, a husband cannot do so to the spirit who looks after his own house and his children. Fourthly, a tie is formed through the arrangements relating to cattle. A man cannot marry using his sister's cattle as bride wealth. A man must not drink milk from the cattle of his sister's marriage. Rules like these involve the requirement that everybody must have a wide range of social links with people who are more distantly related to him than his own close kin. In the fifth place, the joking relationships form another kind of bond. Joking relationships between designated people emphasize amongst other functions the fundamental moral values of the community. The person with whom one has joking relationships is a stranger in the sense that he is outside the particular kind of relationships involved in those specific situations. He is not a member of the close kin, and therefore is not involved in the hostilities or problems with which the close kin involves any individual.

Lastly, there exist cult areas—'land-shrines'—in other words localities to which each individual has his respective ritual ties.

There is therefore a complex pattern of social ties involving a given individual with a variety of different groups. The effect of these conflicting obligations to different groups is that the individual Tongan will find it difficult permanently to mobilize against any other individual or group within the society. Thus, Tonga society is integrated in a complex fashion within itself. Such an integration means that a variety of persons and groups each have certain restricted powers of control over the behaviour of the individual, because of the roles which he is obliged to play in a whole series of relationships. To seek, in one capacity, to act against a particular group would almost certainly involve conflict with other ties which in some way bind the person to that group against which he purported to act. This tangle of obligations leads to attempts to try to find a settlement in terms of some moral precepts, and validated by spiritual powers. In Tonga-land it may be the husband's father's spirit, which is a member of neither spouse's Mukowa, who oversees their house. Mystical power is sometimes strongest where there is least secular power. 'In these powers which lack governmental apparatus—and in many who have this—the role of ritual and religion, and of mystical beliefs, including those in witchcraft, emerges as enforcing respect for social ties which have no force to support them.'[15]

What are known as segmented societies also show a system of checks and balances. Perhaps the most well-known example of this is the Nuer, a Nilotic people whose study by Evans-Pritchard is one of the classics of anthropology.[15a] The main point relevant to the present argument is that the Nuer show a complex pattern of contraposed segments, as indicated in the diagram.

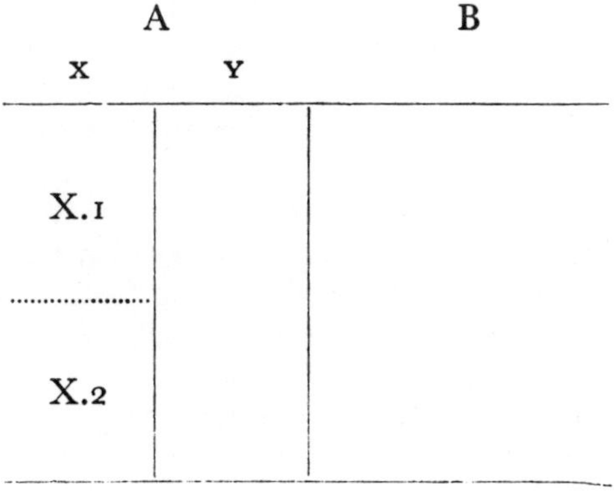

In the first place, the whole people is divided into two segments, A and B. Each of these is again dichotomized, A being divided into X and Y. Any given individual regards himself as having loyalties to Section A in contrast to Section B, but to sub-section X of Section A in contrast to sub-section Y. Both Section X and Section Y are again sub-divided into 1 and 2, so that the same individual will regard himself as being a member of X.1, when contrasted with X.2. This again makes for a balancing of loyalties. The hostility which an individual member of X.1 feels for a member of X.2, is balanced by a common allegiance with him to X as against Y, and hostility which either of them feels as members of X for individuals in Y will again be counterbalanced by the common loyalty which both of them have to A as against B. This balancing is also supported by other kinds of interlocking networks. Thus in the Nuer society there appears to be no need for, and at least there is no, imperative authority. Authority or leadership is of a resticted kind consisting largely of a duty, inhering in the functionary called the Leopardskin Chief, to advise and to make peace.

We next come on to the kind of political system which has been called authoritative chieftainship, where power or authority inhere in a single source, normally a single ruler, who may or may not be assisted by some kind of staff of varying degrees of complexity.

Centralized chieftainships, or monarchies, seem to have emerged in a variety of ways, of which military conquest is one, but only one. Sometimes they appear to have originated in the growth in numbers or wealth of some distinct social stratum, whose leaders have thus been able to acquire political power. An example from Africa is the Gusii of Kenya, who are composed of seven tribes, each inheriting its own part of the Gusii territory. Each tribe is divided into a number of ancestral clans, of which one or two in each tribe are regarded as the founding clans, the first arrivals. The Getutu tribe's founding clan was called the Nyakundi. Since the Getutu territory was safer from raiders than that of other tribes', refugees were apt to pour in to it from the others, and to become clients of the leading Nyakundi men, giving them political loyalty in return for protection. If the refugees were women they became wives of their protectors—who did not have to pay cattle for them, and thus were spared much of the expense of polygamy. Both these factors made for a great increase in the population, and in the political strength, of the Nyakundi clan. They therefore put power behind the traditional legitimate authority of the clan. Traditionally the only elders with the right to judge cases were Nyakundi elders. What we obviously see here is a causal interconnection between prestige and power.

In the foregoing example emerge a type of role (the patron or protector) and a type of political unit (the leader-followers band, providing reciprocal benefits) which have both been of great importance in the generation of political change. They have certainly been important originating factors in centralized chiefdoms or monarchies. Mair[16] cites the Mandari chiefs of the Nile Valley as an African example. Another is afforded by the Germanic tribes described by Tacitus (the ancestors of the Anglo-Saxon invaders of England). These must be seen as one origin of the feudal order of medieval Europe.

Marc Bloch[17] writes:

> Although in the ancient Germanic societies the affairs of the kindred group and the people offered sufficient scope for normal energies, they had never been able to satisfy the spirit of adventure and ambition. The chiefs, especially the young chiefs, surrounded themselves with companions . . . these companions they led in battle and on plundering expeditions, and in the intervals of rest gave them hospitality in their great wooden 'halls' where the atmosphere was congenial for long drinking-bouts. The little band was the mainstay of its captain in wars and vendettas; it supported his authority in the deliberations of the free men; and the generous gifts—of food and drink, of slaves, of gold rings—which he lavished upon these followers was [*sic*] an indispensable element in his prestige. Such, as Tacitus depicts it, is the companionage (comitatus) in first-century Germania; such it is still, several centuries later, as it appears in the poem of Beowulf and (with some inevitable variants) in the old Scandinavian sagas.

Such, too (again with inevitable variants) is it with the Chinese gangs of nineteenth-century Malaya,[18] or the twentieth-century gangs of 'Cornerville', U.S.A.[19] The gang is an archetypal political unit, deriving its dynamic force from *free* allegiance, *personal* loyalty and *reciprocal* benefits—these also, of course, tend to give it impermanence. The chief characteristics of the Germanic and Saxon bands are well described by Dorothy Whitelock, in her book on early Anglo-Saxon society in Britain.[20]

These were, of course, not kin-groups. Their characteristics were, firstly, that they were voluntarily joined, in the sense that a man's birth or status did not automatically prescribe the group which he joined (no doubt he was compelled by the desire for survival in such a world); secondly, that the bond was a personal one between each follower and his chief. Thirdly, the group was for mutual protection; and fourthly, the need for it arose because of the breakdown of hitherto existing political machinery. The political structure of the Roman Empire had broken down; and the earlier kin-groups were insufficient to provide protection in those times. The group was, in fact, 'a hierarchy of personal relations, based upon a system of mutual obligations'—words used by W. F. Whyte to describe the street-corner gangs of early twentieth-century America.[21]

The relationship between chief and follower was regarded as a mutual pact, in that non-fulfilment by the chief absolved the followers from their loyalty. But this apart, the follower was deemed obliged to defend his lord with his life. He had also the obligation to be loyal to his comrades. The followers in such bands entered voluntarily the service of the chief, taking a pledge to be loyal to him while he was loyal to them. Their job was to serve him with their swords; his was to lead them, successfully, and to reward them suitably with spoil, including domains.

Where the chief's own territory is small it can be governed effectively from one centre. But above a certain size, either in area or population, it becomes too large for effective oversight, including such activities as the collection of taxes and the maintenance of order. In such a case some sort of local delegation of authority is generally found; and in the feudal system of the European Middle Ages delegation took the form of setting up reciprocal ties: the grant of domains to his followers, effectively in perpetuity, in return for a vow of fealty. The vassal swore to maintain his lord, the lord in his turn to protect his vassal. But often, since at least the greater vassals were effectively sovereign within their own territories, in most feudal states (England was an exception) the vassal was often the equal of his sovereign. While this system was in its details peculiar to Europe, the general arrangement of a series of hierarchical levels of chiefs, superior chiefs and ruler is found in many states. The relation of ruler, intermediate chiefs and people frequently gave rise to difficulties and is an interesting subject of study to political scientists. One example, which has been described by Gullick,[22] was that of the Malay states in the nineteenth century, before the irruption of British power. These states were greatly influenced by Hindu ideas of kingship. The Sultan or Rajah, that is the head of each state, was appointed to his position through a complex principle of inheritance. The right of accession to the throne was not automatically that of the eldest son of the late ruler, but was held within a narrow range of royal relatives. Accession was in addition effectively subject to the approval of the district chiefs of the state. But these chiefs themselves were hereditary rulers over their own domains; that is to say, they were not dependent upon the will of the sovereign for their own power. Furthermore, within their own districts, each chief wielded more effective power than did the sultan. Indeed the latter was to a certain extent a figurehead, or dependent upon the goodwill of the chiefs, or upon playing one group of chiefs off against another, for his own hold upon power.

But in their turn the chiefs were ultimately dependent upon the goodwill of their own peasant subjects. This was, in part, due to the natural characteristics of the Malay land. Population was small in relation to territory. This meant that the Malay peasant was essentially mobile. In other words, if the chief's exactions in the way of taxes and oppressions were too onerous, the answer always available to the peasant was to move to another district. If he did so in any considerable numbers, the population in the chief's district, and consequently the number of followers which he could draw upon for his own power and status, would decline, and this was an effective ultimate check upon oppression. The sanction against injustice at court was loss of manpower. Population was also the source of a Malay chief's wealth, for it meant greater revenue. Most chiefs derived their revenue from the collection of taxes upon goods passing certain tax barriers, or tax points, which they set up usually near the mouths of rivers in their domains, since rivers were the only efficient means of transport in nineteenth-century Malaya. The income both of a chief and of the sultan was mainly derived from taxation of exports and imports: although secondarily, during the nineteenth century in particular, it was also derived from shares in the financing of tin mines. Both of these however depended upon the control of population.

The Malay chiefs controlled the population in order to control the economy; and controlled the economy because they required the surplus over and above producers' subsistence needs to sustain not only themselves and their retainers, but also the armed following which was the basis of their power. Economic power was, for them, the means to political and military power, which was their ultimate goal.

In the Malay states we can see both centrifugal and centripetal forces working together. The diffusion of power into the districts robbed the sultan himself of effective control. It dispersed power into the districts amongst chiefs who frequently were at loggerheads with one another. Nevertheless, chiefs needed to maintain the sultanate, in order to buttress their own status. Their status, in the cultural norms of the Malay world, was derived largely from the existence of the sultan. This was in fact, as Gullick tells us, symbolized by the periodical gatherings of the chiefs at the sultan's court to do homage to him. The very fact of doing homage to the sultan, the representative of God, was an enhancement of the chief's own status. The chiefs were driven by their own need of acknowledged status to preserve the sultanate, and to maintain a degree of peace and order in the state at least sufficient to permit occasional gatherings at the royal court.

The centrifugal tendency was thus balanced by a mutual dependence of status between sultan and chiefs. A degree of unity was also attained through the religious and cultural ideologies of the Malay people. They were united not only by loyalty to their sultan but also by the feeling of a cultural unity through being a part of the Muslim world. As Gullick says, 'the sense of being all Muslims together played its part in uniting people otherwise divided by many cultural differences'.

While any one village might be culturally homogeneous, neighbouring villages might be very different—there might be villages of people from Java, Sumatra, Borneo, Celebes, and other localities in the Malay world. They needed a strong tie, such as Islam provided. We see here another instance of the role of religion and of ritual as providing a *supra-mundane* unity for peoples otherwise divided by ethnic as well as by political barriers.

Clearly then struggles between the sections and the whole are one of the problems which arise in the development of authoritative chieftainship. Another locus of conflict is the question of succession. For instance, under the succession law of most African tribes, as well as of Malay, no one individual was clearly designated as heir to the throne. Hence at any time there are likely to be several claimants to the throne. Often the rules of succession contributed to produce civil war.

A third source of conflict is the rudimentary character of social stratification in the less technologically developed kingdoms of this kind. The limitations of the economy prevented the growth of horizontal stratification, and the cutting off of a noble class from the ordinary people. This made for instability of power. It is clear that in a political study, we need to know something about the economic basis of chiefly or kingly power.

Two structural principles seem to emerge from the examples so far discussed.

Firstly, in the simplest societies, there is the absence of any permanent or enduring locus of power, which 'flows' from one person to another, according to the immediate situation.

Secondly, in segmentary societies and those represented by pre-colonial Malaya, there is one form or another of balancing of powers and obligations.

Where power, instead of being widely diffused through society, becomes focused in a few sources, or in one only, the question of its legitimacy becomes important. In many instances of authoritative chieftainship (or kingship) the ruler is supposed either to be divine, or at least to have some special relationship to the gods, so that he is an intermediary between them and his people.

An interesting example is the Lovedu, a Bantu tribe inhabiting the Transvaal.[23] Their ruler is always a woman, who is believed divine, with magical powers to control the rain. Thus she possesses an infallible means of bringing prosperity upon her own people, and of punishing its enemies. She has a special relation not only to her people, but to nature.

> The basis of the queen's control over nature is her divinity. So bound up is she with nature that her very emotions affect the rain. The complex of royal institutions includes the conceptions that she must be without physical imperfections, not susceptible to the ills that befall ordinary men; that she cannot die a natural death but departs only by her own volition; that succession to the throne is uncertain since the choice of a ruler must in the last resort be made by the spirits of the tribe; that though she may not have a husband, lest political control become concentrated in him, yet she must bear the heir by a secret consort (a royal classificatory brother) specially chosen to maintain untarnished the purity of the royal blood; that she ensures the regularity of nature and the changing of the seasons; and, more particularly, that her death dislocates the rhythm of nature, bringing drought and famine, the abrogation of law and order.[24]

She thus stands in a special relation to the Order of Nature. But she also stands in a special relation to the Order of Lovedu society, since she is linked in a 'marriage'-relationship with each of the districts into which the Lovedu realm is divided. The heads of districts all send 'wives' to the queen, who thereby becomes son-in-law to these heads, and, by allocating the same wives to other district heads and to royal relatives, she becomes parent-in-law to the latter.

> The use of the mechanism of the social system to align groups into reciprocal relations forges a great network of ties radiating from the queen to all strategic points in the society. . . . Payments of tributes and services to the queen are thus looked upon as the fulfilment of kinship obligations, in return for which the queen not only gives land and protection from enemies, but also transforms the clouds into rain and so frees men from fear and uncertainty. Thus the kinship ties that bind subjects to the rain-queen are interlocked with the values and institutions supporting her divinity.[5]

Lovedu society is thus an outstanding example of the way in which, in many societies, and to various degrees, political power is legitimated by association with the deeply assimilated norms of kinship and of religion. To the question of legitimacy we return shortly.

In all these examples of societies we find a variety, and sometimes a wide and complex variety, of social groupings. There is, however, among them little functional differentiation. We may perhaps conclude that in the simplest forms of society, such as the Australian aborigines, the facts of environment and of population sparsity, and the repetitive nature of the social organization, all go to diminish the probability of political conflicts, as defined above, and therefore the need for specifically political roles, groups and programmes. Neither in these nor in segmentary societies is power located in any particular role or group, nor is there any specific programme of domination. Indeed the function of these kinds of social structure appears to be to diffuse both power and its correlative, obligation, as widely as possible.

Where we come to the beginnings of centralized rule, as in Malaya, there is a certain crystallization of power-roles and groups: chief or king, court, vassals and so forth. As Firth[26] shows, in relation to Tikopia, there may be a clear differentiation of the roles of chief and what may be called lieutenant. The latter, here and elsewhere, may have essential political functions, which are not merely of supporting, but rather of counter-balancing, the chief. In Tikopia, the authority of the chief is in theory paramount; but their social system contains certain institutionalized devices for limiting it. Thus among the functions of the 'lieutenant' (called *maru*) may be formally to convey to the luckless subject a sentence of death which the chief has pronounced on him; but in doing so he may, if public opinion seems to support this, also tell the man to cut off into the bush and stay there until the chief's anger has died down. In this and other ways, the *maru* may in fact support the office of chiefship, by mitigating any excessive action on the part of an incumbent. The role of lieutenant as 'lightning-conductor' is an important part of political activity; and in this respect, at least, the case of Tikopia appears to resemble more politically sophisticated societies. But, in general, the differentiation of the secularly political from the norms and values of kinship or religion is, at this level, still incomplete.

III

Consideration of the political aspects of more complex social structures ('states', for instance) involves taking account of other entities which, although they are relevant in some degree to the study of simpler societies, here emerge into prominence. These are chiefly three: Organization; Communication; and what Almond and Powell call the 'political infra-structure', that is, the complex of more or less informal groups and programmes such as parties, interest-groups, caucuses, lobbying and direct action, upon which the formal structure of government now rests. These three entities are of course interdependent.

The characteristic structure of modern society is the 'formal (complex) organization'. It is found as a structural character of, for instance, civil services, business firms, armies and lunatic asylums, which all, in modern society, necessarily become larger and more important. The essential nature of a formal organization is that it is a system of social relationships, roles and programmes which is *planned for a defined objective*. It is, in fact, in Toennies' word[27] a *Gesellschaft*. A more elaborate, or more inclusive, description is given by Strother,[28] who says that—

1. Organizations are groups of two or more people,
2. In some kind of cooperative relationship to one another.
3. This cooperation implies some kind of collective goal(s) or output(s).
4. The groups exhibit some kind of differentiation of function among members and
5. Maintain some kind of more or less stable and explicit hierarchical structure.
6. Although not emphasized in the classical theories, which tend to treat organizations as closed systems, it would seem essential to recognize that organizations exist in a total field; references to clientele, milieu, inputs, equilibrium and legitimation indicate recognition of this fact.

The study of organizations in Sociology, lately quickened by fecundation from Biology and Engineering, received its chief theoretical impetus from Max Weber's celebrated discussion of legitimate power.[29] Power cannot rest merely on force or the present threat of force; it requires also that those subject to it shall feel some kind of a duty to obey. The bases upon which this sense of duty rests were analysed by Weber, who distinguished three typical grounds: firstly, traditional: 'the belief in the sacredness of the social order and its prerogatives as existing of yore'. Secondly, charismatic: 'the affectual and personal devotion of the follower to the lord and his gifts of grace'; and lastly, legal authority, which 'rests on enactment. . . . The basic idea is that laws can be enacted and changed at pleasure by formally correct procedure.' Weber believed that legal authority was most completely typified in the complex organization known as a bureaucracy. The 'ideal type' of bureaucracy, as described by Weber, is a system planned so as to achieve impersonal efficiency. It is planned to eliminate, as far as possible, human failings, either moral or intellectual. Thus, in the first place, the official is to have no personal pecuniary interest in the cases upon which he works. Appointment and promotion are according to an impersonal system, without room for favouritism. The official's job is his sole, or at least his primary, occupation; thus he should have no conflicting obligations. Secondly, there is a clearly-defined hierarchy of offices, each one having a clearly-defined sphere of competence. Weber also stated that 'legal authority' involved an organization governed by impersonal, written rules and instructions; and that all administrative acts are formulated and recorded in writing: thus there is a permanent 'office' to serve as a basis for systematic continuity of action.

Weber regarded the bureaucratic form as the most technically efficient, and thus, in modern society, the indispensable form of administration—though he apparently regarded bureaucrats themselves as beings even worse than university professors.[30] Being technically efficient, it was rational. But Weber fully recognized a characteristic of modern society which we may call the infection of rational procedure by irrationality. This topic forms an important part of his discussion of the sociology of modern music; it is to be found also in his work on the relations between religion and capitalism. And he was fully aware of the importance of both the traditional and of the charismatic grounds of legitimacy in the modern world.

The gist of more recent work on formal organizations is that, while the formal patterns of authority therein certainly exist and are important, they do not fully describe the pressures for and against compliance which are to be found. Chester Barnard[31] and H. A. Simon,[32] for instance, place an emphasis on the subordinate's exercise of choice in obedience: they use the concepts of a 'zone of indifference' or 'zone of acceptance', beyond which disobedience will follow any attempt on the part of the superior to enforce authority. Simon also points out that the pressures which support authority may be very various: they may include the disapprobation shown for a shirker by his fellow-subordinates, or the unwillingness of most people to take initiatives. Blau, on the other hand, in *The Dynamics of Bureaucracy*,[33] shows that normally a range of quite deliberate variation is introduced by a subordinate into the way in which he carries out a general instruction; these variations being made in order to give him the sense of being an autonomous individual.

One implication of the foregoing discussion is that there appear to exist two concepts of bureaucracy: one, the Weberian concept of a technically efficient, rational system; the other, the concept of a system in the long run inefficient and dysfunctional because of its formalistic rigidity.

But a diachronic comparative study would certainly show a great difference in the objectives for which organizations (including governmental ones) are set up. Comparing those of today with those of, say, three-quarters of a century back, we may express the difference (perhaps over-succinctly) by saying that entrepreneurship has become an organizational goal. Not only is this because of the greater relative importance of the large industrial organization, compelled to innovate; it is also, of course, because social and industrial *development* is a major objective of governments. Basically, the work of an entrepreneur is to solve the novel logistical problems that emerge as a result of technological innovations. But this is essentially the theme of the new subject of Management Science, which, for the older entrepreneur's insights, hunches, etc., substitutes Operational Research and similar techniques which are in principle available to all. While this means that entrepreneurship can (and must) be carried out by an organization, it also means that the organizational form itself must take on much greater flexibility.

Cross-cultural comparison, however, raises other problems about bureaucracy, to which it is not yet possible to provide very full answers. These chiefly concern the conflicts between different bases of legitimate power, or of social cohesion, in different societies or cultures.

Bureaucracies, of sorts, were characteristic of societies other than Western, as the work of Eisenstadt[34] shows. But they differed in important ways from the 'type' of Western bureaucracy. The Ottoman civil service was composed of slaves; and while in some ways this might be supposed ideal, it undeniably differed from the West, notably in that certain moral problems could scarcely have arisen in it, which certainly arise in the 'Western' form.

The problem may be approached in the following manner. One of the undoubted 'functional pre-requisites' of society is that social activity shall be institutionalized: that is, that patterns of action which are customary and to some extent normative shall be established, or perhaps rather, shall emerge. This, *inter alia* means the requirement that new or inchoate means, or new objectives, of political expression shall at some point be able to be put through established channels of communication or action. This would appear to be a minimum requirement of social order: the existence of clear and established 'corporate habits'. The existence, in Western societies, of established forms of party-system, legislature, executive, and so on, is an instance.

The normative character which these have in the West has led to their being established in the 'developing' countries. But this deliberate establishment of forms is done sometimes in the absence of the attitudes and ethos which in their countries of origin support them: no doubt in the hope that the forms, when established, will generate the ethos. This may happen in the long run, but in the meantime the forms often suffer a kind of spirit-possession by values alien to them. In other words, certain sorts of social conflict arise between the 'universalistic' norms characteristic of these, and the more 'particularistic' traditional norms.

Talcott Parsons reminds us that universalistic norms are far from being fully accepted (as norms, apart from the question of practice) in 'modern' societies. *Bon père de famille est capable de tout.* But at least these societies show some willingness to accept the proposition that, by and large, nepotism and corruption are anti-social. Bayley[35] points out that 'corruption', as used here, is a Western concept. In other societies, it may imply conformity to a pattern of behaviour which one's peers, family and friends strongly support and applaud because it normally indicates a primary loyalty to one's kin group. Bayley, asserting that bribery and corruption appear to pervade the entire political structures of developing nations, makes a point that, along with its obvious socially-harmful consequences, it may have, especially in under-developed societies, effects which are to some extent beneficial. Nepotism in government appointments, helping to swell the ranks of the civil service, acts as a substitute for government schemes to provide employment, and thus reduce the disruptive possibilities of large armies of urban unemployed. It helps to tie people to the political system. Nepotism and corruption help to make the bureaucratic system more comprehensible and 'human' by linking it with familiar processes. And bribery is a sort of measure to raise the earnings of civil servants; thus it may help to promote the entry of relatively able personnel.

'Bureaucracy,' says Wolpert, 'by its nature cannot act stably as an independent source of authority. Its canons are efficiency and regularity, which, taken by themselves, do not afford the necessary kind of cement for social solidarity. No modern social order can operate without bureaucracy, but, contrariwise, no social order operates by bureaucracy alone. . . . Only in cases where power and authority are inextricably intertwined can authority have the chance of enduring.'

Political order, where its existence in a society can be discerned, appears to reside either in a balanced reciprocity of perceived interests, or else in authority legitimated in some manner. Authority, whose function 'has been to minimize the scope and range of fear as a determinant of social relationships',[36] has been seen to be legitimated partly by its association with the values of kinship and of religion. These, in modern societies, tend to become weaker. It may be suggested that their place is being taken by the ideology of individual moral self-determination.

If so, this would be something antithetical to bureaucracy, which, like God, fights for the big battalions. We may see here a possible cause of the existence of so-called 'political infra-structures'.

This term involves a spatial metaphor which must be received with caution. It is not necessarily *infra* in the sense of subterranean, inferior, or even grass-roots. Nor is it necessarily *infra* in the sense of supportive. Such a meaning would assume that political activity is generated diffusely, which is by no means obvious: it may often be fostered centrally. The infra-structure may exist as a reaction against the formal institutions. The term is applied to the more informal (but not necessarily less institutionalized), political activities: interest-groups, brokerage and patronage, factions, the underground, and direct action.

It seems clear that all of these are in some sense anti-bureaucratic. Patrons and middlemen, as Boissevin[37] points out, on the basis of his research in Sicily, flourish where the formal civil service channels for getting things done are too remote from the ordinary man. In such societies, it is a necessity of life for a poor man to attach himself to someone more influential, in a patron-client relation; similarly, the second will establish links with someone even more powerful; thus a chain, or network, is set up, bypassing, and more effective than, the formal channels. The relation is symbiotic: the client needs his patron, but the patron needs his clients and middlemen in order to sustain his own power. For this reason, and also because the relation is a *personal* one, it reinforces the sense of self-determination more than does the bureaucratic machinery of the state, which at these levels, in such societies governs only by force.

Interest-groups are a phenomenon of great importance for the sociology of present-day politics. In the first place, they are obviously specialized groups. They are deliberate means of bringing together, out of a fragmented urban-industrial society, categories of people who, typically, have only *that* interest in common among them. Thus they are, at the same time, ways of mitigating the fragmentariness of urban-industrial life, and the powerlessness of the individual as against powerful corporations. Thus one of the earliest, and still one of the most important, kinds of interest-group, the trade-union, was a natural reaction to the rise of modern industry.

The interest-group, perhaps more than any other political

phenomenon, is now regarded as the sign of democratic development. And no doubt it is particularly associated with societies having a stable democratic tradition, where relatively informal organizations are capable of a high degree of permanence, and of negotiating with government departments on a relatively equal footing. On the principle that to set up the form is to generate the spirit, they have sometimes been deliberately established as a means to democratic dialogue (as has been seen in the establishment by Imperial powers of workers' trade unions in their colonies). But in modern society, a group representing any continuing and important interest must, if it is to be effective, itself become permanent, expert, and, very probably, large. (It has been pointed out that the British trade unions would benefit by higher-powered, and better paid, executives.) Interest-groups, like other organs of mass-democracy, demand specialists, and therefore themselves tend to become bureaucratic: the paradox of Michels.

The counter to this has been taken, in the contemporary world, to be direct action (not that direct action is peculiar to the contemporary world, by any means). Almond and Verba, indeed[38] call the machinery of this phenomenon 'anomic interest-groups'. Anomic is hardly the correct term, which might rather be 'amorphic', since the groups rather appear to have a deliberately fluid structure, than to lack principles.

The sociological significance of direct action lies first in the obvious fact that it is the form of political activity in which those taking part have the strongest feeling of immediate, and effective, participation; the gap between means and ends there seems smallest. Thus it is a reaction not only against the anonymity, but also against what is held to be the deviousness of normal politics, and what is held to be its confounding of means and ends. This may be baseless: no doubt mass action is as carefully planned and led as are 'normal' political activities; but for the ordinary participant, it is today virtually the only means of directly and effectively expressing, in the political field, what he feels to be his convictions and his personality. In direct action, politics becomes not only a mass-activity but an expressive activity.

The attention devoted in recent years to the political infra-structure of modern societies has led, by a further turn of the wheel, to a more detailed search for the existence and functions of similar processes in simpler and in 'developing' societies. Properly speaking, such an interest is not new at all: Evans-Pritchard's study of the Nuer appeared in 1940, and Firth's consideration of the complex relations of Authority and Public Opinion in Tikopia was first published in 1949[26]. But what might be called the behavioral study of political systems in modern societies (work like that of Easton or Almond) has at least been followed by more attempts to analyse the specifically political functions of programmes and groups in simpler societies: decision-making processes; conflict-resolution, élites, communication, and so on.[39]

One result of comparative studies, in the political field as in others, is to demonstrate the range of variation which certain programmes, groups, roles and organizations may undergo in their relations with different social environments. We have already referred briefly to the case of bureaucracy. As a further example, Mercier Vega[40] suggests that one explanation of the important role of the Army in South America lies in the fact that it is organizationally stable and technically competent. This technical competence is as much civil as military—engineering, communications, cartography, Indian affairs. This technical competence and organizational stability have helped to make the armed forces a firm pillar and an arbiter between other political groups. Their function, indeed, is less military than political—but this could only be so in countries which lack the political structures for which they provide a substitute.

Lastly, as the same author suggests, the concept of the State itself has thrown up many different varieties. The State which grows up out of a society (as in Europe) differs from the State which exists to create one modern political society out of numerous, traditional societies, based on tribal or on 'ethnic' loyalties, as in Africa or South America. It may be a political, an economic, a cultural entrepreneur. It may be a State-machine dominated by a party, or an individual. Yet all varieties have certain formal resemblances.

In the comparative study of political institutions exists an opportunity of examining the consequences of the diffusion of institutional forms into differing environments, each creating something new out of what it has received.

REFERENCES

1. Almond, G. A. and Powell, O., *Comparative Politics: a Developmental Approach* (1966)
2. The passage is given in Hecksher, G., *The Study of Comparative Government and Politics* (1957), p. 25
3. See Gerth and Mills, *From Max Weber* (1948), pp. 77–8
4. Radcliffe-Brown, A. R., Introduction to *African Political Systems* (ed. Fortes and Evans-Pritchard, 1940)
5. See Middleton, J. and Tait, D. (eds), *Tribes Without Rulers* (1958)
6. Easton, H. D., *A Systems Analysis of Political Life* (1965)
7. Almond and Powell, *op. cit.*
8. Almond and Powell, *op. cit.*
9. Almond and Powell, *op. cit.*
10. Meggitt, M. T., 'Indigenous forms of Government among the Australian Aborigines' (*Readings in Australian and Pacific Anthropology*, ed. Hogbin, I. and Hart, L. R., 1966)
11. Meggitt, M. T., *op. cit.*
12. Miller, W. B., 'Two Concepts of Authority' (*American Anthropologist*, Vol. 57, 1955)
13. Langness, L. L., "Some Problems in the Conceptualisation of Highlands Social Structures' (in Hogbin and Hart, *op. cit.*)
14. Colson, E., *The Plateau Tonga of Northern Rhodesia: Social and Religious Studies* (1962)
15. Colson, E., *op. cit.*
15a. Evans-Pritchard, E. E., *The Nuer* (1940)
16. Mair, Lucy, *Primitive Government* (1962)
17. Bloch, Marc, *Feudal Society*, trans. Manyon (1961), Vol. I, Chapter XV
18. Blythe, W. L., *The Impact of Chinese Secret Societies in Malaya* (1969)
19. Whyte, W. F., *Street Corner Society* (1955)
20. Whitelock, Dorothy, *The Beginnings of English Society* (1952), Chapter II
21. Whyte, W. F., *op. cit.*
22. Gullick, J. M., *Indigenous Political Systems of Western Malaya* (1958)
23. Krige, J. D. and E. J., 'The Lovedu of the Transvaal' (in *African Worlds*, ed. Forde, D. See also Krige: *The Realm of a Rain Queen*, 1943)
24. Krige, J. D. and E. J., 'The Lovedu of the Transvaal', *op. cit.*
25. Krige, J. D. and E. J., *op. cit.*

26. Firth, Raymond, 'Authority and Public Opinion in Tikopia' (*Essays on Social Organisation and Values*, 1964)
27. Toennies, F., *Community and Association*, trans. Loomis (1955)
28. Strother, G., 'Problems in the Development of a Social Science of Organisation' (*The Social Sciences of Organisations: Four Perspectives*, ed. Latané, Mechanic, Strauss and Strother, 1963)
29. Weber, M., *The Theory of Social and Economic Organisation*, trans. Henderson and Parsons (1947)
30. Mayer, J. P., *Max Weber and German Politics* (1947)
31. Barnard, C., *The Functions of the Executive* (1938)
32. Simon, H. A., *Administrative Behavior* (1945)
33. Blau, P. L., *The Dynamics of Bureaucracy* (1963)
34. Eisenstadt, S. N., *The Political Systems of Empires* (1963)
35. Bayley, D. H., 'The Effects of Corruption in a Developing Nation' (in Etzioni, A. (ed), *A Sociological Reader on Complex Organisations*, 2nd edition, 1969)
36. Wolpert, J., 'Towards a Sociology of Authority' (in *Studies in Leadership* (ed.) Gouldner, A. W., 1950)
37. Boissevin, J., 'Patronage in Sicily' (*Man*, N.S. Vol. I, 1966)
38. Almond, G. A. and Verba, S., *The Civic Culture: Political Attitudes and Democracy in Five Nations* (1963)
39. See, e.g., Banton, M. (ed), *Political Structures and the Distribution of Power* (1965) and Bailey, F. G., *Stratagems and Spoils* (1969)
40. Mercier Vega, Luis, *Roads to Power in Latin America* (1969)

5.

Marriage and Kinship

I

'MARRIAGE' is an institution: a pattern of rules and customs in respect of some objective (or objectives). 'The Family' is a group. 'The Kin' may be a group, or a looser aggregate (perhaps a network). And, finally, 'Kinship' refers to another, but a related, institution: one might, as an approximation, say that it stands to 'the Kin' as 'Marriage' stands to 'the Family'.

Marriage may be defined as the pattern of recognized usages governing establishment and continuance of the family group. Thus, as an institution, it creates a number of well-known roles: husband, wife, father, child, grandfather, mother-in-law, which in most societies have more or less clear patterns of expectations attached to them. Marriage involves groups, of which the family is clearly the most important: so much so, that a good deal of the discussion on marriage resolves itself into discussions about the family group. Marriage also involves programmes: the prescribed forms for entering into, and for terminating, a marriage, are examples.

Kinship may be defined as a system in accordance with which people are regarded as holding certain statuses and having certain rights and obligations in consequence of their 'relationships' established through the circumstances of parentage or marriage.

A person's kin consist of an aggregate of people related to him in a way which is determined by the custom, or convention, of the society. For example, in a patrilineal society, a kin-group is formed only by those who are related through males; a man's father is of his own kin, but his mother (although in some senses she is his closest relative) is not of his kin. At any moment of time the kin-group is the living members of the *lineage* of those who descend through males from some real or mythical ancestor. (With such forms as matrilineal, or as radial kinship, the principles are different.) This may suggest that the social functions of the kin-group are different from, and not necessarily wholly consistent with, those of the family. But the point to notice here is that kinship is determined by conventional 'rules', of which a considerable variety are to be found in different societies. Not only is the kin-group not coextensive with the family, but it is also normally much larger, ramifying through collaterals, and stretching back through ancestors.

These definitions will of course be taken as provisional, something to start off with. But we shall not, for the moment, define the family: we shall take it that everybody thinks he knows what this term means.

There are a few commonplaces about the family which can well form the introduction of this chapter. To call them commonplace is not to admit that they are true.

Firstly, the assertion that the family is the most important of all human groups. Why is it the most important? The first answer to this is, because it is essential to the survival of the human species. Robin Fox[1] suggests that *all* human beings are born prematurely, since this is the only way that so big-brained a creature can be born without injury to mother or infant. Therefore it cannot at birth, nor for a long time after, fend for itself. It therefore depends during this time on maternal care; and since a succession of children will keep the mother occupied, she will need, at the least, some male or males around.

The second answer is that the family is essential for the survival of human culture. It is essential to *social* existence, since unlike many of the lower animals, man is not equipped at birth with a pattern of innate responses sufficient and ready to see him through his life: what innate equipment he has is largely potential, and needs not only maturation but training. In particular, of course, human society depends upon a complex system of symbolic communication, of which ordinary language is a part, and this has to be socially learned. Parsons,[2] writing at some length, regards the structure of the elementary family (of parents and a small number of children) as being functionally important here. We shall return later to this point.

The contention that the family is an essential human group has never, so far as we know, been experimentally tested (the

Israeli *kibbutz* system hardly constitutes a rigorous test) and it is not clear how it could be. We are left with the argument that in every known society, *some form* of group, to which the name family may be plausibly given, is found.

The second 'commonplace' assertion is the double one that, although in simpler societies the family and kin-groups are of paramount importance, in modern society the importance of neither is paramount, and indeed that of the kin-group is slight. This is a half-, or perhaps a three-quarter, truth. We have, in the first place, to be clear as to the sense in which it is intended to be taken. If it means that the range of functions for which the family may act as a mechanism has narrowed, this is, as we shall see, probably true—though we must not exaggerate the extent of the change. If it is less 'important' in the sense that authority-relations within the family, and the expectations attaching to the roles of 'child', or 'wife', or indeed 'husband and father', have become less rigid, or less clearly ascertainable, this is probably true, too; but it is not clear that it is relevant to the question of the family's importance. If it means that marriage, and the setting up of a family, are less popular today than before, there seems little evidence for such a belief.

II

Arguments as to the place of the family group in society are complex, and require some understanding of the varied forms taken by what is generally called the family. An elementary discussion of these forms is given in the following paragraphs.

1. What is the simplest structural form of the family? One might have proposed the elementary family of parents and children. It is worth noting, however, that Robin Fox[3] contends that the real 'irreducible and elementary social grouping is surely the mother and her children'. This unit *has* to survive, if the species is to; but it is not strictly, or universally, necessary for adult males to be in constant association with the mother-child unit. And it is of course true that in modern societies, family groups consisting only of widow, or divorcée, and children ('denuded' families, as they are sometimes called) are

going concerns. However, what Fox contends has perhaps greater importance in that it helps in the analysis of more complex forms of family structure.

2. The elementary (or 'nuclear') family is typically a group comprising one married couple with their own children.

This is of course the form which is characteristic of modern societies; or rather, what is characteristic of such societies is that there the elementary family sets up its own separate household, often at some distance from its parents or relatives. It is regarded, for fiscal and similar purposes, as a separate unit. It appears to be the expected or ideal behaviour to do this immediately upon marriage, and inability to do so is looked on as deprivation. (There are, however, some 'normal' exceptions, even in modern societies, as we shall see.)

In other societies, 'neolocality', this insulation of the elementary family, may not occur. Nevertheless evidence shows that, even there, the elementary family can be looked on as forming a distinguishable sub-system of a larger group, and that the role of husband or wife may often be in conflict with the obligations to other kin. There will be more about this later. In other words, there is conflict between the claims of the *conjugal* group, and those of the *consanguine* group. The former is the family-group which is based on the marriage-tie (as is the elementary family). The consanguine is the form of family group which tends to emphasise blood-ties—or, more correctly, lineage-relationships—more than marriage-ties.

Now it is clear that conjugal groups are relatively transitory. Typically they include two generations: when the elder generation dies, or when the younger gets married, the 'family of orientation' of the latter (that is, the family into which they were born and in which they were socialized) ceases to exist, and the younger generation set up new 'families of procreation' —those in which they will beget a new generation. This in its turn will become the family of orientation of this new generation: there is a continual succession of new families.

3. The consanguine family does not die: generations succeed one another in the same family. Since the most important link here is the tie uniting people belonging to the same lineage, it

follows that marriage does not cause the younger generation to leave the parental family: instead, the young person brings his or her spouse back to live there.

Of course it would be impossible for *both* the young men *and* the young women to bring their spouses back: it could happen in one family, but could not be generalized throughout a society. What happens is that in societies where consanguine families are customary, custom also lays down who shall remain: usually either the young man remains, and brings in his bride, so that their children will be born in the father's family's house (patrilocality); or the girl stays with her parents, and brings her bridegroom in, so that their children will be born in the mother's family house (matrilocality). Patrilocality is normally (and naturally) associated with the reckoning of descent through the father alone (patrilineality); while matrilocality is normally associated with matrilineality, the reckoning of descent through the mother alone.

These organizing principles cause the consanguine family to become, typically, a more complex group than the conjugal. In a patrilineal society it will comprise, at one stage in its cycle, the father and mother, their married sons and these sons' wives, and the unmarried sons and daughters (the married daughters will have gone off to live with their husbands' families). At a later stage, after the old parents have died, the same family will consist of a number of brothers, each with their wives and children. How many of these brothers live together will depend on such factors as whether the family land, or family residence, is large enough to support or contain them: if not, one or more will hive off and eventually generate consanguine families of their own. But this, if it happens, does not mean the break-up of the original group, which continues as a going concern down the generations. The pattern will be of a complex group consisting of several elementary families, inhabiting the same house or the same compound (depending on the residence-customs of the society), cooperating closely in the household tasks—including the rearing of the various elementary families' children—bound by kinship ties, and under the authority of one family head (the old father or the eldest brother in a patrilocal group). This complex group is generally called an 'extended family'.

There is thus a connection between 'conjugal' and 'elementary', and a connection between 'consanguine' and 'extended'. 'Conjugal' points to a different characteristic from that connoted by 'elementary'; nevertheless the nature of the conjugal tie is such as almost necessarily to lead to an elementary family-structure. It is the same with consanguine and extended families.

In the conjugal, elementary family, the roles, obligations and pressures tend to be different from those in the consanguine, extended family. The size, complexity and permanence of the latter make for an insistence upon traditional role-playing; it offers little scope for innovation. Furthermore, in such a group, roles tend to be 'multiple'—which means that, for example, the same individual may, *within the one group*, combine the roles of son, brother, husband, father and uncle. This, too, is likely to make for a conservative social structure. In the conjugal-elementary family, on the contrary, the structure is simpler and looser, the pressure to conform to tradition is less, there is more mobility in every sense.

4. We have now to introduce another complication, which is, however, not very difficult. In both the extended and the elementary family, each of the husbands may have one wife only. This condition is of course known as monogamy. But there may also be *polygynous* extended families. Polygyny is the system, or custom, by which a man is *permitted to have* more than one wife simultaneously. In a polygynous extended family, each and every husband may have all his wives, and their children, living with him in his part of the composite household.

But the elementary family may also exist with polygyny. An example known to the author may illustrate: it is of a Chinese millionaire in Malaya who installed his two wives (and one recognized concubine) each in a separate house; the three houses being in three different towns, about two hundred miles distant from each other. The facts illustrate several important aspects of polygyny. Not everyone could afford three large houses: but often, perhaps usually, one of the main objectives of the practice of polygyny is to increase, or at least, to display, one's social and economic position. Wives are status-symbols. This inference appears to be supported by the fact that while, as Murdock[4] tells us, polygyny is the most approved form of marriage in some three-quarters to four-fifths of the societies studied in his samples, the proportion of societies in which it is actually the *most common* form is very much smaller. Another objective of polygyny is to give companionship and domestic assistance to the first wife, and for this reason the wives may live in the same household: the group is then a polygynous extended family. But against this can be set the danger of conflict and quarrels, either between the wives—or, much more likely, between the wives' sons. The danger was *not* successfully avoided in the present case, and the resulting developments would have interested Balzac. A third point is that in polygynous societies a general principle is recognized that wives shall receive approximately equal treatment, though special *honour* may be given to the first wife. This principle will in practice be affected by such factors as the beauty, fecundity and strength of will of the different wives. In the present case, this principle was recognized in the testament of the husband, who predeceased his consorts: the houses, which he bequeathed to each wife severally, were of approximately equal value; but a larger monthly allowance was bequeathed to the principal wife. Also the principal wife's house contained, as was proper, the ancestral altar, and an additional sum was alloted to her to carry on the proper ceremonies. (On the other hand, concubines, though recognized, should not have equal status with true wives; and in this case the concubine was bequeathed insufficient funds to keep her house in repair.)

Polygyny is, therefore, a normative system involving obligations, not only on men but on women. Islamic law and custom permits polygyny, as did Chinese; but Islamic law restricted the number of wives a man might have to four; further, it enjoined him not to take more wives than he could support. Favouritism is everywhere frowned upon. For their part, wives are expected to live together in harmony. This last norm may well be associated with the widespread custom of 'sororal polygyny', whereby a man, having taken a woman as his principal wife, later takes her sister as his second. The social advantage of this system is held to be that, since sisters are more used to one another's ways than are unrelated women, they will get on better together.

5. Another form of marriage structure is polyandry: the union of one wife with several husbands. Murdock[5] shows this form of marriage arrangement to be extremely rare: in a sample of 565 societies, only 4 societies were found to practise it. With such an incidence, only tentative explanations for its existence can be put forward. It has been suggested that polyandry is a response (one possible response, among numerous others) to conditions of poverty: where natural resources are so sparse that a man cannot produce enough to support a wife and children of his own, he may join in with some other men in sharing the upkeep, and the services, of a woman. This may be plausible in some of the few known cases; less so in others. In any event, poverty cannot be the sole condition of polyandry; and what the other conditions may be is impossible to tell.

The polyandrous system has suggested a terminological problem: are we entitled to think of polyandrous groups as being instances of 'marriage' or 'family' at all? The answer would seem to be that if we look on the mother-child dyad as the essential family-unit, this system does qualify.

6. The 'joint family'. This is a variant of the extended family which is characteristic of Hindu society. In it, adult brothers live together, with their respective families of procreation. As well as maintaining a common household, they also hold property in common—indeed, many such joint families are trading firms, having a legal corporate existence, usually with the eldest brother as manager—and assume joint responsibility for the education of younger siblings.

7. Lastly may be mentioned the 'stem family'. In this type of family-structure, the sons, on growing up, leave the parental home to set up their own neolocal households—all except one, who brings his wife to live with his parents. Thus the stem-family may be regarded as an intermediate type between the elementary and the extended: unlike the first, it is typically a three-generational group, but unlike the second, it excludes the families of collaterals. The name (*famille souche*) was invented by Frédéric Le Play, the French sociologist, in his studies of European working-class families,[6] and it may be regarded as a form adapted to a regime of peasant small-holdings, where

a succession of male generations is necessary to work the land, but where the size of holdings is insufficient to support more than a few people. Levy[7] however notes it as a typical form in China also, and suggests that the requirements of ancestor-worship are responsible for the three-generation form there.

The foregoing discussion suggests that the family may be defined as a group of persons, and also as a set, or sets, of roles, the character of which differ in different societies according to the functions which the family fulfils.

III

Exogamy and Incest-taboo

All known societies have rules which forbid a man or a woman to marry any of those persons with whom he stands in certain relationships. Thus the English Book of Common Prayer forbids a man to marry his grandmother, his mother, his sister, his daughter, and certain others. Such rules are known to anthropologists as rules of exogamy ('marrying out'). Of course, it would also be a criminal offence for a man to have sexual relations, quite apart from marriage, with any of these relatives; but this would be a different act. Incest is the name given to sexual intercourse, irrespective of marriage, within the 'forbidden degrees'. All societies have incest-prohibitions, also; though which relatives stand within the 'forbidden degrees' may vary somewhat from society to society.

Let us take the incest-prohibitions first. The fact that some system of prohibition is universal in human societies, but very far from being so in animal societies, suggests that it may be related to something in respect of which human beings differ from the majority of animals. A number of different explanations for its existence have been put forward: these may be divided into two main classes, biological explanations and cultural explanations.

The first class are based on the character of the human physical make-up. One such explanation is that inbreeding, particularly between parent and child or between siblings, is harmful in that it greatly increases the probability of the appearance of deleterious recessive characteristics; and that while it would also increase the possibility of the appearance of advantageous recessives, the former greatly exceed the latter, and in a slow-breeding animal like man, this would mean a drastic reduction in the breeding population, and therefore gravely affect its survival-capacity.

Another biological explanation is to the effect that for early man, few in number, with a short life-span, producing relatively few offspring, who were widely-spaced and had a small chance of survival to adulthood, intrafamilial breeding was a virtual impossibility, and the tendency to breed-out became implanted in the race.

Cultural explanations for the incest-taboo have several variations. One is that unregulated sexual competition is disruptive for any group, and that therefore it must be prohibited within the family group, which is of fundamental importance to the survival of the human race. Another is the theory that the taboo is a formal expression, either of the sexual indifference of kinsmen to each other, or of the horror of sexual relations between kinsmen. The last explanation is somewhat implausible as it stands, for one thing because an action which is the object of *universal* indifference or of *universal* horror hardly needs to be formally prohibited. Secondly, it is not the case that these sentiments *are* universally felt. But, as Fox says,[8] it is unnecessary to bring in universal sentiments here. If any particular sentiment is very widely, but not universally, held, rules and sanctions would be necessary to coerce the minority who do not hold it.

The trouble with some of these explanations is that to explain why a practice is advantageous is not to explain why it has come to be followed. The explanation in terms of genetic consequences may be true, but it does not follow that primitive man would have grasped it. As Aberle and others suggest[9] the prohibition may have been *selected* through efforts to solve a cultural problem such as the elimination of conflict within a family, although since it was also adaptive on biological grounds, it *may be* that species or races of man which adopted it had a greater likelihood of survival.

On the other hand, it is perhaps best to see *exogamous* rules (that is, those relating to marriage) as *positive* injunctions to form socially approved ties with members of a different group.

On this view, what we have is a process of forming 'marriage-alliances' with groups who are potentially hostile: a group will give its daughters in marriage to men of the other group, and will marry their daughters in return. This exchange of women should help to reduce tensions between the two groups, and increase the strength of each. Fundamentally simple, the system is capable of being greatly complicated (in some tribes), because of other rules, such as of unilineal descent or unilocal residence, which have to be worked into the pattern. The problem is discussed by Fox.[10]

IV

Kinship and the Family

One of the most impressive differences between modern Western society, on the one hand, and both simpler societies and ancient civilizations such as India and China on the other, is the difference in the relative importance of wider kin-relationships. In many simpler societies the extended family is the preferred and commonest type of family group, while the family or families that exist at any point of time are regarded as links in a temporal lineage-chain. Birth gives anyone a clearly-defined status in a kin-group, with rights and duties equally clearly-defined. Duties towards one's own kin are often paramount. Further, the rules of the society may enjoin specific privileges and obligations between specific pairs of relationships. Thus among the Trobrianders of New Guinea, the mother's brother occupies a position of special authority, with special duties of supervising the upbringing of his sister's sons.

In England, on the contrary, the extended family has never been a customary form, for the last thousand years at any rate. The importance of the kin has varied, but it is doubtful if it ever, at least since the Norman Conquest, denoted a clearly-defined group, with clear and distinct obligations. Today, although the kin-network is by no means without importance, it is an amorphous and fluctuating aggregate, whose function is ill-defined.

The number of kinship systems known to anthropologists is

so great that it would be futile in this chapter to attempt anything even distantly approaching a complete account. Anything of the kind could only be given in the form of statistical tables of the incidence of various isolated customs or rules; and the disadvantage of such a procedure in the present connection is clear. Those who want something of the sort may consult Murdock's *Social Structure*[10] and *World Ethnographic Sample.*[11]

Here we shall compare three different examples. One is the traditional Chinese patrilineal and patrilocal system. The second is the matrilineal and matrilocal system of Jelebu, one of the Malay States. In both cases, the wider-kin ties have been, till recently, ties of as great an importance as those of the family proper. The third is the contemporary British family system. This is, when compared with the other two, to a much greater extent a conjugal, and an insulated, group.

It will be seen that two of these societies are of major historical importance. Jelebu, as a political unit, has hardly that degree of importance; but, like the others, its marriage system is of great theoretical interest. Lastly, all three systems have something else in common: for a considerable time they have been subjected to influences from within and without, which have promoted substantial change. The nature and effects of that change themselves constitute important sociological problems.

The Chinese Family

Recently students have pointed out that the 'ideal' family pattern of Chinese society: the form which has traditionally been held up as a model in Chinese literature, was in fact the family system of only a minority of Chinese—of the gentry and scholar class, well-to-do and able to influence the diffusion of cultural norms. The system or systems customary among the bulk of the population, the peasants, may have been very different. Some work has been done on the study of these in recent years[13]; more however is known about the gentry system.

The ideal (and to a large extent the actual) Chinese traditional family structure was closely associated with Chinese religious, ethical and political norms, which laid great importance on piety to the family ancestors and duty to the Emperor. Accordingly the traditional family was patriarchal; it was also patrilocal, and patrilineal. Traditional Chinese society permitted polygyny, though a distinction was always made between principal wife and secondary wives, the former enjoying greater honour and prestige. The taking of concubines was also recognized and tolerated.

Ideally the Chinese gentry-family was a multi-generational extended family. It comprised the head of the family and his wife, or wives, all his sons, their wives and children, and all unmarried daughters. The ideal was to have a large number of generations under one roof. But the actual size of Chinese families seems to have been much smaller than this would imply. Olga Lang, basing her conclusions on a number of studies of rural and urban families, suggests that the average size of an urban upper class family in the first half of the twentieth century was between 6 and 7 persons, of a rural landlord family about 9. (For wage-earners and lower middle-class the size ranged from 3 to 5 approximately, and for poorer peasants, about 4 to 5.) Such information as is available suggests that gentry-family size did not greatly differ at much earlier ages. In this respect, that is, the ideal did not correspond with the reality, which was affected by economic, rather than moral, factors.

In other respects we may suppose that ideal and reality corresponded more closely. One of these was the matter of paternal authority. In scarcely anything was the social ethic of pre-Revolutionary China more insistent than on the principle of social authority, exemplified in the duty of subjects to the Emperor and, more important because more immediate, the duty of children to father, and, in general, of junior to senior. The *Three-Character Classic*, a schoolbook written in the tenth century A.D. and of immensely wide diffusion, which, like some nineteenth-century Western schoolbooks, combined the functions of instructor in reading and in morals, is insistent on the point. 'A child should know how to obey his parents. When Hsiang was nine years old, he used to get in and warm the bed for his parents. Children must respect their elders. When Jung was four years old, he voluntarily gave up the bigger pear to his elder brother,' are two of its verses, and the theme is repeated, with greater or less sophistication, throughout Chinese literature. One might suspect that what was emphasized so assiduously was in fact only achieved with difficulty; but on the other hand there is plenty of evidence from contemporary Chinese settlements outside China, of the continuing strength of the traditional authority-pattern.

Ideally, the father-son relationship was based on awe, respect and fear. It was the central role-relationship in the family, and exemplifies the general point that the more important the relationship is to family and kin, the less it is a relation of affection. The son had towards the father the duty of respect and obedience; the father the duty of educating and training his sons; but it would be truest to say that this was not a duty towards his sons, but rather towards the lineage, since only if the sons were duly trained could they be relied on to carry out the prescribed ceremonies to the ancestors. As the son grew older, the relationship grew more equal, particularly with the eldest son; when the head of the family grew old, he might hand over the effective command of the household to his eldest son; but respect and deference were always his due.

Extreme deference was due also to the patriarch's principal wife.

The tradition was for daughters to be treated affectionately; and this was perhaps related to the fact that, to their father's family and lineage, they were less important. Their destiny was to leave this family on marriage, and to take their obedience and loyalty to their husband's family.

Marriages were of course arranged by the parents, generally through a middleman; they were the subject of bargaining, in which the bridegroom and certainly the bride, had little or no say. On marriage the bride coming into her husband's parents' household, fell under their authority: and the authority of her husband was far inferior to that of her mother-in-law: within the family, the consanguine relationship was more important than the conjugal ones.

The extended family group formed part of a wider kin group. This was a patrilineal lineage-group. Notionally, it consisted of all persons bearing the same surname, who were supposed, by a generally accepted or at least tolerated myth, to have descended from one ancestor. For many purposes (though not all) the effective group was the *local* group of those with the same surname: the Wang's or the Li's living in one's own town or district, rather than all the Wang's or all the Li's. Freedman proposes the term lineage for the local group. The term clan is often used for the wider, non-local group. Both translate the Chinese *tsu*.

It will be seen that, as contrasted with the kinship system of Britain or the United States, the Chinese system was a clearly defined one. The 'rules' for reckoning it could be clearly understood. Each lineage might almost be called a corporate group: typically it possessed its own house or temple, where the tablets of the lineage ancestors were displayed, and where social or business meetings of the lineage representatives could take place.

For the lineage or clan had a far greater economic and political importance in China than the kin in England or the U.S.A. In Chapter 3 it was remarked that the Imperial system of law administration was defective and suspect. Some of the functions it should have performed were taken on by commercial guilds; but the family unit, and the clan or lineage, were the chief loci of power in Imperial China. The *tsu* had funds; and the weight of religious and moral tradition and the relative immobility, for most, of Chinese society, gave it power. It helped to maintain the ancestral tablets and ancestral graves. It exercised welfare functions, and helped to pay for the education of promising, but poor, boys of the lineage. It loaned money. In all, its object was to maintain the existence and welfare of its families and their members, but also to exercise judicial and corrective powers over them. In the absence of an effective State apparatus, either centrally or regionally, the domestic unit took over political, as well as economic, functions. The great importance attached to its functions in these respects no doubt partially accounts for the stress laid on the authority to be exercised by parents and elders, and on the duty of giving respect and obedience to them.

Among the more interesting aspects of the study of social institutions is the analysis of their responses to change. Some attempt has been made to study the Chinese family under Communism; but although the topic is clearly of immense importance, it suffers from the drawbacks, first, that it is difficult to obtain adequate data; and secondly that the period involved is somewhat short for changes (which are likely to be extremely complex) to show themselves clearly. In the meantime, some useful material can be derived from the study of family and marriage systems in Chinese settlements overseas.

A visitor to one of the territories of Chinese overseas settlement—Singapore or Malaya, for instance—must be impressed with the strength of Chinese tradition. At any rate up until the beginning of the Second World War, the traditional family system seems to have constituted a model for at least the well-to-do Chinese in the South Seas. Ties were maintained with the homeland, genealogies preserved, and ancestral tablets exhibited in the clan temples which were erected in the major towns, and this was the more interesting in that at least the vast majority of the Chinese who emigrated were not from 'gentry' families, but from poor ones—poor peasants, often—who had emigrated to try and better their position. Those who grew well-to-do or wealthy seem then to have accepted the lineage and family institutional norms as part of a process of what might be called 'embourgeoisement'.

In some respects, however, it was functional for their purposes. The wide clan, consisting of all with the same surname, without reference to locality (and it should be pointed out that the number of surnames in China is much fewer than in most Western countries) was very valuable as a sort of credit and guarantee organization for its members. Dewey has discussed this.[14] A Chinese living in Singapore and wishing to trade with Indonesia, would find members of his own clan living in Indonesia, and these he could rely on to extend him credit and to protect his interests. This strongly-rooted sentiment of clan solidarity made the group in this respect a very practical organization, carrying out familiar tasks.

In another respect, however, the social environment of lineage and of family had changed. In China much of its importance had been as a political organization—a substitute for a state judicial and administrative system. But in at least some territories of emigration (Malaya or Singapore, for instance) the colonial government, at least for most of the twentieth century, maintained a judicial and administrative system which was tolerably efficient. Therefore one of the bases of family and lineage authority became eroded, and the authority became supported by sentiment (and perhaps by the sense of personal advantage of the head). But it now came into conflict with other social factors. The Chinese in South-East Asia were to a large extent immersed in an urban, commercial environment—which, indeed, the immigrants had largely helped to create. Although it remained quite common for a boy to go into his father's business, it was no longer necessary to do so: other work was available, and therefore a young man had a chance of being economically independent. Indeed, work in a Government office enjoyed a higher prestige than business. Secondly, the world-wide movement for women's rights caused young brides to put pressure on their husbands to be independent of the parental roof. Finally, this was more and more made possible, and necessary, by the housing situation in the cities which favoured small family units.[15]

The resultant situation appears to be a transitional one.[16] The force of tradition appears to be considerable: a Westerner living in such territories would feel the sense of obligation to parents to be much stronger than in his own society; but it is often expressed in the phrase 'The old people would feel sad if we didn't. . . .' In other words, the old people can, in general, no longer enforce what they think right. Extended households are probably not rare; but it is probable that many of them are temporary; the young people reside with their parents (and it may be the girl's parents, not the boy's) for a while after marriage, out of respect, and then move away.

Similarly in the choice of marriage partner, deference is given to the wishes of parents; and for this reason it may be difficult to go against them; but in general, economic and social pressures no longer compel the young people to obey.

A situation of extreme complexity has developed. It is, however, in several ways comparable to that in the West. In the first place, the changes are the consequence of modernization: that is, of the development of a predominantly industrial-commercial society, in an urbanized setting, and the development of social and regional mobility and of generational independence associated with these changes. In the second place, it is a movement from predominantly consanguine to predominantly conjugal ties, in which, however, there is still an appreciable degree of attachment to the wider kin. More and more, the trend, as elsewhere in Asia, is towards the elementary family in which the primary link is between husband and wife, and their primary duty is to their own children.

The Matrilineal Family

Jelebu is a district of Negri Sembilan ('The Nine States') which is itself a state of West Malaysia. The Malays are Islamic, and Islam promotes a patrilineal, patrilocal system; but the ancestors of the Malays of Jelebu came in from Sumatra, bringing with them an exceptional system of matriliny, which still largely persists.[17] Under it, a man, on marrying, will go to his wife's family's homestead, and either build a house of his own within it, or else live, for a time, with her family before building his own house. He is thus largely under their influence: in particular, under that of the wife's mother's brother.

As in all traditional Malay societies, marriages are arranged by the parents: this time less with an eye to lineage considerations, than because the system consorts well with the general ideology that young people, and girls in particular, are irresponsible and lack judgement. (The life prescribed for them before marriage makes it difficult for them to be otherwise.)

We noted previously the tendency for conflict to arise between the claims of conjugal and consanguine relationships. Where the society is matrilineal, the grounds for conflict are increased. In all known societies, the principle is that the male is dominant in his own household. In other matrilineal societies, such as the Trobriands, of which Malinowski has written, there is no ideology which conflicts with the rule that this male shall be the mother's brother. But Islamic society in general, and Malay society outside Negri Sembilan, holds firmly to the belief that the husband should be master in his own house. In Jelebu this principle conflicts with the view that the husband is an intruder, of inferior status, in his wife's family's homestead.

As with the Chinese patrilineal system, so the matrilineal, matrilocal system of Jelebu found its strength, in earlier times, in a supportive legal-administrative system. It was not that the family or lineage group had any specific political functions, as the Chinese one had. In fact, there is little concern with lineage;

the ancestors have no specific importance, and there is little concern about perpetuating a descent-line. Its strength was that it was supported by the traditional norms of the customary law. When, as the result of the growth of a colonial administrative system during the twentieth century, the customary law became less and less meaningful, the inconsistency between the matrilocal rule and that which emphasizes a man's responsibility for, and control over, his own wife and children, became manifest. Other social factors began also to affect the situation. With better communications, wider job-opportunities became available, and the man could go away (to join the Federal police-force, for instance) out of the range of the matrilocal system, and the influence of his wife's family.

This leads us to consider one important aspect of kinship-structures: the tension (found particularly in unilineal systems) between the claims of the kin-group and those of the elementary family which forms a link in its chain. Any idea that elementary or conjugal families are, as it were, dissolved into the wider kin-structure is in need of amendment. Thus Firth, writing of Tikopia,[18] shows that while in normal times a man fully recognizes his obligations (to provide food, etc) to a wide range of kin-members, in times of emergency (such as a famine) these obligations quite definitely give way to the claims of his own elementary family. Fortes also,[19] under the name of 'complementary filiation' discusses, with reference to the Tallensi of Africa, the relation of the intimate mother-son link to the links and obligations of both parties with the wider kin-aggregate.

Probably the general consideration here is that the two groups have inherently different objectives: the kin-group is a political one, concerned with power and balances of power, whereas the elementary family is very largely a group whose primary function is the display and development of mutual affection: an 'expressive' group, in the sense we have earlier given to that word.

IV

The British Family

The third of our three family types is the contemporary British family.

This may be summarized as follows: monogamous; mainly conjugal and elementary; typically neolocal.

There seems little evidence to suggest that the British family was ever anything but an elementary one; Laslett [20] produces data which seem to suggest that in the seventeenth and eighteenth centuries its average size was small. But in the first two-thirds of the nineteenth century a very rapid increase took place in the population of England and Wales (and to a somewhat smaller extent, of Scotland). The economic and social factors associated with this increase are not entirely clear, but it is safe to say that it was an aspect of the Industrial and Agricultural Revolutions. A diminution in the rate of population increase began around the last third of the nineteenth century, and continued till the mid-twentieth. These population changes are reflected in statistics of family size.

There is little doubt that, apart from changes in size, the British family (like the family in other Western societies) has experienced profound structural and functional changes over the past century, and these changes are probably still continuing. What seems at present clear is that marriage is no less sought-after than it has ever been, if the statistics of those entering the state are relevant evidence. The most recent report of the Registrar-General for England and Wales (1967)[21] shows that, whereas in 1911, out of 1,000 women aged 15–49 years, 502 were married, in 1967 the corresponding figure was 697, an increase of more than one-third. What is as significant is the fact that this increase took place chiefly in the younger age-groups: between 1911 and 1967, the proportion, out of 1,000, for women aged 15 to 19 had increased from 12 to 78, an increase of six-and-a-half times; and for those aged 20 to 24 from 242 to 571, an increase of just over two-and-a-third times.

Marriage therefore seems to be popular. After looking at advertisements in magazines and on T.V., one might be inclined to think that the Family, like Christmas, was invented by consumer-goods manufacturers: and this is not wholly improbable. The factors, however, are no doubt more complex than this. One of the predominant reasons must be that it is easier now to get married than it was, say, fifty years ago: the development of loan-schemes for house-purchase; of schemes for the building of rented housing by local government bodies;

and of hire-purchase schemes, have all reduced the burden of capital outlays on the home, which was previously so much of an obstacle to marriage; and higher real incomes and medical and welfare benefit schemes have reduced the cost, and the anxiety, of having babies.

Nevertheless families are smaller. Accurate comparisons are somewhat difficult to establish here; but the Family Census which was taken in 1946, on a 10 per cent sample of the population of Great Britain, as a part of the investigations of the Royal Commission on the Population, showed that in the case of marriages which had taken place in the period 1870–79, nearly four-fifths had had three or more children born to them, and over two-fifths had had seven or more (one-sixth had had ten or more); but in the case of marriages taking place in the year 1925, only one-third had had three or more children, and only one family in twenty-five, seven or more. Twice as many families of 1925 were childless, as compared with the earlier period.

These figures may somewhat exaggerate the difference in average family size, since they do not take account of deaths among children and young people, which were of course greater in the earlier period. A considerable disparity must, however, remain. It is worth noting that the difference is not (wholly) accounted for by the size of Victorian *working-class* families. Middle class and professional families were also large. While systematic data on this matter are lacking, the evidence of biographies and the like make it clear that a distinct tendency this way existed. For instance, Charles Darwin, born in 1809, was one of a family of six; he married in 1839 a woman who was one of a family of nine; they had ten children.

The trend towards small families was confirmed by the 1951 census, which showed that, of all married women aged 15 to 49 years of age, fewer than one-quarter had had three or more children, while 30·5 per cent had had only one child, and 21·8 per cent had borne none. Even among the women aged 30–35 who had been married 10 to 14 years, only 40 per cent had had three or more children, while 34·1 per cent had had one or none.

The immediate cause of this change was no doubt the dissemination of birth control knowledge and facilities; but the remoter causes may be summarized under the term 'modernization'. The Royal Commission on the Population[22] suggested a network of interrelated factors: prominent among them is the growing independence of women, since late Victorian times, and the belief that they should have a greater say in such matters as the spacing of births. Probably another factor was the generally increased standard of living between the early nineteenth and the mid-twentieth centuries. A first consequence of this seems to have been the great population increase of the first two-thirds of the nineteenth century, due to a decline in the death-rate; it may well be that a second and later consequence was a raising of people's social and economic aspirations, and, as a result, decisions to limit family-size, in order to fulfil these aspirations. Other factors, such as housing shortage, and, particularly in the 1930's, political and economic insecurity, no doubt contributed. It should also be borne in mind that a high Victorian birthrate may have been a compensation for high infant mortality.

Not only is the modern family smaller, but its duration is more and more at the discretion of the partners. One of the remarkable features of the contemporary marriage system in Britain is the great increase in divorce. In 1938 the number of decrees made absolute in England and Wales was 6,250; in 1960 this had increased to 23,868, and in 1967 to 43,093.[23] The interpretation of comparisons over time has to take account of changing legislation. It was not until 1857 that divorce was allowed, in England and Wales, by normal process of law; even then it was difficult. In 1937 the Matrimonial Causes Act considerably widened the grounds for divorce, and in 1949 the Legal Aid and Assistance Act gave financial assistance to those who needed it in order to undertake proceedings. But the changing law is itself a reflection of changing attitudes, and of changing social structure. In Victorian times the social mechanisms available for 'keeping a marriage together' (apart from the difficulty of legal proceedings for divorce) were the lack of alternatives to marriage; the current norms relating to marriage, and the pressures of kin and neighbourhood. The divorced woman was an outcast from society, whether the divorce was due to her adultery, or not. Nor would she have any means of support, except, sometimes, a possibly resentful parent. Secondly, it would be reasonable to say that the mid-nineteenth-century view of marriage was that its prime object was not the happiness of the partners (at least not of the wife) though this was a desirable secondary object. Rather, to be married was a social duty, for which the wife's reward was respectability and protection. Thirdly, in a society less mobile than the present one, kin and neighbourhood pressures could be applied more effectively to support these norms, and at least to keep intact the legal bond.

It would certainly be untrue to say that there are no longer any economic obstacles to divorce; but certainly among younger age-groups and those without children, they are fewer. At the same time, there has been an obvious change in norms and in neighbourhood pressures, and these, while in some ways making the marriage relationship easier, have in other ways made it more unstable. Perhaps it may be said that there is a tendency for the partners to look upon a marriage as an experiment, rather than a permanent step. This suggestion may very well be supported by statistics of the Registrar-General showing a very substantial increase over the past thirty years in the numbers of remarriages of widowed and divorced persons: these increases are particularly great in the youngest age-groups.

In a large proportion of marriage-systems (including, as we saw, the traditional ones of China and Malaya) marriages were or are arranged by the parents, with the bride and bridegroom-to-be allowed only a small say, if any. The reasons for this practice are various. In part it results from the greater importance attached in many societies to the lineage, rather than to any individual family, and the desire to see that alliances suitable to the interests of the lineage are secured. A variant of this is the practice of seeing that both bride and bridegroom bring into the alliance not only their own presumably desirable persons, but a reasonably substantial amount of property as well. This may result in difficult and protracted bargaining over marriage-portions.[24] The proviso may be in order to ensure that they can contribute to the economic undertakings of the wider kin-group, but also so that they may not become a burden on their parents. There is a third reason: a proper-sized marriage-portion is a sign of status: it shows not only that the father can put up an amount suitable to his position, but also that he has the weight to elicit a proper one from the other party.

In contemporary Britain, certainly for the vast majority of people, choice of mate is at the discretion of the young man or woman themselves. Some of the factors associated with this change have been indicated already. They include the greater economic and social independence of younger people; and the growth of the view that marriage need only be temporary and experimental, not permanent. It is also connected with changes in the nature of the wider kin-group, which, as we shall see, is no longer a decision-making collectivity. Also, it may be suggested, the ability of which parents may feel themselves possessed to see differences between the suitability of one young person and another has been reduced, first by the much-advertised generation-gap, and secondly by the prevalent feeling, induced by the swift rate of change in human affairs today, that success is unpredictable, and that one boy is just as likely to hit the jackpot as another.

If we now turn to the relations between the elementary family and the kin, we see that one of the most important characteristics of the British kinship and family systems is that relationship is reckoned 'bilaterally' (or 'radially'). A child will consider his mother and her relatives as much related to him as his father and his relatives—as much, and no more. Apart from such very special matters as entailed estates, the only thing which a child now customarily takes from his father, rather than from his mother, is his surname: but this is not mandatory, and a man on marriage can if he likes take his wife's surname, and this can be handed down.

The fact that kinship is bilateral (instead of, as for instance in traditional China, unilineal) means that 'the kin' can in Britain never be a group possessing a corporate unity down the generations. For Ego's kin will be the relatives of Ego's father and Ego's mother; but the kin of Ego's children will be Ego's relatives plus the different collection brought in by Ego's wife. Thus each generation brings in (at least in principle) a further accession to the aggregate of kin. Clearly, in a bilateral kinship system, a person's kin-aggregate is different from the kin-aggregate of any of his cousins, uncles, aunts or parents. It is an aggregate personal to the individual (and his siblings) although it overlaps those of other near relatives. Furthermore, the social significance to an individual of any given relative lies less in the particular relationship involved than in the amount of social interaction which they have, or the distance they live apart. Relationship-roles, apart from the parental role, have few clearly-defined duties attaching to them.

But kinship is by no means unimportant, as various recent studies have shown.[25]

As is well known, the surveys carried out by Young and Willmott in Bethnal Green, and by Kerr in a poor working-class area in Liverpool, showed the existence of kinship ties embracing groups of nuclear families. One species of grouping to which the authors drew particular attention was that formed by a woman and her one or more young married daughters, all living with their families within easy reach of one another. The evidence of Young and Willmott was to the effect that to the younger families the existence and activities of the old lady had important social functions. Apart from such specific tasks as minding the children of the younger families, and so helping them to cope with daily life, 'Mum' and her house provided a centre where the daughters could maintain their links with one another. The authors make the point that the tie between mother and married daughter is the important inter-family bond; those between mother and son, or between father and son, are much less so; probably in part because the links between a son and his parents are not nowadays, in the main, links of dependence; whereas the young married women, in Young and Willmott's and in Kerr's samples, depended to a considerable extent on their mothers for advice and help in household affairs.

Young and Willmott propose the term 'extended family' for this relationship between nuclear families of the older and the younger generations. But this seems an unfortunate misnomer, since not only do the various nuclear families not occupy the same residence-unit, but the head of the older-generation family exercises no authority over the members of the younger. It might be said that the 'Bethnal Green pattern' acts as a sort of substitute for the extended family in societies where this kind of family, in the normal form, could scarcely exist. Eugene Litwak,[26] discussing a similar kind of relationship as found in the United States, calls it the 'modified extended family'.

What has to be noticed is the fugitive and essentially labile character of the bond. Kerr points out that in the area she studied, the relation of dependence was less likely to exist where the young wife was somewhat better educated. In Bethnal Green, the links between the younger married sisters tended not to survive the death of the old mother. And above all, resettlement, even when the distance moved away was not very considerable, was, according to Young and Willmott, sufficient to break the link.

The existence of a socially-significant network of kin, surrounding the nuclear family, has been pointed out by other investigators, such as Firth[27] in respect of London, and Williams, in respect of a rural area in South West England.[28] In these examples, the metropolitan and the rural areas show a considerable degree of resemblance, which is perhaps to be expected from the fact that the greater part of Britain is urban-dominated. The characteristics of the kinship system revealed may be summarized as follows:

1. The number of individuals recalled and recognized as kin by conjugal pairs tends to be perhaps surprisingly large for a society which has recently been popularly regarded as composed merely of isolated nuclear families. In Firth's survey, taken in a South London borough in the late 1940's, out of the twelve conjugal pairs about whom most information was gleaned, nine recalled over one hundred relatives each, and four over two hundred each. These relatives extended for the most part over only five to six generations: the network was shallow but wide. Williams found a very similar state of affairs.

2. The recognition and acceptance of kin ties is to a large extent a matter of individual choice. The kinship system is not forced upon the individual (except presumably when he or she is a child); it is rather a system which is composed by the individual through a process of personal selection.

3. To a certain extent, the closeness of ties may be related to degrees of genealogical nearness, but this is not necessarily so.

4. Firth suggests the importance of what he calls 'pivotal kin': that is, certain individual members of any conjugal pair's kinship-network, upon whom they rely for information about

other members. Such individuals, either because of their genealogical position or because of personal qualities, become communication-centres.

5. The bilateral or radial aspect of kinship is very marked. It was usual, in the surveys, to find that each member of a conjugal pair would regard the kin of spouse and self as equally 'their' kin. While the system is patrinominal, Firth, like Young and Willmott, regarded it as matricentred; the link between mother and children (especially daughters) was the strongest one, and on the whole more seemed to be known about maternal than about paternal kindred.

6. The importance of kinship lies partly in an exchange of services, but partly lies in more intangible forms of mutual support: support in forming opinions and judgements, companionship, exchange of information. Williams discusses its importance in forming something like a corporate body at important *rites de passage*, particularly funerals. He indicates that, in the district which he studied, the various funeral roles of bearer, mourner, etc, were conventionally allocated according to genealogical nearness to the deceased.

We may add the following points, not emphasized by the writers just referred to:

7. The relations for which the norms are most clearly defined are those within the nuclear family: husband-wife, and especially parent-young child. Duties and rights here are of course supported by legal sanctions. Duties to elderly parents, on the other hand, are supported by moral norms of comparable strength to those enforcing the care of young children, but are not enforced by legal sanctions. The conflict between moral norms and the physical and social obstacles of insufficient housing space and the double burden which the care of aged parents, as well as of her children, would impose on the married daughter, has made this one of the most difficult areas of the contemporary kinship system.

8. The role of parent remains a 'specific' role (in Southall's terminology) but almost all other kinship-roles are extremely diffuse: for example the role of 'uncle' has few specific expectations attached to it, in contrast with the role of mother's brother among the Trobriand Islanders. Consistently with this diffuse-

ness, British kinship terminology is imprecise, as Radcliffe-Brown points out: for example, the term 'uncle' covers four different relationships. The role may sometimes be so diffuse, the expectations so vague, even in fairly near relationships, that a role can hardly be said to exist: can 'cousin' be a role?

9. Except in very rare cases, kinship no longer has the function of indicating descent, or of giving a status in society, with associated rights and duties.

The Functions of the Modern Family

Talcott Parsons tells us that it is essential to the fulfilment by the family of its major functions that it should be a general-purpose, non-specialized group. But there has nevertheless been, in modern society, a narrowing of the range of activities normally associated with the family, and a shift of emphasis. These changes are of course associated chiefly with the fact that, since the Industrial Revolution, production, welfare and training have tended to be organized outside the family. But, in addition, changes have taken place, since the end of the nineteenth century, in the self-sufficiency of households. It is enough to point to the development of packed and processed foods, and of the variety of forms of service industry and of commercial recreation (and with them the decline in household size and the virtual disappearance of domestic servants, who sixty years ago were one of the most familiar of suburban phenomena) to indicate the basis for revolutionary changes in the structure and internal relations of the British family. Families of all social classes now need—and in fact must—be less self-sufficient.

As compared with the nineteenth century, the economy of today is more diversified and less preponderantly 'heavy'. Consequently more work-opportunities are available for women outside the home. (But it was the 1914–18 war which first convinced the public that women were capable of working outside their homes, other than as servants or unpaid welfare workers.)

One may summarize the consequences of these changes by saying that today in only a minority of cases (such as farming households) is the family a productive unit, in which the younger generation are likely to be trained to take their place. More and more, its economic functions are reduced to those of an ultimate consumer, organizing the allocation of fixed sums of housekeeping money.

At the same time as its economic functions have diminished, the importance of the twentieth-century family as a public administrative and fiscal unit has increased in Britain. Although kinship and the State tend in some degree to be antithetical systems, the Governmental organization tends to use the family as an agent. This agency becomes more important with the growth in significance of direct taxation, and also with the growth of welfare services. The legal obligations which parents assume towards their children today very largely mean the obligation to ensure that these children are duly exposed to the educational, medical and welfare services which are provided by the State.

Apart from this, the family in modern society appears to be important on two main grounds:

1. It is the group within which mutual affection and companionship between its members, and therefore the psychological protection of each of them, are fostered.
2. It is the unit for the care and socialization of children.

Its success in either capacity depends to a large extent upon its success in the other capacity. There are, indeed, a number of relationships between these two functions, and between them and recent changes in the social and population structure of Britain. The trend towards a smaller number of offspring, better spaced, not only means a greater likelihood that those which are borne will be better cared for; it also means that the mother's health and mind will benefit from having less drudgery; and this, combined with the longer expectation of life today, and the tendency to have one's children earlier, means that she has more leisure to cultivate herself as a person. But this is not only more possible, but also more necessary, in the first place so as to fulfil adequately her parental role. Parsons very truly, if somewhat obviously, points out that it is desirable (and particularly desirable in the small nuclear family) that parents should be mature people, with interests outside the family, so that the child's socialization, which begins inside the family, shall be led out of it into the wider society. But in the second place, the other function of the family, that of mutual companionship and protection, also requires that the wife should be a person rather than an unpaid household drudge. And once again, increased life-expectancy of both husband and wife increases the need.

Titmuss, in an interesting article, points out that the working class man combines the authority or prestige-role of head of the family with the role of wage-earner, in which he is subject to the possibility of unemployment through redundancy, etc. He points out the severe psychological effects which the consequent role-conflict may have.[28a]

For today the socialization of the child within the family depends less than it did in Victorian times upon the use of formal, tradition-backed precept. Formal training, of any kind, is now entrusted to specialized educational institutions, rather than to amateurs: the task of the family is rather that of encouraging the child to use these facilities: more fundamentally, it is that of convincing the child that *a normal social life is worth living*. And this can only be done with difficulty, as Bowlby has indicated,[29] when the normal family relationships and roles, upon which the child bases his security, have been upset. Today this function of the family is both more necessary (presumably) and also more difficult, because of the absence of support from a kin-group or from institutionalized social tradition.

Over the past century, certain trends may be discerned in the structure and functions of the British family, as of the family in the United States and, to some extent, those of other Western societies. These, which have in part been noticed or implied earlier, may be summarized as follows:

1. A change from a large to a small group;
2. A change from a stable to a mobile group;
3. A change from an adult-centred to a child-centred family;
4. A change from an integrated authoritarian group to an individualized and more permissive group;
5. A change from a neighbourhood-enclosed family to one with loose kin and neighbourhood ties, and largely insulated.

These changes are of course associated with the rise in importance of the functions of protection and companionship, and the relative decline of the function of perpetuation of the lineage, and that of transferring and allocating wealth, which were important, at least among well-to-do families, in previous centuries.

The family, like other social groups, requires to be supported by ritual, symbolizing not only recognition and approval by society (the public wedding ceremony) but also symbolizing the unity of the group, the interdependence of its members. Bossard and Boll[30] on the basis of their field research on a large number of American families, discuss the importance of the 'rituals' which go to make up the daily life of the average family. These may vary from formal programmes, such as family prayers, to simple and informal ones such as the custom of putting father's slippers to warm by the fire against his coming home, or taking him up a glass of lemonade at night. They have in common that in each case the action was felt by the doer, and by the other members of the family, to have a weight of meaning, to be actions which not only acknowledged, but willingly accepted, family ties. They were actions which continued to be done, because it seemed proper and necessary to continue them: they had an importance for the life of the family: an emotional weight.

Bossard and Boll write of American families, but it seems in accordance with general experience to suggest that these rituals are a feature of family life in other societies. Therefore certain conclusions which the authors come to after surveying the evidence of informants covering three generations, are pertinent. It appears to them that, while these symbolic affirmations and supports of family union were by no means dying out, changes in them could be detected, and that these changes were in the direction of greater simplicity, less formality, less rigid and authoritarian prescription; less dependence on tradition; the rituals were more the individual creations of individual families; less with the aim of symbolically teaching control and repression, and more that of liberating and guiding potentialities.

These changes are clearly related to changes in the structure and functions of the Western family itself.

The two social factors which have most affected the nature of the contemporary Western family are the decline in importance of the lineage as a means for the transmission of social status and of property; and the assumption of many of the functions of social training and protection of its citizens, young and old, by the State: a tendency towards the substitution of specific legal obligations supervised by the State, for the more diffuse moral and religious obligations embodied in the Christian religion. One consequence, mentioned earlier, is that parents come to have specific duties towards their dependents as agents of the State. But this apart, the chief consequence is that the primary purpose of the family comes to be looked upon less as instrumental, and more and more as that of developing ties of personal affection between its members, so as to protect them from the more and more anonymous, impersonal pressures of an industrial society. It is to much less an extent than formerly an agent of social control in the interests of a lineage, or of a relatively consensual society or class: rather it is a place of relaxation: it is a place for expressive activity. The progressive extrusion of expressive activity from the economic system has gone more or less concurrently with the extrusion of instrumental activity from the family system—though it is not suggested that the causal connections are direct ones.

Clearly, the degree to which these expressive purposes can be achieved will vary, and in particular will be restricted, for poorer families, by environmental limitations: these will include, not only 'sub-standard' accommodation in the usual sense, but also the lack of scope for individuality imposed by the requirements of corporation landlords in high-density housing. This is likely to provide a social problem of considerable importance.

REFERENCES

1. Fox, Robin, *Kinship and Marriage* (1967)
2. Parsons, Talcott and Bales, R., *Family, Socialisation and Interaction Process* (1956)
3. Fox, Robin, *op. cit.*
4. Murdock, P., 'World Ethnographic Sample' (*American Anthropologist*, Vol. 59, 1957)
5. Murdock, P., *op. cit.*
6. Le Play, F., *Les Ouvriers Européens* (1877–9)
7. Levy, Marion J. Jnr., *The Family Revolution in Modern China* (1949)
8. Fox, Robin, *op. cit.*

9. Aberle, D. F., *et. al.*, 'The Incest Taboo and the Mating Behaviour of Animals' (*American Anthropologist*, Vol. 65, 1963)
10. Fox, Robin, *op. cit.*
11. Murdock, P., *Social Structure* (1949)
12. Murdock, P., 'World Ethnographic Sample', *ut. sup.*
13. Freedman, M., *Lineage Organisation in Southeastern China* (1958) and *Chinese Lineage and Society* (1966)
14. Dewey, A., 'Trade and Social Control in Java' (*Journal of the Royal Anthropological Institute*, Vol. 92, Part 2, 1962)
15. See Freedman, M., *Chinese Family and Marriage in Singapore* (1957)
16. See Ward, B. E. (ed), *Women in the New Asia* (1964), especially articles by Wee, A. E. and Foong Wong
17. Swift, M. G., *Malay Peasant Society in Jelebu* (1965)
18. Firth, Raymond, *Social Change in Tikopia* (1959)
19. Fortes, M., *The Web of Kinship among the Tallensi* (1949)
20. Laslett, P., *The World We Have Lost* (1965)
21. *Registrar-General's Statistical Review of England and Wales for the year 1967*, Vol. II (1969)
22. *Royal Commission on the Population* (1949)
23. *Registrar General's Statistical Review, ut. sup.*
24. See, e.g. Arensberg, C. and Kimball, S., *Family and Community in Ireland* (1940)
25. Young, M. and Willmott, P., *Family and Kinship in East London* (1957)
Willmott, P. and Young, M., *Family and Class in a London Suburb* (1960)
Kerr, M., *The People of Ship Street* (1958)
Willmott, P., *The Evolution of a Community* (1963)
Firth, R., *Two Studies of Kinship in East London* (1956)
Williams, W. M., *The Sociology of an English Village: Gosforth* (1956)
Williams, W. M., *A West Country Village* (*Ashworthy*) (1963)
26. Litwak, E., 'Extended Kin Relations in an Industrial Democratic Society' (in Shanas, E. and Streib, G. F. (eds), *Social Structure and the Family*, 1965)
27. Firth, R., See Note 25
28. Williams, W. M., *A West Country Village* (*Ashworthy*) (1963)
28a. Titmuss, R. M., *Essays on the Welfare State* (1963), Chapter 6
29. Bowlby, John, *Maternal Care and Mental Health* (1951)
30. Bossard, J. H. and Boll E., *Ritual in Family Living* (1950)

6.

Artistic Institutions

I

ALL LITERARY, and all artistic creation of whose fruits we have any record, constitutes social activity, since the very experience of it by others is a social transaction. The sociology of literature, or of art, consists in an attempt to find partial explanations of artistic forms or styles through the discovery of intelligible relationships (that is, those which depend on our understanding of the *meaning* of actions) between artistic and other social activities. In view of the complexity of artistic creation, any such explanations are likely at best to be partial, but should not be neglected on that account. Such attempts are intellectually fruitful, if they can show, with a high degree of probability, connections between some artistic productions in any given society, and some other social factors, not necessarily all.

The sociology of art, which of course includes the analysis of artistic institutions, is based upon two postulates, which are, for instance, discussed by Leenhart.[1] These are, first, that artistic activities resemble religious, political or scientific activities in being integral parts of *social* reality. The artist creates because he is a social being. Secondly, artistic products and services enter economic (and political and other) markets. Society is the place of artistic and literary consumption: the place where artistic and literary products are bought, or rejected, admired, or disparaged; bring, or may bring, power or prestige. Thus, the sociology of art has an intelligible field of inquiry. But, of course, statements like these are mere starting-off points. The central difficulty lies in the fact that sociology is concerned with generality, with types of social action, with structural regularities. It tends to deal with those relationships which may be made subject to generalization and normative regularity; which can be typified, or can be considered under the aspect of roles or institutions, that is, sets of expected or prescribed actions or relationships. In contrast, the critic of literature, music or painting is generally thought to be concerned chiefly with the characteristics of an object which are novel and unique. *Hamlet* and *War and Peace* obviously have much in common with other plays or other novels: they are composed of words; they deal with the actions of people in societies, they have a certain common structural element. Yet what is important about *Hamlet* is not that it shares more or less the same vocabulary and grammar with *Caste* or *Chu Chin Chow*; it is, rather, the Hamletness of *Hamlet*: that which gives it its unique quality and value. What common ground is there for the two scholars to occupy?

Yet at almost all periods, and certainly today, it is the case that literary critics, and critics of the visual arts, are keenly alive to the social testimony of works of art. How is society expressing itself through the poet or novelist? In what ways are painters able to say something about social structure? Critics, historians of art and literature, and sociologists are all finding a field of interest in topics of the kind admirably formulated by Leach: 'Why did the Victorian age have a Victorian taste? And why was it able to persuade the Victorian artist to produce Victorian art?'[2]

Because of the immense importance of Art in the life of mankind, some attempt to discuss its sociological problems ought to be made here. A sociological study of art encounters, however, very considerable difficulties. Among them is the fact that, in contrast with the subjects treated in earlier chapters of this book much of the groundwork is still to be done. There are few detailed studies of the relations of artists to their social groups, even in modern societies, and although in the past two or three decades a great deal of ethnographical material has been collected about primitive art and music, or the art and music of non-Western civilizations, the volume of material available to the theorist does not compare with that available for the comparative study of religion. It is, indeed, in an early stage. The ethnology of plastic art requires in its practitioner the ability to see the sculpture both as a work of art in its own right, and also as something deriving significance from its place in a living culture. The ethnology of music requires the means of securing perfectly accurate recordings, not possible till the advent of transistorized tape-recorders. Unfortunately, the growth of means of appreciation goes *pari-passu* with the disappearance of the material itself: or rather with a profound change in styles, processes and roles.

To explore the problem of the Sociology of Art, it may first be fruitful to look at the similarities between art and science. This is an age which at least appears to us to be dominated by science and technology; and it would not therefore be surprising to find those who are not scientists seeking to use the language or the vision of science to clarify their own fields of work. A new journal *Leonardo* appeared in January 1968; it was to be a kind of forum where practising artists can speak to each other about matters of common vocational interest. Such a purpose is itself a sociological curiosity. But more important was the journal's policy, expressed by the editor as follows: to 'reflect the developing worldwide impact of contemporary works of art on mankind on a planet . . . where the diversity of community life is being given a unifying basis by the universality of scientific and technological achievements'. In the light of this statement, it was interesting to see, in the first issue, how a number of the contributors were attempting to explore concepts, or ways of interpreting existence, which seemed to them to be common to both Art and Science. Among these, for instance, was the concept of organization, which is obviously prominent enough today, both in these two and in other disciplines. It was clear that these artists had found, in what they took to be the way scientists looked at nature, fruitful means of formulating their own visions of existence. The dominant intellectual interest is thus influencing other manners of understanding the world.

Science and art are both parts of the culture of a society. Art, like science, is, in the first place, a vision or an experience within an individual. But in both cases this vision or experience is largely affected by influences from the society in which the individual lives. It may well also be an influence upon other individuals. And for these influences to take effect, there has normally to be some sort of organization, whether in the form of scientific foundations, departments and industrial concerns, or in the form of machinery for the dissemination of works of art (these include publishers, printers, reviewers, dealers, critics), or indeed for the training of writers and readers. The existence of this organization means that both scientific and artistic vision become enduring social entities, elements in a continuous complex series of social relationships.

The sociological study of art has, for its materials:

1. A number of art objects (novels, plays, paintings, etc), each of which is the expression of a vision of existence through some commonly understood medium, such as language.
2. Historical data about the organization of the production and dissemination of these art objects, and about readership, audiences, the evaluation of art, etc, and the conditions which have affected them.

That is, it involves both a certain degree of critical analysis of art objects and of stylistic resemblances among them (just as the sociology of science involves some acquaintance—the more the better—with science itself) but in addition the study of social and economic history, to identify the social factors which may turn out to be related to elements of style and/or content.

Science can be and has been discussed as a social system. Now it is certainly true that no sociological research could explain the genius of Newton. But few sociologists have ever held that it should. The scope of sociology, as of most disciplines, is limited. Art is in a somewhat analogous position. The creation of a great work of art is, to the artist himself, an unpredictable reorganizing of his experience and outlook. And it brings to those who appreciate it a recatalysing of their own experience. The quality of uniqueness is its significant feature.

But at the same time, another aspect of artistic (as of other) activity requires to be noticed. In his book, *The Structure of Scientific Revolutions*,[3] T. S. Kuhn speaks of 'puzzle-solving activity'. In his view, much of scientific activity (including work of high quality) consists in discovering elegant solutions to problems the terms of which are set by the 'paradigms' (the current general theories) in their field. According to Kuhn, at any given period the predominating theories in physics, chemistry, or other sciences dictate, not only the kind of problems tackled, but the methods used and the sort of answers looked for. The general acceptance of these great theories entails a 'network of commitments' on the part of scientists which constitutes the 'rules of the game', and success follows a neat and aesthetically satisfactory compliance therewith.

Science is not art; but still it might be felt that artistic activity holds something not quite dissimilar: in any period much good painting, or fiction, may be described as neat solutions to problems set by the current 'rules' (standards of taste, 'styles', pervading ideas as to what artists ought to do, and the like). These at least influence the kind of problems tackled, the methods and techniques, and the range of variation in the 'answers'.

This example may lead us into topics of considerable importance to the sociology of art. In the first place, there is this matter of common language or common code of interpretation: since artistic activities are, like scientific, religious, political and other action, integral parts of social reality, they use to a certain extent one another's language or code of interpretation. But which uses whose? The direction, nature and concomitants of this sharing are matters for sociological study.

The second topic is that of the forum or market place. Society is the place where art is appraised and consumed; the place where paintings and the like are admired, disapproved or neglected; bought or not bought; judged, by critics. But between whom is this commerce? Who appraises, and for whom? To whom does the maker appeal? In what sociologically relevant ways do criteria of judgement differ in different periods? Who takes part in this 'commerce'?—to use the word in a wide sense.

Between them, these two ideas (the notion of artistic and other social activities as having common fates, and the idea of social milieux as the 'consumers' of art) succeed in making Art a distinctive *social* activity, and in at least raising the possibility that its relations to the other elements of society can be investigated in something of the same way as can those of science. As there are religious 'styles', 'styles' of politics, and what Kuhn calls 'paradigms' of science, so there are styles of art, not only in the narrow sense, but styles of art-distribution and consumption. In principle, it is a reasonable activity to seek for relations among them, and between them and other aspects of social structure or culture, and to seek for some common element. Indeed, it could be said that the *perception* of these relations initiates the sociological problems of art. The central fact of sociology, says Cohen[4], is the problem of social order. And order emerges *as a problem* when relationships are perceived.

This twofold aspect of art in society cuts across another distinction, also well known, but also important enough to mention. It is that in all the major cultural activities, such as religion, science, art and others, we have an intimate relationship between innovation and tradition.

It is reasonable to define a work of art as an expressive organization which constitutes the formulation of a vision of existence—a vision by the individual artist. But in all societies, simple as well as complex, this individual formulation emerges from a professional tradition—a corpus of techniques to command one's resources, and of manners of interpretation. This need not, often will not involve anything like a face to face group; it may be an ambiance of admired examples and of judgements and preferences, which teach an artist how to form his vision and which give him a code for expressing it. Obviously we have here another relation—and again a complex one—between the individual and his society—a field for aesthetic and ideological tournaments between Self and Others, between Present and Past. An excellent illustration of this relationship comes in the passage in E. L. Gombrich's *Art and Illusion*[5] in which he writes of John Constable. Gombrich tells us:

> Even when he renounces the picturesque, it is still in terms of pictures that Constable thinks. Of his native Suffolk he writes: 'It is a most delightful landscape for a painter. I fancy I see Gainsborough in every hedge and hollow tree.' And indeed it is not hard to show that the vocabulary which Constable used for the portrayal of these East Anglian scenes comes from Gainsborough.

And on another occasion Constable speaks of a Dutch painter's work:

> 'a truly sublime Cuyp, still and tranquil, the town of Dort is seen with its towers and windmills under the insidious gleam of a faint watery sun, while a horrid rent in the sky almost frightens one, and the lightning descends to the earth over some poor cottages with a glide that is so much like nature that I wish I had seen it before I sent away my "Salisbury".'

> Constable [says Gombrich] was convinced Cuyp had made a valid discovery. He had examined Cuyp's rendering of lightning and found it like nature . . . a configuration which, in the context, became a valid cryptogram for that unpaintable glare.

The painter that is, uses a 'language', a social vehicle. Or may we say that out of this tradition he 'generates' his own language. The tradition in this last case is specifically a painting tradition; but as we have seen, it may be affected through 'commerce' between different intellectual modes and between different people, groups, publics.

II

The sociological study of art embraces, of course, a wider field than that of artistic institutions. It may be useful to mention, very briefly, the scope of the former, before proceeding to discuss the latter at greater length. The Sociology of Art, then, may be held to include the following topics:

First, how does society define the term 'art'? What characteristics at any given period, are held to be *important*? And what sort of activities are held to be among the 'arts'?

The lack of distinction which Bentham saw between poetry and push-pin suggests that while poetry, music, painting all express, to a greater or less extent, a vision, or rather an experience, of the nature of existence, this expression is only a social entity insofar as it is permitted: that is, understood as art: the sanction is incomprehensibility.[6] To what Western societies now commonly regard as 'art', there are numerous activities which are peripheral: games, jokes, the skilled employment of language to promote one's own interests, and frustrate those of others, or gratuitous vandalism, for instance; while just within the scope of today's art come activities such as stochastic painting or music by computer, which in another period would very likely have been looked on as jokes, or games, or indeed sheerly evil: so emotive is the field of expression, or appreciation. The study of these norms and customs, and of other factors linked to them, may well constitute an important field of sociology.

Kristeller[7] tells us that the terms 'the arts' or 'the fine arts' did not receive the meaning which is today attached to them until the eighteenth century. This was the beginning of a period when the theory of art (whatever its practice) was of a formal and 'classical' turn, and the limits of what counted as art were fairly clearly defined. Today the limits are ill-defined, and one would be inclined to say that it is the frontier-regions of art which are now of most interest—were it not difficult to know which is frontier and which centre. Of this theme there is one special part—the relation of art to industry—which will be given some more consideration later on.

Secondly, what is the social meaning and function of artistic production? How is it related to the other elements of the Social System?

This is probably the field in which the greatest quantity of theoretical and empirical work has been done.

The Introduction to the *Critique of Political Economy*[8] contains a passage generally regarded as one of the most important formulations of Marxian theory: that in which Marx sets forth the relation of 'superstructure' to 'substructure'.

> In the social production which men carry on, they enter into definite relations that are indispensable and independent of their will; these relations of production correspond to a definite stage of development of their material powers of production. The totality of these relations of production constitutes the economic structure of society—the real foundation, on which legal and political superstructures arise and to which definite forms of social consciousness correspond. The mode of production of material life determines the general character of the social, political and spiritual processes of life. It is not the consciousness of men that determines their being, but, on the contrary, their social being determines their consciousness.

The passage is not, of course, unambiguous: the word 'general' in the last sentence but one may perhaps be regarded as hedging. Still less downright is Engels' letter to Borgius, written much later.[9]

> Political, legal, philosophical, religious, literary, artistic etc. development rests upon economic development. But all of them react one upon the other, and upon the economic basis. It is not

the case that economic conditions are *alone the active cause* and all else mere passive effects; rather their action is reciprocal on the basis that *in the last instance* economic necessity always prevails.

What, at least, is plain is that Engels asserted an *inter*-action between artistic and other social elements. Later writers have attempted to study in detail the nature of this interaction. Goldmann, for instance, seeks to demonstrate a 'homology' between the structure of society at certain periods, and the structure of the works of major writers (representative writers of those periods). So, in *Le Dieu Caché*[10] he finds a relation between the social position, in seventeenth-century France, of the *noblesse de robe*, completely dependent upon the whim of an absolute monarch; the theology of Jansenism, with its conviction of the helplessness and dependence of man in face of a transcendant and inscrutable God; and the poetical recreation of this theology in the plays of the Jansenist Racine. In a later work, *Pour une Sociologie du Roman*[11] Goldmann puts forward the idea of a homology (the word is his) between the structure of capitalist society and the structure of the nineteenth- and twentieth-century novel.

Goldmann accepts R. Girard's interpretation of modern society as 'degraded'. Modern society is permeated by the ideology of exchange-values; but since creative artists are dedicated to use-values, there ensues a sort of alienation between the artist and society. Indeed, while in earlier times the artist was the spokesman of society as a whole, under capitalism truly creative artists can only be the spokesmen of particular groups within society. The fundamental hypothesis of Goldmann's structuralism is therefore that the structures of the universe of the work of art are homologous to the mental structures of certain social groups.

It is inconceivable, says Goldmann, that so complex a form of art as the novel, practised for so long, so widely, and by such diverse practitioners—to such a degree indeed that it is the characteristic literary form of today—should not bear some significant relation to the 'most important aspects of social life'. But a sociological study of the novel should not be concerned with its content, which, at least in the case of the finer novelists, reveals little of significance. The resemblances which should rather be looked for, he tells us, are *structural* ones. What does this mean? The chief illustration which Goldmann gives is that the novel is characterized by the presence of a 'problematic hero' who is defined as a 'personage whose existence and values confront him with insoluble problems of which he is unable to form any clear and rigorous understanding (this last trait distinguishing the hero of the novel from the tragic hero)'. The modern novel describes the search by a 'problematic hero' for authentic values in a degraded world; values which are not those 'which the critic or the reader regards as authentic, but those which, without being manifestly present in the novel, organize in an implicit fashion the totality of its universe'.

Furthermore, there is a 'homology' (which Goldmann clearly thinks important) between the *stages* of capitalist development and the form or nature of the hero.

In the early stage, the individualistic 'captain of industry' stage, the typical novel-hero was an individual. The second phase of capitalism, that of trusts, monopolies, finance-capital, and state-intervention, of the decline in importance of the individual in economic organization, and consequently, in social life generally, is reflected in the novel, first by a form in which the hero is not the individual but the group, the collectivity; and by a second, apparently later, form marked by the dissolution of the individual personality of the hero; by the absence of a hero.

These are what appear to be Goldmann's most prominent ideas. If some comment is to be attempted, it would be, first, that his fundamental notions seem to have been picked up here and there in an over-hospitable manner. The term 'dégradation', to take one example, is borrowed from the work of the existentialist philosopher Rene Girard. To employ a term originally used in a cosmological and implicitly evaluative context as if it were scientifically descriptive may well lead to begging the question: the sociologist ought, for example, to enquire whether, or in what precise sense, the present age is more 'degraded' than were others. But this need not be pursued.

The three types of hero, too, seem highly dubious. But we are left in the air because of the lack of cases to support the arguments. In fact only three writers are effectively discussed —Robbe-Grillet and Sarraute, cursorily, and Malraux at some length. Clearly the matter of 'sampling' is important, all the more in that it is not impossible that some novelists (especially French ones) should read sociology, and accept from it ideas as to how they ought to write; and thus the situation becomes (in the language of military journalism) fluid.

The example of Malraux seems anyway to have been an unhappy one: Malraux' novels are said to be examples of the replacement of the individual hero by the collectivity; but Goldmann's own full and interesting discussion suggests that Garine, Kwatow and the others are individuals, and are no more simple effluents of a collectivity than are the characters of *Plain Tales from the Hills* (but the application of the theory to Kipling might prove interesting).

It is inconceivable, as Goldmann says, that there should be no relation between the novel and society: but the difficulty is to find the illuminating connection. It is doubtful whether 'structural' approaches, at least as used by Goldmann, are helpful. How, for one thing, is the existence of the *héros problématique* a fact of structure, and not of content? Structure is a blessed word, and has been the target of criticism by sociologists themselves. One is tempted to say that it arises more out of the need to seek somewhere, somehow, a meaning in social relations, than out of success in finding one.

An interesting comparison might be made between Goldmann on the novel and Max Weber's work on the sociology of music. Weber did not devote to the study of art that enormous, detailed attention which he gave to religion. But in one short essay, called *The Rational and Social Foundations of Music*[12] he presents a thesis of extreme interest, and worked out with remarkable erudition.

Weber attempts to demonstrate what may, following Goldmann, be called a 'homology' between the structure of Western music and that of other aspects of Western society. Just as the development of Western capitalism was, he held, marked by the progressive development of 'rationality', and just as the development of administrative systems was marked by the growth of rational organization on bureaucratic lines, so Weber essayed to show that 'rationality' was a characteristic of modern Western music, and of Western alone, as he strives to show by comparison with non-Western systems. Here Weber is seeking to demonstrate the existence of structural homologies (but he does not use this word) within a particular society, and, by implication, of systems of concomitant variations between different societies.

The Rational and Social Foundations of Music is a work of some difficulty. It remained unpublished until 1921, after Weber's death; and though first written in 1911, does not seem to have been made ready for publication by the later year: it starts abruptly and stops abruptly, and some parts of the topic receive much fuller treatment than others which seem equally important. Further, as is common with Weber, the style is clotted with implication, allusion and erudition. Nevertheless, for its learning and originality, it has good claims to attention.

The article considers briefly a number of topics: the rise of professional musicians, the development of modern musical instruments, such as the piano; but its main theme is the nature of music itself: or rather, the contention that Western music—that is, at the stage it had reached by about the end of the nineteenth century—was a 'rational' system, and that its possession of this quality of 'rationality', to a degree previously unequalled, rendered it unique among the musical systems known to history or ethnology.

Now 'rationality' is an extremely important concept in the sociology of Weber; unfortunately, however, his use of it is by no means free of obscurity. But two things seem clear: first, that, as used by Weber, rationality is an attribute of social systems; and second that it has reference to the *means* chosen to attain ends, not to the quality of the ends themselves. 'Rational' action is that which is chosen as being, and which is, the most effective to attain given ends.

It is important, further, to note that Weber regards 'rationality' as being a characteristic of modern capitalist society, in the sense that the justification of forms of behaviour and organizations is sought less and less in tradition and more and more in their efficiency in securing the aims which the society is deemed to have. To take an example from the field of political organization, Weber considers that typical feature of modern society known as 'bureaucracy' to be rational, since it is, in his view, the form of administration most technically efficient to achieve the society's purposes. Thus a bureaucracy is more efficient as a tax-collecting system than is, say, tax-farming by feudal lords, since bureaucrats are impartial, technically qualified, not personally involved, and so on. Social action is thus rational when the means utilized are (and are chosen because they are) efficient to achieve the end in view.

It would seem that our ability to use the term 'rational' in any such way as this depends upon a clear consensus as to the nature of the end which the action or system seeks to serve. There are various general difficulties in Weber's use of the term; but we are concerned here with his use of it to characterize musical systems.

In the work under consideration, Weber does not define rationality. But, since the meaning of it discussed above pervades his other writings, it is to be assumed that he is using it in the same sense here: in other words, that he is asserting that there is a certain quality which is common to Western economy and administration and to Western music. This is an assertion for which very likely a *prima facie* case might exist, since both are parts of the same society; and it is an assertion that many might be tempted to wish true. It must be asked on what grounds Weber holds it.

1. Weber instances the Western system of musical notation. This permits the recording of both simultaneous relations and relations of succession of a very high degree of complexity, and thus makes feasible (other factors also cooperating) the composition of highly complex music. Further, it not only makes musical compositions permanent but also stabilizes them, since the scope for variation and improvization on the part of the performer necessarily becomes more limited.

2. Weber also discusses equal temperament in the tuning of musical instruments. He concludes that this, at the expense of a slight diminution in the fineness of discrimination of small intervals, permits the simultaneous playing of a variety of musical instruments, and thus makes possible the composition of music of a high degree of ordered complexity.

These may both be regarded as means towards the composition and the playing of music of a high degree of complexity, and therefore, provided that it is agreed that compositions showing a higher degree of such complexity have greater aesthetic value than those showing less, to speak of them as rational is presumably consistent with Weber's general use of the term. But he goes further.

3. The structure itself of Western music is, he says, 'rational'. It is so through being based on tonality, on the diatonic scales, and through these upon a complex 'vertical' harmonic texture, based on triads, their inversions, and so forth. While the musical systems even of some 'primitive' societies are polyphonic, the harmonic quality of modern Western music is immeasurably more developed than is the case with any other system. This is so although Western music is not only harmonic but melodic, and melody requires the presence, in a musical structure, of notes which cannot be 'rationally' assimilated into the harmony. That is, there are always what Weber calls 'irrational' elements, in tension with the others. 'Chordal rationalization lives only in continuous tension with melodicism, which it can never completely devour.'

Today we should have to add that it is also in conflict with the greater awareness of what Dunwell calls 'the intrinsic interest of sound-groups themselves' rather than of 'their function as a musical language'. But Weber might perhaps have replied that Impressionism tends to give way to formal system, and that the major musical influence today is not Debussy but Schönberg. But the real point to be made is that what in fact he *did* say seems to place a new meaning on the word 'rational'. What Weber is telling us is that the 'grammar' of Western music permits us (or rather permits those capable of doing so) to generate relatively complex bodies of harmony from relatively simple basic principles. If he did mean this, and supposing for the moment that it is true, then it has nothing to do with the means-end relationship, which seems to be implied by his general use of the concept of rationality.

This seems to be clear from a contrast between the so-called 'rationality' of music and the rationality of economic or political structure. Rationality in an economic or political system is something called forth by the external needs of the system, and moreover, in ways we can understand: we can see *why* honesty and competence in a bureaucrat should be rational. We can see why, in a sense, he *has to be* honest: it is so as to be efficient for given ends. But music has no 'end'—does not have to 'be' anything: not even heard: though it does require that men should be familiar with the experience of hearing. A book by the German novelist Hesse tells of a certain group of adepts whose task in life was to devote themselves to the creation of patterns and structures of the utmost complexity, formed out of glass beads. Music is a *Glasperlenspiel*. Its acoustic 'raw material' is given by Nature, but the musical use made of it—the rules of sequence and simultaneity of tones—is a matter of convention (followed for purely aesthetic reasons). And the conventions change; and what we now know is that we are today just as capable of appreciating Schönberg (that is, of relating him to the values of our world of experience) as of appreciating Debussy, or Brahms, or Palestrina.

The 'homology', it may be suggested, lies, not in a greater growth of 'rationality' in music, similar to the rationalizing of political or economic structures, but in an increasing trend towards experiment in organization, which may be detected in all forms of social activity: in the process of scientific theory-building, in social engineering, and in art. In this respect, to this extent, expressive organization parallels instrumental organization: both are anti-paradigmatic. But while in the latter this represents rational procedure, since it provides the opportunity for a technically efficient relation of means, which are limited, to ends, which are given, in expressive activities, such as music, means are not limited and ends are not given. Where 'all choices are open' because no laws are acknowledged, artistic creativity is impossible, since creativity means denial. Thus 'artistic styles' come into being to give a framework. What is rational in instrumental activity may be irrational, or rather, may be destructive, in expressive activity.

III

Thus, thirdly, the sociology of art is concerned with art as an institution: that is to say, with norms such as styles, fashion and taste; with roles; the role of artist, of executant, of patron, of middleman; and with programmes, such as training.

How far is it possible to speak of the artist's 'role'? A role obviously depends upon the existence of some degree of specialism; and, although some writers on primitive arts have suggested that in the more simple societies specialism in the arts is non-existent, this seems improbable, since at any level above the most rudimentary some kind of differentiation, if only by age or sex, is an essential element of social structure. One of the problems here is, exactly at what stages of differentiation are we entitled to speak of 'specialism'? Is it when the performer is paid regularly, is given gifts, or is simply acknowledged as an artist of more than the average talent? If the latter, it is scarcely to be supposed that any society exists in which such a degree of specialism is absent.

The problem is somewhat more difficult, and more interesting, when we approach the question of the existence of professionalism. We normally speak of a professional as being someone who is supported, either whole-time or at least for a substantial part of his time, by the rewards given directly for his work. But here again, both in our own society and in others, there is a significant range of degrees of professionalism. A person may be partly supported by part-time fees; on the other hand he may be able fully to make his living by the occupation in which he calls himself a professional. But as Merriam[13] points out, while all musicians are specialists in some sense, and while some musicians are professionals, one of the most important criteria is the degree of acceptance by society as a specialist or a professional. The true specialist, says Merriam, is a social specialist; he must be *acknowledged as an artist* by the members of the society of which he is a part. And Merriam goes on to point out that this is the ultimate criterion; without it professionalism would be impossible. This is again to make the fundamental sociological point that the existence of the artist depends upon the existence of his public.

The ethnological literature has a good many scattered references to the existence of specialist artists (musicians, sculptors, etc). Their professional status—in the sense we have used the word above—is often described and discussed; although the data lack the detail and precision that one would like to have. One of the most explicit discussions is that of Nadel relating to the Bida drummers.[14] Drumming in Bida, says Nadel, is a full-time occupation. Sometimes a drummer will practice a little farming, in addition, but this is not frequent. Drummers are organized in companies who take in new members as the old members retire. These novices serve an apprenticeship as minor performers in the company. When they are proficient they become fully-fledged members of the drumming craft. There seems to be an element of heredity in the occupation: the sons of drummers mostly follow the paternal profession; singers and dancers, on the other hand, are often not the children of singers or dancers. While drumming is a profession, singing and dancing in Bida are vocations.

Thus in this society the distinction between music and drumming seems to be allied to an organizational distinction. In the one case the entry into the profession is to some extent on hereditary lines, in the other heredity appears to play little part. Other instances show a relationship between the type of occupation followed and the particular social relationship into which the artist enters. Writing about Dahomey, Herskovits[15] states that those following the occupations of brassworker and of maker of appliquéd cloths were the retainers of the Dahomean king. These specialists were essentially courtiers both by position, by affiliation, and by their personal loyalties to the monarch. Thus their dependence upon the king determined their place in Dahomean society. From this it followed that geographically these workers were confined to the capital, since there was their only market. On the other hand, woodcarvers were, as Herskovits says, more democratic, because any man could be a woodcarver. There were specialist carvers, but the entry to the specialism was not restricted by administrative requirements.

As we should expect to find, then, the condition of specialism or of professionalism in simpler societies depends to some extent on what may be called political circumstances, that is, on the existence and the requirements of central or important power groups, rather than on general demand; the artist exists, indeed, often as a retainer of the king. Rose Brandel,[16] speaking of the music of the Bakuba of the South Central Belgian Congo, gives another instance of this relationship. Here the musical bard may be attached to the retinue of the king, and may serve as a royal historian and, as she says, a general poet-laureate. The Bakuba, who ruled a large empire in the sixteenth century, had a royal court with a 'master storyteller' and a 'keeper of the royal traditions'. The work of these bards was to extol the royal lineage. This form of political activity is, as is well known, widespread amongst pre-industrial societies. It also had obvious connections with the role of the bard in other types of society, as the official, or at least accredited, retailer of the heroic legends of the nation or people.

Another important question concerns the social status or prestige of the artist. Is he regarded as of a high prestige, or is he regarded as a deviant? Malinowski, speaking of Trobriand society, gives evidence to suggest that the status, at least of outstanding singers, was such as to excuse in them behaviour which in other people would be regarded as a grave crime. The role carried with it the privilege of behaving in ways which are not normally permitted by the community. Among the Basongye, too, Merriam tells us that musicians were of a definitely low status, the butt of jokes; considered to be lazy good-for-nothings. The current opinion there was that they exist only for music, and nothing else is of importance to them. Nevertheless, the Basongye musician is regarded as a very important person, because the work which he does is essential for the maintenance of the society. Without the possibility of singing and dancing, the life of Basongye society could not continue. The musician's status is low, but his importance is high. Because of his high importance he is permitted to follow a role which puts him outside the requirements of normal behaviour. And in fact we are told that the commission of what in others would be regarded as crimes, is often overlooked in the musician.

The artist's training, in pre-literate societies, is, as one would expect, largely a matter of apprenticeship to an individual. Himmelheber,[17] speaking of the Guro or Atuto woodcarvers of West Africa, states that the customary thing is for the boy to go as an apprentice, either to his own father, or to another relative such as an uncle, or to somebody unrelated but well known for his expertise. Himmelheber suggests that apprenticeship to one's own parent is the preferred thing, at least on the part of the parent, since it gives him opportunity to use his son's abilities, then or later. In other cases, apprenticeship may be not to an individual, but to the group which the novice joins. The Dahomean drummers offer an example of this type of training, which may therefore be said to approach the idea of a school.

There is thus some evidence of the existence of full-time, or largely full-time poets, musicians, and plastic artists who are employed in some fashion or other by powerful individuals, if not by the community in general. However, as Merriam says, it is difficult to find in the ethnological literature sufficient detail as to the condition of employment, the rates of payment, and similar factual material. Merriam's conclusion is that complete professionals seem relatively rare in non-literate societies, and this is supported by Brandel who says 'it should be remembered that the "professional" musician is the exception, not the rule. Most music-making, especially in the less organized, spread-out areas of Central Africa, is a product of layman, community activity, en masse.' Artistic roles would therefore appear to be somewhat less differentiated in simpler societies than in modern ones. It is evident that the existence of specialism and professionalism, or at least the degree to which these exist, must be dependent upon the degree of specialization in the society in general, and therefore upon such related matters as the standard of living, the wealth of the society, and the level of technological development.

The role-expectations attaching to the role of artist in Western societies show, as is well known, a considerable degree of variation, and indeed of ambiguity. Painters in Tudor England were often little more than craftsmen, taking orders and carrying them out according to the client's specifications.[18] The same man might paint his client's portrait, and repair the gilding on his family tomb. England was behind the times: in sixteenth-century Italy, the artist had become an individual, and resplendent abilities, it was felt, should command a resplendent style of life: Popes hastened to pick up the brush that Titian dropped—or at least the story was received with approval. From nineteenth-century Britain comes an equally significant anecdote. A Harley Street physician, an eminent barrister, and Sir J. E. Millais, R.A., were chatting at their club with the Prince of Wales. His Royal Highness asked each what he earned. After the doctor and the barrister had quoted figures, Millais gave his: the Prince was surprised to find that it was considerably the highest.

There are several ways in which this anecdote—current at least, and probably true—is significant. The first is that by then it was possible—at least for the future Edward VII—to have got the idea of a 'typical' painter—with whom one could institute statistical comparisons of professional incomes. The second is that the story was told by Millais himself: the artist was not now either a patron (the Renaissance ideal) nor a client (generally the reality) but a middle-class man, a bourgeois. To some extent this development was the surprising consequence of the Royal Academy, which, designed to make the British artist into Raphael, made him instead into Podsnap: a fairly liberal Podsnap, with an agreeable vein of sentiment, humour, highmindedness, and a certain superficial keenness of observation. Thirdly, the reaction produced the artist as Bohemian, as necessarily deviant in a society searching for moral respectability. But this image of the artist is not peculiar to Victorian, or even to European, society, as we have seen.

IV

But before considering any further the role of the artist, which can hardly be effectively separated in discussion from the question of artistic styles and the technologies of production and distribution, we ought to turn our attention to something which bears closely on these last topics: that is, the question of literacy (and its counterparts in music and painting)—the question of channels of communication. Styles, the role of the performer and the public, and the character of the communication process are, naturally enough, closely related. In the field of verbal art, the transition from preliterate to literate stages makes a fundamental difference in the form of the art. In music something similar is the case. With the plastic arts, the situation is different and perhaps more complex. Accordingly, it will be well to deal with each art form separately.

Taking the case of literature, the first transition is from the artist as a bard to the artist creating art-forms. In *The World of*

Odysseus[19] Finley tells us that since heroic poetry such as the Homeric epics (and also the productions of bards in contemporary Yugoslavia) is always composed orally, by bards who are illiterate, and is recited to a listening audience, themselves mainly illiterate, there is need for some device whereby the memory of the bard, and the attention of his audience, may both be sustained. These circumstances affect the structure of the poem itself. It is distinguishable from literary epics by the constant repetition of phrases, lines, and whole groups of lines. Athena is 'owl-eyed', Achilles 'city-sacking'. But as Finley tells us, this is no simple monotonous repetition. There are a number of different epithets for Achilles, for example, and the choice is determined by the requirements of metre and syntax. About a third of the entire poem consists of lines, or blocks of lines, occurring more than once in the work.

The reason is, that the repeated formula is an indispensable thing. The bard composes in front of his audience. He does not remember lines and repeat them. Lengthy composition in these circumstances makes a tremendous demand on the concentration of the bard, and of his audience. The fact that it can be done at all means in the first place that the bard himself must be a specialist, a professional with long training. He therefore has at his command a large stock both of available incidents to use as material for composition, and also of formulae to bring in to reinforce his poem as the occasion arises. But also repetition of familiar matter is essential for the audience as well. Just as a child, in order that it shall understand the way in which the plot of a story is unfolding, requires to have repetition of incident and repetition of comment, to save it from becoming tired and losing interest, so in the same way the illiterate audience needs to have the expectation of repeated epithets, repeated descriptions, and repeated events, as well as repeated personages turning up again and again in the story. They give the audience something, as it were, to rest upon so as to get a brief second wind.

Though oral literature is vast in amount, and reliance upon oral techniques is unlikely to hamper its composition, the last paragraph will remind us how important for literature is writing. We may divide societies, from our present point of view, into those which are pre-literate, those which are characterized by restricted literacy, and thirdly, those in which there is a development towards universal literacy. As Goody points out,[20] over the past two thousand years the vast majority of the world's peoples have been neither literate nor non-literate—they have been on the margin, living in societies which are characterized by restricted literacy. Much of Asia is in this position; much of Africa also; and for many centuries up until the beginning of the nineteenth, a great deal of Europe. The characteristic of such societies is that although in them the majority of people can neither read nor write, they are closely influenced by the great literate traditions—of China, of India, of Islam—which by indirect means have influenced the outlook of the illiterate peasants.

Factors restricting literacy are partly of a technical and partly of a sociological character. The former include the questions of the medium—to what degree the materials for writing are cheap and easy to come by and to use. For instance, paper is more administratively convenient than clay for official documents. There is also the question of the presence or absence of mechanical means of paper-making, of printing, or of distribution of printed material. Another question is that of the nature of the graphic form. Ideographs are more difficult to memorize than are phonetic alphabets. Among sociological factors are those leading to the conscious restriction of opportunities for learning to read and write. These may arise where groups of people with political power have an interest in maintaining a monopoly of the sources of their power. Occupational groups such as priests may be found to do so. Again, ruling classes may find it desirable to restrict the opportunities of the subject classes to become acquainted with sources of information.

The consequences of restricted literacy are, in the first place, the predominance of mnemonic learning. Even where the reading of books is used, it tends to be the case that learning by rote, or learning to memorize, is valued more highly than the ability to read out of a book. Thus the use of the book is restricted. Books, when used, are read to be memorized—there are large oral residues, as Goody says, in literate culture.

A further sociological consequence of restricted literacy is the emphasizing of social (class) and cultural contrasts between classes or groups within the general culture. Allied to this is the continuance, or indeed the growth, of a folk art, that is to say a sub-culture, having its own literary products and its own means for disseminating, or for handing down, or for passing from one to another these literary products. The folk culture is a sub-culture different from, but not wholly divorced from, the high culture of the society. In this it exhibits an interesting likeness to the conditions of religion in the same kinds of society.

In Europe and in the Anglo-Saxon countries mainly in the nineteenth century, and in the other countries of the world mainly in the present century, the main trend has been towards the development of universal literacy. In regard to literacy, any comparison between different areas at the same time, and in the same place between different times, is a difficult thing to make. This is because of the problems of the definition of literacy, and of the practical assessment of its extent in any society. What, in fact, is meant by 'literacy'? Does it mean the ability only to read? Or does it mean the ability to read, and to write as well? If it means the ability to read, then what degree of ability should be the measure? Is it to read a simple sentence, for example, or the ability to read an official form, or the ability to read a novel? We have here the problem of functional literacy, that is to say the concept of literacy as being the ability to use one's knowledge for purposes of practical use in the contemporary world.

Whatever the definition is, how does one measure the extent of literacy? Does one take the subject's own statement, or does one offer him some sort of objective test? Here further difficulties arise. When one is dealing with persons who are alive, testing is at least possible: not so with the dead. Cipolla,[21] Schofield,[22] and other writers have suggested that, for eighteenth- and early nineteenth-century England and Wales, the only measure which has any real reliability consists of the use of the parish registers of marriages. These do appear to offer something approaching a reliable measure of the extent of adult literacy. The register had, of course, to be signed by the bride and bridegroom; or, if they could not write their names, they were required to make a mark on the register form. The proportion of crosses offers some indication of the extent of adult illiteracy.

There are objections to the idea that this is a completely reliable method; nevertheless it is the best available.

Judging by such a measure as this, in mid-eighteenth-century Britain about 50 per cent of the adult population was literate.[23] By the early part of the nineteenth century, the increase in literacy seems to have been relatively small: perhaps from about 50 per cent to about 60 per cent. The increase was very much slower in England than in many Continental countries. Partly this was due to past attitudes; to the fear on the part of the upper classes that if many of the lower orders were educated 'there would be no more servants, who would clean shoes or attend upon horses'.[24] Partly it was due to the fear entertained by the governing classes, of sedition and rebellion. But thirdly, there was in England of the early eighteen-hundreds no very pressing need for a literate population. England, as the originator of the industrial revolution, developed comparatively slowly its economic and technical potential. This means that for some time it had a use for unskilled labour. Later comers to industrialism, such as Germany, who were able to build upon a higher base than England, developed faster, and therefore had a more pressing need for skilled and educated workers.

Louis James, in an interesting study of working-class reading,[25] shows that, as a result of the development of literacy in the early part of the nineteenth century, there arose amongst the urban proletariat a specifically working-class literature. This was new, in the sense that it was written for a population which had lost touch with the rural folk-culture, and had also experienced a growing gap between themselves and the new governing classes. There had, in fact, emerged the 'Two Nations' of which Disraeli wrote in *Sybil*: the nation of the educated, well-to-do middle-class, buying three-decker novels at one and a half guineas—the public which patronized Macaulay, Thackeray, George Eliot; and on the other hand, the mass of the population, having wages of thirty shillings or less per week, who bought, not books, but rather journals like the *Family Herald*, the *London Journal* or *Reynold's Miscellany*. These were, in Wilkie Collins' words, the public 'which lies right out of the pale of literary civilization'. It was by far the larger public of the two.

Increasing education and a rising standard of living have

tended since then to widen the scope of the educated public, or if the phrase is preferred, to change the attitude and the interests of the working-class public. We must however note, that this development of literacy in the matter of verbal communication is also paralleled to some extent by the development of musical literacy. Mackerness[26] writes of the existence of an urban folk music in late eighteenth-century and early nineteenth-century Britain. This urban folk music, again something different from the rural folk culture, comprised ballads and broadsheets. Such ballads or broadsheets, of which examples are given by Mayhew,[27] partook somewhat of the nature of news-sheets, spreading news of events of various kinds, or else they were versifications relating to interesting or harrowing events. The existence of these ballads or verses, Mackerness suggests, indicates two significant things. In the first place, he regards it as being evidence of a fair degree of literacy among the masses before 1840. While this may be so, one has to remember the fact that such a broadside reaches a considerable number of people is not evidence that all of them read it. There may be one person who reads it out aloud to a group, so that the whole group gets the benefit without being able to read it themselves. Secondly, Mackerness suggests that it is evidence of the existence of a large number of secular melodies which the majority of the populace could be expected to know by heart, so that the tune to which the ballad was sung would be readily known.

The relations between increased literacy, the nature of art forms, and the role of the artist are evidently intricate, and it is impossible here to do more than indicate a few connections. In the first place, a book which can be possessed, read silently, re-read and referred back to, permits and requires a different vision and a different form from something which is merely heard. Secondly, the opportunities for the stimulation of the writer by his audience are, at least in the case of the novel, of a much more distant and roundabout, and a much less intense kind. This was true even of periodical literature, although here a certain amount of 'feed-back' could be derived from the sales-figures of periodical parts. In the case of books, of course, the nineteenth century saw the reviewer, in journals such as *Blackwood's* or the *Quarterly*, interposed between the writer and a mainly silent reading-public (silent, that is, to him, though recommendation and criticism flowed from reader to reader, and doubtless affected sales). The influence of the reviewer and critic (one form of the role of middleman in the arts) in nineteenth-century Europe is well known, and is an illustration of the increased complexity of 'programmes' of art production in industrial society.

But it is equally true that he represents only an intermediate stage of development: one in which the processes of production and distribution are not all under the control of the producer (since the reviewer is a wholly—or largely—independent sales-promoter), and also a stage of limited, rather than mass, production. For if we have regard to the shrinkage of space for reviews in today's periodicals and the immensely larger number of book titles now published, we see how the review has become inadequate as a general medium of sales promotion. At the same time, changes in the nature of readership, and of book-production, have made possible the development of new techniques—blind buying of paper-backs in supermarkets, direct approach to key consumers, and so on. It is guesswork, but fairly reasonable guesswork, to say that further stages in the development of industrial society are likely to be accompanied by still further stages in the organization of the marketing of literature.

The earlier stages of the development of literacy were—at least in England—marked by a class-division: between literary productions whose price largely restricted them to a middle-class readership, and popular periodical literature for the new working classes. In between came a flourishing trade in reprints, whose prices, nevertheless, must have made them more available to lower-middle readers than to the poor. (No Acts empowering British local authorities to provide free libraries came into force till the mid-nineteenth century.) But the growth of what is sometimes called mass-culture is obviously a consequence of the technology of pictorial communication.

V

The case of the visual or plastic arts differs from those of music or of literature in that there is nothing of what one might call notation to be learned; though there is, of course, iconology. This leads us to the question of what sociological comparisons between painting and the other arts are relevant to our immediate concern.

The resemblances between painting and literature are obvious. Both incorporate visions of existence. Both innovate, but do so within a stylistic and ideological tradition. And both look to a public, and indeed to a market.

The contrasts, however, are equally important. Up to the present at any rate, the painter's or sculptor's work, unlike that of the poet, novelist or musician, is primarily a unique object, in which there can be property and possession. This has various consequences. For the sociologist, it has the consequence that it is easier to identify the producer-consumer relationships. For the consumer himself, the painter is a more suitable subject for patronage than is the writer. For the producer, there is a closer dependence on the taste of individuals or of a narrower group than can be the case with the writer. The second contrast is, that painting or sculpture can symbolize status, prestige and power. It therefore has a particular value for the patron. In the third place, painting is not discursive; it is much easier for the painter than for the novelist or poet to avoid taking up political positions, although he need not avoid them, if he does not wish to. A fourth contrast is that, as compared with the writer, the painter or the sculptor requires more fixed capital (a studio) and more running capital (expensive paint or stone). Further, the writer can, to some extent, compose mentally while doing something else: the painter can only create in front of a canvas. Consequently the serious painter has to be a whole-time worker, while the writer can be content to earn less, or can if need be, depend for his living upon other jobs.

The sociological problems of painting are linked with changes in forms of stratification and power; and secondarily with technological changes that were associated with these.

It will be useful to start with a brief comparison between the social position of the painter in Britain in the sixteenth century and in the nineteenth century. The earlier period saw the painter in Britain still in the position of a craftsman. In Italy, the Renaissance, involving as it did a cult of the individual such as was applied to painters by Vasari in his *Lives*, enhanced the social position of the painter. The all-round individual was the ideal of the time. This ideal was exemplified in artists such as Leonardo and Michelangelo. But this change in status spread slowly elsewhere; and in sixteenth-century England, the typical artist was still a non-innovating craftsman. The trade was dominated by its Guild, the Painter-Stainers company. The artists were generally grouped in family businesses. There was, on the whole, little specialization. Furthermore, the predominant patronage, which was that of the Crown, was designed to promote the idea of State power. Thus these social conditions were mirrored in the type of painting most prevalent at the time. Portraiture was the most common form of painting, and consisted almost wholly of the portraits of royalty and of courtiers. Furthermore, the portrait was less an exploration of character than a symbol of rank. The typical Tudor portrait showed little exploration of the facial character of the sitter whose face might well have been a mask rather than flesh.[28] The painter dwelt chiefly upon the details of the richness of the dress and jewellery of the sitter.

By the mid-twentieth century the position of the painter has of course changed very markedly from this. He is today an individual professional person. Painting is regarded as the expression of an individual vision (although the vision is fed upon knowledge of an exceptionally wide range of stylistic precedents). Hence since painting is the expression of an individual vision, problems arise both of the training of the painter for this particularly uncertain vocation, and problems also of the evaluation of his work. Economically, the painter is supported by a continually growing public demand for painting, and also by the possibility of employing his talents in commercial design, in addition to, for many, art teaching. On the whole the career of the painter, though still precarious, is less precarious than in previous ages. For the young artist, publicity can be obtained through the art schools, of which he is a student. Otherwise his works are sold either through exhibitions or through the dealer. Furthermore, for the established artist there is now an international market in works of art.

In the early and middle nineteenth century the painter's position was midway between these two. His position was changing, as an aspect of the general social change which had been continuing, perhaps from the seventeenth century. But it was certainly different in say 1830 or 1850 from what it had been a hundred years before and from what it would be a hundred years later. The changes in class and power relationships, which had been continuing through the early nineteenth century, led to changes in the sources and in the types of demand for painting. These in their turn led to changes in the organization of the distribution of works of art.

Briefly this change may be said to be one away from patron to public, with the state itself making a brief appearance as patron. It is well known that throughout Europe, until approximately the end of the eighteenth century, the source of demand for paintings had been firstly the Prince and secondly the wealthy nobility. This was the case in Italy, in France, and also in England. The Netherlands formed to some extent an exception to this general principle. In Britain the Tudor monarch and the courtiers, and later the landed nobility and gentry, were the major buyers of paintings, whose characteristics had therefore to be such as this restricted group accepted.

In Britain this patronage did continue into at least the early nineteenth century, and not without considerable benefit to painters: Lord Egremont, and also Sir George Beaumont, at the time of Turner and Constable, were amongst the most enlightened patrons which this country has seen. But there was, from the end of the eighteenth century onwards, a very definite social change in the market for paintings, and this change in the market goes step by step with changes in the character of painting itself.

To take the question of state patronage first. During the early part of the nineteenth century, certain movements were set on foot which represented a deliberate effort on the part of the government (the modern State, that is, not the monarch) in the first place to promote art, and in the second place to elevate by its means the general tenor of life in the country. The activities of the Victorian state in the fields of social welfare are, of course, well known. The same urge to improve the social conditions of the masses is undoubtedly to be seen in its attempts at artistic patronage. It must however be said that in the short term at least the results of the latter activities were less successful than those of the former. The most notorious was a scheme to commission artists to produce paintings to decorate Barry's new Houses of Parliament. It was a fiasco, largely because the directing committee was composed of earnest amateurs, *au fait* neither with the techniques of painting, nor with what was up-and-coming in art fashions. It gave official patronage a bad name.

The more important development of that time was the movement from art 'patron' to 'customer'.

'Patronage', as the term has been applied in the arts, has had a variety of meanings. A patron may, like the Archbishop of Salzburg with Mozart, maintain the artist exclusively, if not adequately, and exercise first claim on his time: the artist is his employee, courtier and servant. A patron may commission more or less munificently, encourage, sustain when necessary (but not completely maintain) and sometimes give more or less welcome advice on technical matters: the case of Sir George Beaumont. Perhaps the supreme examples of this group are the rulers (including the Popes) and their families in sixteenth- and seventeenth-century Italy.[29] Or the patron may commission a few works annually, from different people: as, in the field of music, do the Arts Council, some other foundations, and some business firms today in Britain.[30] These three classes obviously stand in very different relations to the artist: the third, which is characteristic of today's practice, is scarcely different from that of 'customer'. But in the nineteenth century the typical relationship of the painter with his market was that he painted pictures (naturally this does not include portraits) without any special commission in mind, and sold them to somebody with whom he was previously unacquainted, through the medium of exhibitions or of dealers. This however is to make too sharp a distinction. In fact, during the nineteenth century personal relations between painters and buyers still continued, though to a less extent, and painters who were making their way in their profession sometimes had cause to be grateful to the buying policies of discriminating customers. Furthermore, painters like Rossetti owed some of their undoubted commercial success to the fact that the trend of painting which they were interested in also appealed to the known tastes of individual buyers.

And yet these tastes were different from those of a century earlier, and they were also the tastes of members of a different social class. This leads us to consider, in the following pages, an important relationship between the content of a work of art, the market conditions for it and the role of artist in supplying his market.

One characteristic which will strike all those who are acquainted with English nineteenth-century painting, is the overriding importance of *subject* in the painting of this period. Even in works where the formal composition seems to many a very charming one (for instance Egley's *Omnibus Life in London*[31])—even here the picture tells a story: something is happening in it; there is a past and a future, in which we are interested; it is a stage in a game of consequences.

This fact has attracted much attention among art historians. Oppé noted it emphatically in his chapter on art in the book *Early Victorian England*.[32] Humphrey House in a paper in the book *Ideas and Beliefs of the Victorians*[33] says, 'the world of their pictures is a world in which you expect things to happen. The pictures seem to refer to what has gone before, or what will come after.' It can be illustrated extensively from the paintings of the time, at various levels of achievement. We have Hunt's *The Awakening Conscience*, Martineau's *The Last Day in the Old Home*, the *Past and Present* series of Augustus Egg, and Ford Madox Brown's *Work*.[34] The importance of the manifest subject—the idea that every picture, or nearly every picture, told a story, is not perhaps unique to this period; but it is an outstanding fact in it. No doubt we may trace this back to the eighteenth century through Hogarth, but what budded in Hogarth blossomed here.

But it is not just that the picture has a story, but that the story has a moral. Moreover, it is expected to have a moral: for we find that the tenor of much contemporary art criticism is to the effect that the mission of art is moral elevation through the influence of the subject matter. A passage in the *Art Journal* of 1840 gives this advice to painters:

> One of the points that requires the most consideration is the choice of subject. Much more depends upon this than artists are sometimes disposed to admit . . . subjects of effective interest . . . and often conveying a fine moral, are to be found without

degrading the pencil to the commonplace . . . by attracting the attention of that class which may be uneducated and perhaps even coarse and vulgar, even they may be improved.

The *Art Journal* is said to have brought in £50,000 for its proprietor. The fact is relevant: by such criteria as we have, sentiments such as these were popular.

We see here, then, one implication of the importance accorded, in this period, to a picture's subject: art takes its place as a vehicle of moral control. Indeed for many, the only passport which entitled art to circulate in society was its homilectic capacity. And so we find the themes of family and sexual morality; of prudence in conducting one's affairs; and also the theme of 'My Station and its Duties'.

The solitary figure of Hogarth apart, this insistence on the moral distinguishes the first half of the nineteenth century in Britain from previous periods and places, British, French, Italian or Dutch; and it is quite alien to any style of easel painting after the Impressionists: one certainly does not associate it with the work of Kandinski or Jackson Pollock.

Furthermore, it was not satirical, bitter or terrifying, like Gilray or Goya; nor was it intended to be only ephemeral, like a cartoon in a periodical: its qualities were that it was permanent, like furniture, earnest and respectable: and very limited in range.

Pictures are in this period concerned with characters: with morally responsible individuals. In a very particular sense, painting was a socially significant activity. In this sense, and in the sense about to be discussed, there is an interesting nineteenth-century parallel with socialist realism. Socialist realism is concerned with the social education of rising classes. This was also the avowed aim of the nineteenth century.

The aim was quite explicitly stated by an important man of the time, Thomas Wyse, M.P.

> The arts which flourish [he told a meeting of painters in 1842] are those which rise out of the feelings and taste of the great body of the people, which reflect them, which appeal to them; which in fact are no other than a more perfect exemplification, in other forms, of their intellectual and moral being . . . the education of the middle classes renders inevitable the education of all above and below them. But to effect this, more than ordinary exertions

> and sacrifices are necessary. It is the duty of each and all to contribute to them. Everyone in his position—the artist in his, the legislator in his—is bound to advance, to extend this education by . . . elevating the national taste, by correcting the national prejudices.[35]

Such a view of the purpose of art was entertained not only by critics and educationalists, but by artists themselves. And not merely to improve their fortunes with the public. Take the case of Ford Madox Brown, a painter who did not in any way permit himself to earn success through compliance. When exhibiting his painting *Work*, now in the Manchester Art Gallery, Madox Brown himself wrote a description or explanation of it running to approximately 2,300 words. The description did not concern itself with what today would be regarded as the essential pictorial qualities of a picture. It described the people, or the human types, assembled therein, in terms of their moral meaning; the moral and social significance of navvy, rich man, philosopher. It might well have been written, if not by Samuel Smiles, at least by Charles Kingsley. This was what Brown regarded, and felt his public would regard, as the important thing.

Work, like *The Road to Ruin*, *The Awakening Conscience*, *The Hireling Shepherd*, *The Last Day in the Old Home*, and many others, are, as it were, sermons on moral themes. They are obviously directed to the prosperous middle class (obviously, because this class is depicted, and this class bought them). If we look for intelligible relationships with other elements of that society, we surely find them first in the whole Evangelical movement with its appeal to the well-to-do, its insistence on the examination of conscience, and upon moral earnestness. Not only the Low Church, but the Broad and the High, contribute. In his sermons, Thomas Arnold, Headmaster of Rugby, may be described as using the concepts of social class, social mobility, and social control, in order to educate the sons of the new rich in the moral nobleness of the ideal English gentleman. To the station of the true English gentleman pertained duties and standards, and while these were to be inculcated through the sermon and educational precept in the first place, the painter was expected not to remain indifferent.

Art is thus regarded as one of the mechanisms of social

control in a society characterized by rapid social mobility. In ages where social mobility has ceased, the purpose of art is regarded as something different. But in the early and mid-Victorian times, people felt themselves to have a moral duty to examine and to improve themselves, and equally a duty, by exertion in their calling, to improve others. The artist, too, had a social duty.

But in another view, its public worth is economic. 'Independently of the beneficial and elevating influence of the fine arts upon a people, every pecuniary outlay, either for the purpose of forming or extending collections of works of art in this country, has been directly instrumental in creating new objects of industry and enjoyment, and therefore in adding, at the same time, to the wealth of the country.' So said the Select Committee set up in 1841 to consider 'the promotion of the fine arts'.

From the end of the eighteenth century and onwards, the public for a painter—at least for the more successful—was widened to include not only the well-to-do middle classes, but also the much less affluent. Engraving, has of course a long history; but it was in the eighteenth century, and apparently with Hogarth, that the trade in the reproduction of paintings grew to something like the proportions which it attained in the nineteenth century and later. Hogarth, by reproducing large numbers of his works in copper engraving, extended the market for his paintings, and therefore became independent of the rich individual patron. In his own words, he 'reposed on the million'. Furthermore, Hogarth's copyright act of 1734–35, by protecting the property of the artist in his painting, ensured him remuneration in respect of engravings which were sold.

The dissemination of engraved reproductions continued through the latter part of the eighteenth century and into the nineteenth. It provided a means whereby certain entrepreneurs both vastly enlarged the market and also obtained for themselves large, though short-lived, fortunes. John Boydell, Lord Mayor of London, for example, cashed in on the economic opportunities of a new market, and new applications of the technique of copperplate engraving. His 'Shakespeare Gallery', a collection of paintings commissioned by Boydell from leading artists, for the purpose of being engraved, was, in the words of

Boase, undoubtedly one of the most elaborate schemes of patronage in the history of British art. But it was, of course, a different kind of patronage from the seventeenth- or eighteenth-century sort. Ultimately the patron was the multitude of less-well-off people.

It is hard to know whether the effect of the trade in copperplate reproductions was to enhance or to diminish the popular knowledge of art. It was beneficial in that it provided at least some acquaintance with masterpieces and semi-masterpieces, at a time when the acquaintance of the ordinary man with originals was virtually non-existent. (Public galleries did not come into existence in Britain until the mid-nineteenth century.) The number of those who were brought into contact with the visual arts therefore vastly increased; but the great majority of contacts were at secondhand, and furthermore, owing to the characteristics of reproductions, this secondhand acquaintance was an acquaintance with only certain aspects of the original painting. The characteristics of copperplate engraving ensured that only what was, as it were, the story of the painting—the characters, their attitudes and so forth—could be reliably reproduced. There was no possibility of reproducing colour, nor of reproducing methods of laying on paint. The interest of many Victorian painters, and of their publics, in the content, the story, the iconographic aspect, must partly be due to this fact.

The businessmen and industrialists who constituted the new type of customer of contemporary schools of painting such as the pre-Raphaelites, were attracted to contemporary painting, partly because there was no doubt that contemporary paintings were genuine, and not fakes. But also they were led to purchase through the efforts of the rising class of art dealers.

During the nineteenth century the dealer as an economic type comes in to take his place between the painter and the public. The origins of the art dealer lie much farther back: the seventeenth century, at latest. In the eighteenth, people like Gavin Hamilton and others were using a knowledge of Italian society gained in various ways, to acquire and import, to some extent as a sideline, old masters for the market which still existed amongst the aristocracy and landed gentry of Britain. (The market was such that it seems also to have been profitable to manufacture them.) But during the course of the nineteenth century another source of dealers was coming into existence; people such as print-sellers and the like were also acting as buyers of pictures and as go-betweens. The house of Thomas Agnew, for example, arose out of a firm of carvers and gilders, looking-glass and picture-frame manufacturers, opticians, ancient and modern English and foreign print-sellers, dealers in old coins, medals, and all kinds of curiosities. Ernest Gambart, a dealer who was celebrated in connection with the pre-Raphaelites, was originally a print-seller who acted as middle-man between painters and their new public. The dealer was the outcome, as it were, of a wider public and also a different public with different tastes, furthermore a public which was less knowledgeable, or believed itself to be less knowledgeable, than those who had gone before.

The art dealer thus unites three socio-economic types. In the first place, he is the broker who finds markets and makes deals between interested parties, neither of whom is fully cognisant of the market. In the second place he is an entrepreneur. 'A dealer,' said William Agnew, 'can seldom afford to initiate taste, but a dealer with flair can anticipate the circumstances in which taste changes, and by so doing accelerate that change.' In the third place he is a capitalist. He is one who can accumulate stock-in-trade and hold it for a good market. Both the French and the British dealers of the nineteenth century performed services to painters by buying their work at a reasonable price and holding it until they could get a better price for it. Thus they relieved the painters of the anxiety of holding their own work for sale. A later stage came in the development of the dealer when he sought to control the sources of his supply, by advancing money to painters in return for the right to a monopoly of their pictures. In the twentieth century, with the growth in the number of painters regarded as important, the widening of the market (both in the sense that it had become international, and because of the greater volume of money available for buying pictures) and the growth of specialist knowledge and of the tendency to regard pictures as investments, the dealer came to occupy a predominant position in the art world.

VI

These inter-relationships are part of a wider network. The ideas behind much of nineteenth-century British art resembled some of the ideas behind the contemporary earth- and life-sciences. Briefly, the resemblance was this: that a picture such as *Work* or *The Hireling Shepherd*, while it conveyed a moral message, was also the delineation of a collection of objects (men, moths or sheep) carefully and accurately depicted. The organizing principle of the picture was not a formal design, but something which lay outside the picture: the moral meaning. There is, it may be suggested, an analogy with some ideas of pre-Darwinian geology and biology.

Humphrey House, in his most interesting contribution to the symposium *Ideas and Beliefs of the Victorians*, has a very nice phrase to describe this state of mind: 'facts loved with a lingering passion.' This may be the attitude of the Victorian businessman, holding nature accountable, so to speak. House goes on: 'This is all partly because the style of vision is the vision of ordinary life. The world of Victorian Art is the world of the plain, practical man, in which things happen and are done. It is an art to suit a practical age and be bought by practical patrons.' This may be true; but there is rather more to be said.

This chapter began by referring to the borrowings that take place today between Art and Science. This was a characteristic of the early nineteenth century too. But the borrowings, the inspirations, were naturally of a very different sort.

Let us take the example of John Constable. We mentioned earlier what Gombrich regards as the influence of a tradition of painting upon Constable's style. This is inevitable; but it is not what Constable would have regarded as the main significance of his work. Time and again, as we see from Leslie's biography[36] or from his letters, collected by Beckett,[37] Constable asserted that the work of a painter was a science. 'In such an age as this, painting should be *understood*, not looked on with blind wonder, nor considered only as a poetic aspiration, but as a pursuit, legitimate, scientific and mechanical.' And: 'Painting is a science, and should be pursued as an inquiry into the laws of nature. Why, then, may not landscape painting be considered as a branch of natural philosophy, of which pictures are but the experiments.'

Now we must remember that the sciences which Constable had in mind, when comparing his own work to Science, were Botany, and particularly Geology and Meteorology. The growth patterns of vegetation, the relation of the appearance of landscapes to the appearance of clouds—it was this rather than Physics or Chemistry to which he referred. The distinction is important, because of the stage of development which the former had reached. They were, of course, in the pre-Darwinian period; in the collecting, naming, classifying period: and it is certainly significant that it was a contemporary of Constable's, Luke Howard, in his book *The Climate of London*, who first collected extensive and systematic meteorological readings of that area, and first gave to the principal cloud formations the names familiar to most of us.

'Facts loved with a lingering passion' must certainly have well described the work and outlook of many of the geologists and biologists of the period. To use a figure of speech, it was the *objects* contained within the frame of their subject matter (new molluscs, hitherto unknown birds, strange rock-formations)—the objects themselves which fascinated them rather than the prospect of finding any *intrinsic* principle to organize their relations. This seems to be analogous, in its own field, with the importance of subject in visual art.

Connected with the stage of development of science was the nature of the scientist. The early and middle nineteenth century was a period when the scientific amateur flourished. He was important because patient, accurate observation and collection still had an important part to play, even if not linked to extensive theoretical knowledge. A characteristic example was Thomas Edwards (born 1814) the shoemaker-naturalist of Banffshire, who though he had no formal education, was made an Associate of the Linnaean Society in recognition of the copiousness and accuracy of his observations on the biology of the Banffshire coast. Edwards' life was written by Samuel Smiles, and this also is important. Although Edwards, for most of his life, achieved little recognition, this sort of vocation was recognized and held in esteem. It had, for the men of the nineteenth century, a moral value, indeed a religious value, and evidence of this is provided by a long line of Anglican clergyman-naturalists, from Gilbert White of Selborne, before our period, to Charles Kingsley, at the end of it.

The religious value, quite obviously, was that to study the works of the Lord was to glorify Him. Thus Kingsley: 'Science is on the march—listen to her divine words, for what is she but the voice of God?' But popular theology of the time included not only the idea of the Earth (as well as the Heavens) telling the glory of the Lord, but also its correlative, the idea of the impropriety of attributing to raw nature an inherent organizing power of its own; therefore the necessity of an external power to produce organization, and thus the ascription of organization to the power of the Deity. This is the essence of Natural Theology: as the existence of a watch necessarily implies the existence of a watchmaker, so the wonders of Nature necessarily imply a Creator and Orderer of Nature.

There is surely a rather interesting parallel between the idea of Nature as a collection of raw data, objects, which owe their structure to an external operant, the Deity; and the idea of a picture as a collection of representations which owe their significance not to any formal composition but to something 'external' to the painting: the moral meaning. This parallel is suggested with due caution, but it seems worth considering.

VII

Two other comments may finally be made.

First, the kind of Victorian picture exemplified by *Work* or *Past and Present* or *The Awakening Conscience* does for its age, with a solemn ponderous insistence, what sociological journalism would do today. Common morality was then dogmatic and superficial, otherwise it could not have been expressed in pictures, which cannot be compelled to argue. Changes in social attitudes are liable to demand changes in the appropriate media.

Secondly, the sociology of art must surely include a discussion of the application of artistic creativity to the design of mass-produced goods; the design of elegant and attractive posters, office-machines, table-forks, tube-stations and fire-engines.

The origins of Industrial Design do not concern us. It was known to Wedgwood and Boulton; but as a movement showing continuous development, hardly existed before the late nineteenth century. Today it is a practice of considerable importance internationally, with Institutes and Journals, and absorbs much of the energy of schools of art, besides their more able products.

What are the effects on artistic roles and programmes?

The first point to make is that it would be a most unnatural situation for artists to be in if they were unable to contribute to the design of manufactures. Freedom at the expense of isolation is a Greek gift. Furthermore, there is some excuse for thinking that an acquaintance by painters or sculptors with sciences such as engineering or psychology may be fruitful for art itself. The problems lie, first, in making an activity which is essentially expressive into one which is essentially instrumental. Moreover, the artist in a *complex* industrial organization works in a situation where design-policy may be influenced by his advice, but cannot be decided by him. It is decided for the most part on grounds of saleability: a concept notoriously difficult for him to cope with. 'The Company's responsibility is not to the individual artist to let him have an opportunity to show the world who he is, it is a responsibility to its employees, to its customers, to its shareholders, and indeed to the community as a whole, and the artists who want to be creative have got to justify themselves in that context. This is not always a popular conception with artists and designers.'[38] So, it is true, had the traditional artist; but with him, failure to sell *now* did not necessarily mean failure to sell *later*, or failure to be an artist. The unsuccessful industrial designer has no such comfort.

While typically the artist works as an individual, the designer tends to be part of a team, and, further, his role tends to be integrated into an industrial system: his work is part of that system. The writer was once told by a design consultant that he had been commissioned by a certain firm to redesign the firm's notepaper. One thing led to another, and before he had finished, he found he had had to reorganize their whole office procedure to go with the notepaper. The story is unlikely to be true literally, but at least is parabolically true: there is an immediate connection between Graphic Art, Industrial Design, the entrepreneurial activity known as 'Design Management' and Organization and Methods; and the individual has to have some expertise in all fields.

The existence of Industrial Design offers to the visual and plastic artist—to a minority directly, to others indirectly—the stimulation of new forms and new processes, novel roles and programmes integrating art and society.

The foregoing chapter attempts only a tentative sketch of certain issues in the sociology of art. Much more detailed work, in the form of monographs on particular societies, periods and schools, must be undertaken before anything like adequate or cogent sociological generalizations can be made. What has been suggested is that the comparative study of societies shows some evidence for changes in the nature of artistic roles in different societies, though these changes seem to be less marked than with instrumental roles. There is some evidence for the existence, in more developed societies, of a greater degree of role-differentiation, and certainly evidence for the emergence of new distinct roles. There is evidence for the belief that the rise of new social groups is associated with changes in taste, and therefore with changes in the concept of the artist's role. Lastly it is related to changes in programmes for the distribution of art products.

In this much of the data has been taken from Britain. Studies have also, however, been made on other societies—for instance France [39] and Italy[40] and these show, not of course the same *kinds* of change, but associations between changes of some kind in artistic and in other social factors. These should form bases for further inquiry.

REFERENCES

1. Leenhart, J., 'The Sociology of Literature: some stages in its History' (*International Social Science Journal*, Vol. XIX, 1967)
2. Leach, E. R., Comment in a discussion; see *The Artist in Tribal Society*, ed. Marion Smith (1961), p. 111
3. Kuhn, T. S., *The Structure of Scientific Revolutions* (1962)
4. Cohen, P. S., *Modern Social Theory* (1968)
5. Gombrich, E. L., *Art and Illusion* (1960)
6. See Douglas, Mary, 'The Social Control of Cognition' (*Man*, new series, Vol. 3, 1968)

7. Kristeller, Paul O., 'The Modern System of the Arts' (*Journal of the History of Ideas*, Vols. 12 and 13, 1951–2)
8. The passage will be found in Bottomore and Rubel: *Karl Marx: Selected Writings in Sociology and Social Philosophy* (2nd edition, 1961), pp. 67f
9. See Engels to W. Borgius, 25 January 1894 (in *Marx-Engels Werke*, 1968, Bd. 39, p. 205). The recipient has previously been given as H. Starkenberg.
10. Goldmann, Lucien, *Le Dieu Caché* (1959) [trans. Thody, P., *The Hidden God* (1964)]
11. Goldmann, Lucien, *Pour une Sociologie du Roman* (1964)
12. Weber, M., *The Rational and Social Foundations of Music*, trans. Martindale, Riedel and Neuwirth (1958)
13. Merriam, A. P., *The Anthropology of Music* (1964)
14. Nadel, S. F., *A Black Byzantium* (1942)
15. Herskovits, M. J., *Dahomey* (1938), Chapter 35, Vol. II
16. Brandel, Rose, *The Music of Central Africa* (1961)
17. Himmelheber, H., *Negerkünstler* (1935)
18. Mercer, Eric, *English Art 1553–1625* (*Oxford History of Art*, 1962), Chapter 4
19. Finley, M. I., *The World of Odysseus* (1954)
20. Goody, Jack (ed), *Literacy in Traditional Societies* (1968)
21. Cipolla, C., *Literacy and Development in the West* (1969)
22. Schofield, R. S., 'The Measurement of Literacy in Pre-Industrial England' (in Goody *ut. sup.* 20))
23. Cipolla, C., *op. cit.*
24. Cipolla, C., *op. cit.*
25. James, Louis, *Fiction for the Working Man, 1830–1850* (1963)
26. Mackerness, E. D., *A Social History of English Music* (1964)
27. Mayhew, H., *London Labour and the London Poor* (1851–62), Vol. I, p. 273ff
28. See Mercer, Eric, *op. cit.*
29. Haskell, Francis, *Painters and Patrons* (1963)
30. See, e.g. Osborne, A. (ed), *Patron: Industry Supports the Arts* (1966)
31. Reproduced in Lister, Raymond, *Victorian Narrative Paintings* (1966)
32. Young, G. M. (ed), *Early Victorian England 1830–1865* (1934), Vol. II, Chapter 2
33. House, H., 'Man and Nature: Some Artists' Views' (*Ideas and Beliefs of the Victorians* [B.B.C. Talks], 1949)
34. Reproductions will be found in Bell, Q., *Victorian Artists* (1967), Maas, J., *Victorian Painters* (1969) and Lister, R., *op cit.*

35. The speech is reproduced in Pye, John, *Patronage of British Art* (1845), pp. 176ff
36. Leslie, C. R., *Memoirs of the Life of John Constable Esq., R.A.* (2nd Edition 1845)
37. Beckett, R. B. (ed), *John Constable's Correspondence* (Suffolk Records Society), Vols. 4, 6, 10, 11
38. Pilkington, Sir Harry, address to International Design Congress (Council of Industrial Design), 1961
39. Moulin, Raymonde, *Le Marché de la Peinture en France* (1967)
40. Haskell, Francis, *op. cit.*

7.

Religion

I

Henningsen[1] speaks of four categories of interpretation of reality: 1. positivistic and rational interpretations; 2. magical concepts, which set man up as a 'determinator of his own destiny and that of other people'; 3. fatalism, which explains the course of man's life as dependent on 'determinators inaccessible to outside influence'; and, finally, 4. religious ideas, which interpret human life as dependent on causative forces which *are* accessible to outside influence. Thus a religion properly speaking involves belief, not only in the existence of such influences, but in the possibility of man's forming a positive relationship with them.

Considered as abstract types, these four categories are useful. Actual instances are not so clear-cut. The distinction between what Henningsen calls fatalism, and religion, is blurred (as he himself recognizes) not only by the existence of societies which postulate deities, but regard them as uninterested in the affairs of the world, but also by the frequent coexistence of 'fatalistic', 'magical', 'rationalist' and 'religious' beliefs, not only in the same culture, but in the same individual. This simply means that most people who are not logicians are content to deal with the different concerns of their lives pragmatically and without seeking for any comprehensive system. For analytical purposes, his distinction is a valuable one, and so is the definition of religion as involving a positive inter-relationship. This is to be preferred, for instance, to Tylor's definition of religion as simply 'the belief in spiritual beings'. Tylor certainly did not mean to deny the importance, for the sociologist, of religious *behaviour*; he held that belief in the existence of spirits 'leads naturally, and it might almost be said inevitably, sooner or later to active reverence and propitiation'.[2] He was concerned, however, to find a wide, rather than a narrow definition. But those who followed him, and particularly those whose interests lay in functional explanations, urged that he had over-emphasized the cognitive element in religion, and paid too little attention to emotion and conduct: that his explanation was not, on the face of it, a sociological one.

Among those who rejected Tylor's definition was Emile Durkheim, who, in the *Elementary Forms of the Religious Life*,[3] provided a sociological accout of religion which is still of great significance. A definition of religion, said Durkheim, must take account of two classes of activity: of beliefs, and of rites, which depend on beliefs. But all 'religious' beliefs presuppose a division of the universe into the two great categories of the sacred and the profane, which are mutually exclusive. Sacred things are of two kinds, or rather sacredness has a double aspect: under the one aspect, it inspires respect, mixed with love and gratitude; but it may also inspire horror and fear. Yet these are only two varieties of one class (varieties which may at times pass into one another). The class of the sacred is set apart radically from the class of the profane, that is, the ordinary, everyday.

Religious beliefs, for Durkheim, are the representations which express the nature of sacred things. The use of the term 'representations' implies an emphasis which Durkheim regarded as fundamental: religion was a group activity. This Durkheim held to be the characteristic which distinguished Religion from Magic: the magician is an individual, working alone. 'There is no Church of Magic.'[4] But the practice of religion is *essentially* a group activity. For when Durkheim defines a religion as 'a unified system of beliefs and practices relative to sacred things . . . beliefs and practices which unite into one single moral community called a Church, all those who adhere to them'[5] this was, as it were, a step towards a most important conclusion of his argument: that the 'sacred', the gods or spirits or the like of which men formed ideas, were symbolizations of 'the moral power on which [a man] depends and from which he receives all that is best in himself: this power exists, it is society'.

> Religion is a system of ideas with which the individuals represent to themselves the society of which they are members, and the obscure but intimate relations which they have with it. This is its primary function . . . for it is an eternal truth that outside

of us there exists something greater than us, with which we enter into communion.[6]

Against this remarkable (and, for its time, extremely pregnant) theory, several criticisms may be levelled. First, while Durkheim relies upon data drawn from the Australian aborigines, his observations about the nature of religion appear to be intended to have a general application. But it is not clear that what is true (if it is true) of an 'elementary' form of religion, in a simpler society, can be assumed true of all forms of religion. This introduces the second criticism, which is concerned with Durkheim's use of the word 'society'. An obvious defect in Durkheim's method lay precisely in his use of simple and undifferentiated societies. Certainly it is everywhere true in an important sense that religion *is* a group activity, and that engaging in collective rituals is apt to reinforce very strongly the feeling of what may be called 'the community of believers'. But a study of religion in more complex societies shows that its relation to the processes of socialization is far more complex and ambiguous than Durkheim's words suggest. Thirdly, Durkheim's assertion runs some danger of being platitudinous, if it means simply that group communion, as such, promotes the feeling of group unity: this would be true of most forms of collective action, not simply of religious ones; it would be true of a lynching-party, for instance.

It would appear that Durkheim's work *assumes* that the significance of religion lies in its function of socialization. But it is by no means clear that, even for sociology, this is the aspect which most deserves attention. Further, it needs always to be remembered that, if religion has a function (or functions) for society, it also has a purpose, or purposes, for the individual. Religion, to the religious person, means *ultimately* a relation between him and something which is non-human; it is not a social conception. Nevertheless, these 'individual' purposes may be as important to the sociologist as are the 'social' functions of a creed or rite.

And, while it is necessary to appreciate the common features of different religions, it is also necessary to remember that the differences between different religions may be profound. All attempt to give answers to the problems of evil and suffering;

man, as Geertz says, needs *some* answer; but the answers given by Theravada Buddhism, by Christianity and by Manichaeism are different. The causes of such differences (so far as they can be discovered) and their results, form important sociological topics.

Durkheim perceived religious activity to be symbolic. And for more recent writers, such as Geertz, religion is 'a system of symbols which acts to establish powerful, pervasive, and long-lasting moods and motivations in men by formulating conceptions of a general order of existence, and clothing these conceptions with such an aura of factuality that the moods and motivations seem uniquely realistic'.[7] A symbol is something, usually apprehensible by the senses, which by common agreement 'stands for' something else. Or rather, a symbol may often be multivocal, recalling a multiplicity of referents. This, of course, gives to many religious, as well as artistic, symbols their power. Symbolism in religious ritual is something which has recently been studied by social anthropologists in several important works.[8] This fact raises the question, how far does the efficacy of religious ritual depend on agreement about the significance of symbols, and what is the bearing of this upon the place of religion in 'modernized' societies?

It seems as though the contemporary sociological attitude towards religion is combining ideas derived from Tylor with ideas derived from Durkheim. For Spiro, religion is an institution consisting of 'culturally patterned interaction with culturally-postulated superhuman beings'.[9] Yet 'culturally patterned interaction' is of course different from mere belief. It finds room for the idea of *dependence*, for the *need of a relation* with beings which are not merely of this world. As A. D. Nock says, religion is concerned with matters in which man is not his own master—with the uncanny—but where the 'secret workings of nature are capable of being influenced by his actions', and are due to 'forces which operate in virtue of wills and emotions comparable with those which prompt his own operations'.[10] Or, in the words of Festugière, 'man feels an invincible need to believe that there is somewhere a god who thinks about him'.[11]

These definitions, taken from the work of men who have studied a variety of different faiths, indicate that religion involves not merely the existence of a belief, but also of what may be called the need for completion. The role of religion as a psychological or social phenomenon is that it assists men to adjust to the facts of contingency, of powerlessness, and of scarcity. It tries to provide an answer to the question of how it is that things seem to be so irrational, at the command of blind chance. Why is it that man is so powerless? And why is he continually frustrated and deprived, and a prey to suffering? The aim of religion, as it appears today and in the past, is generally not how to teach men to avoid suffering: often the contrary; rather it is concerned with the problem of how to suffer: that is to say, the problem of finding a meaning in inevitable suffering. Furthermore, it addresses itself to the problem of a rational basis for conduct in a world which too often seems wholly irrational. It does so by postulating another order of existence which complements the material one. In this order of existence, certain ultimate moral or cosmological truths are embodied which act as guides for his action in this world.

Joachim Wach[12] sets forth four fundamental criteria of religion. In the first place, religion is 'a response to what is experienced as ultimate reality; that is, in religious experiences we react not to any single or finite phenomenon, material or otherwise, but to what we realize as undergirding and conditioning all that constitutes our world of experience'. Secondly, religious experience is 'a total response of the total being, to what is apprehended as ultimate reality'; in this it differs from the moral judgement. Thirdly, religious experience is 'the most intense experience of which man is capable'. And lastly, religious experience 'involves an imperative, a commitment which impels man to act'; and in this it differs from aesthetic experience.

Any definition has to be in exceedingly broad terms, because of the manifold differences between the beliefs and practices of different religions. We can see, however, that three elements are involved in religion. In the first place, it involves patterns of worship: that is to say cults. In the second place, it involves patterns of ideas and definitions: that is to say beliefs. And thirdly, it involves patterns of associations and organizations: social structures.

The question of definition leads us directly to a discussion of the social function of religion. Here we must repeat the difference between function and purpose. The purpose of a religion to the religious man is not necessarily what the sociologist would regard as the function of the belief. And while the believer is generally certain about the purpose of religion for him, the sociologist has good reason to be cautious over statements about its function.

It has been suggested[13] that the functions of religion are the following. In the first place it provides support, consolation and reconciliation with what may be regarded as the true purpose of existence. In the second place it offers a transcendental relationship providing security and a feeling of identity. Thirdly, it sacralizes the norms and values of established society. In the fourth place it provides standards of value by which institutionalized norms may be examined and found wanting. In the fifth place it promotes self-understanding and self-definition.

Two comments may be made here. The first is that, broadly-expressed though they may be, these formulations leave out a good deal. Religions may be sources of support and of consolation—placebos for natural terror, as Petronius suggested; or for social despair, as Marx said; or salvation from indwelling unworthiness—but they may be also sources of the most intense anxiety and despair. Religious movements may unite or divide. Religious institutions may either succour or oppress.

Furthermore (the second comment) while the totality of known faiths throughout the world shows an enormous variety in detail, the range of variation—the amount of apparent contradiction—within any one faith is equally significant. This fact, beloved of 'atheists', has important sociological causes and consequences.

Thirdly, there is one extremely important omission. The function, not of 'religion' but of '*a* religion'—some particular creed or cult—has often been to induce in its followers a sense of group-unity. A group may see its religion as giving a sacred character to its group-identity, its own existence and that of its faith being mutually dependent, and thus political conflicts may be fought which are religious *through being* political.

In the study of religion, the relation of sociological to historical analysis is important. The diffusion of faiths is a salient fact of history. It has had the most complex causes and results. Thus Mithraism, from Persia, spread through the Middle East, and to Rome, and from Rome to many parts of northern Europe. The reason for its spread is partly a social one. It was, for different socio-political reasons, the religion of slaves, of the middle class and officials, and of soldiers. And it spread with the spread of the Roman armed forces and the development of Roman bureaucracy. The great world-religions have been missionary religions and have traversed wide areas of the globe, influencing the cultures, economies, and politics of the regions to which they spread. The most glaring example of such a movement is, of course, that of Christianity. The world-wide spread of this religion, which has taken place in successive movements over long periods of time, has occurred partly through deliberate missionary entrepreneurship, but partly through the Church reaping the fruits of trade and conquest. Perhaps equally important is that of Islam throughout the Middle East, Asia, North and Tropical Africa. Here we see a diffusion which is linked not so much with armed conquest as with the trading and economic pressure of a more developed culture. Also its basic tenets are at once consistent, insistent, and easy to grasp. Thirdly, Buddhism, from its original home in North India, spread to Ceylon, to China, to Japan, to Tibet, and to South-East Asia. The results of this spread include important influences upon the art, language, and social structure of all those regions. But another result was profound changes or developments in the nature of Buddhism itself. The Buddhisms of China, Japan, and Tibet are different in important respects from one another, and from those of Ceylon or of Burma. Where a faith is brought to regions with widely different culture patterns, not only does it suffer a change; it moreover often develops offshoots in which the original body of ideas and practices have been mingled with those of the indigenous beliefs, the earlier strata of beliefs and creeds held in the country. Thus we see such a movement among Christian groups in Africa,[14] or we see admixtures of Islamic elements with those of Hinduism or of early Animism in the countries of South-East Asia. This is an important two-way movement which has evoked considerable attention from sociologists of religion.

Religions often emerge because they set themselves up within the pale of earlier religions. Often this is done as a criticism, a denial, or a defiance of the established religion, and an attempt to do away with what is thought to be its degeneration from an earlier ideal. Thus, the Protestant sects in fifteenth- and sixteenth-century Europe grew up as a criticism of Catholic Christianity, and an attempt to go back to what were felt to be the pure forms existing in early Christianity. On the other hand Christianity itself arose as a criticism of aspects of Judaism.

II

Social Factors Affecting the Existence and Development of Religions

If by a religion we mean, in accordance with the previous definitions, a body of beliefs and practices relating to superhuman powers with which the community of living persons can and must enter into relationship, then there is no known society without some form of activity which may be called religious.

Modern studies of the religions of primitive societies strongly suggest that Durkheim's insight was of extreme importance: that the function of religious ritual precepts, for example those of totemism, was to reinforce the feeling that the collection of people in which one lives is a moral community. In this connection we may regard religion as being, like other social institutions, a means of orientating a person in society. It performs the extremely important function of relating any given individual to the remainder of his human community, of showing him the duties and the ties by and through which he becomes a member of his group; and it also shows him how his group is itself related, for example, to the ancestors from whom it descended and the non-human powers with which it is related. It does this through a system of beliefs; but it does it also, and perhaps more importantly, through a system of ceremonies and rituals. Hence appears to arise the significance of totemism as a social force. In an important article Fortes[15] points out that totemism typically involves a series of regulations (usually prohibitions) relating to the eating of particular sorts of food. A particular group is prohibited from eating the flesh of a particular animal, or from eating a particular plant.

Though rationalizations in the form of myths may exist to account for these prohibitions, they are essentially arbitrary ones. Two considerations are important here. In the first place Fortes points out the peculiarly compulsive character of arbitrary precepts. Those which are simply enjoined, without being explained, typically have greater compulsiveness. The second point in this connection is the fundamental character of eating, and therefore its importance as a symbol of society and of symbiosis; and therefore its importance in connection with totemism.

> The roots of [a man's] identity lie in his membership of the community of his co-religionists; and his apprehension of his identity is focused upon arbitrary food taboos believed to be divinely ordained, and symbolizing, to him, his rights by descent and his consequential moral commitments, to being a Jew or a Brahmin, or a Moslem.[16]

In the same way ancestral cults, so frequently found amongst the religions of primitive peoples, emphasize the community of the living group by reason of its connection with the dead ancestors, and also, through the fact of the belief that the ancestors are deified or quasi-deified, the relationship between the living world and that of superhuman powers.

Such forms of religious belief and practice tend to support the solidarity and the stability of simpler societies. It must be acknowledged that we are not at present in possession of adequate data about the development and the organization of religion in simpler societies. We are beginning to realize, however, that many such societies have undergone social change in times past. And we can connect with such changes the emergence of new forms of religious behaviour. Particularly in recent years, a good deal of attention has been paid by anthropologists to the development of religious movements within societies who have come into contact with Europeans. This is because the emergence of movements of whose origins we have some information has usually been a response to European contact. But Europeans have rarely been the first contacts of such peoples, and it is likely that this process has gone on before their advent. Islam often preceded them in Africa, and Buddhism in the nations of Asia. What we seem to get in these circumstances may usually be called, in the terminology to be defined below, a cult. That is to say it is usually something which is different from, but not actively hostile to, the traditional religion. These movements may be of a considerable variety in terms of size, duration and organization. An example can be taken in the form of the Yakan or Allah-water cult, which Middleton[17] describes amongst the Lugbara of East Africa. The cult centred upon the drinking of 'Allah water', which was believed to make the drinker invincible in battle. The cult appeared towards the end of the nineteenth century and was apparently derived from a neighbouring African people. Its original importance was that it gave the Lugbara a feeling of power as against the tribes with whom they fought, and also as against slavers. Furthermore it seemed to have become a response to conditions of famine and disease. The 'Allah water' itself was regarded as dangerous. It was brought from outside the Lugbara territory with precautions similar to those which attended the procuring of other magical materials. In this phase the Allah water appears to have been a magical material with medicinal properties, and its use was, so to say, directed outwards, that is against other tribes and external dangers. As time went on, however, the cult changed in its form and purposes. In its second phase, it became less a means of protecting oneself against hostile tribes and against slavers, for these after the coming of Europeans became of less consequence, and more a means of reconstructing the social organization of Lugbara society. The leaders of the cult used it as a means of superseding the traditional lineage organization. One of the tenets of the later cult was that the dead ancestors would return. The consequence of this belief was to diminish the prestige of the *living* elders of the community. In other words, the cult became a means of contesting the traditional authority structure of the Lugbara society. It was, as Middleton says, an attempt at a return to the original paradise.

From this we see that religious movements often arise as a response to conditions of social change. Either they reject social change and make for a return to the previous form of social organization, or they reject the existing social organization and make for a new one; either a return to something in the past, or to something which has not yet existed upon earth. They are weapons in what are essentially political struggles.

The Allah-water cult was as, we have seen, in part a reaction against dangers from powerful neighbours. In this respect it is related to many cults of simpler peoples. Lanternari[18] has referred to these as 'religions of the oppressed'. They include, for example, the Peyote cult and the ghost-dance cult amongst the North American Indians, and the Cargo cults of Oceania.[19] The common characteristic of all these is that they came as means whereby the people concerned could throw off the yoke of those, for the most part Europeans, whom they felt to be oppressors. Thus the Cargo cults, which generally arose during or shortly after the end of the Second World War, typically took the form of a belief, suddenly arising in a particular tribe, that at some time in the near future their ancestors, or the gods, would arrive bearing with them weapons and supplies which would enable them to drive away the Europeans. These weapons were commonly to take the form of European rifles and other material which had been shown to be so effective. A form of answer to the need was, so to speak, 'acted out'. It therefore was charged with great emotion and for a time was functional in raising hopes and uniting a group. The efficacy of it was, of course, short-lived in time.

These cults in which the religious consolation takes the form of the hope of betterment in the world through supernatural intervention form one kind of religion of the oppressed. The other, of course, is that in which the redemption or the salvation of the individual is something to be hoped for in another life rather than in this. Of these again there are many examples, among them the so-called Mystery Religions which were found in another period of social change, the end of the ancient world.

Warde Fowler tells us that the original religion of the Romans was one resembling very much what anthropologists show to be the religions of simpler peoples today. It was a religion which centred upon the family and the small tribal group. It was one which emphasized the rituals centring upon the fields, the homestead, and the home itself. The original superhuman entities which the Romans recognized might be described as sacred places or sacred beings whose function was to protect the home, the hearth, or the fields from which the Roman family and society derived its existence. Later in the development of Rome there appeared, according to Warde

Fowler, deities brought in by traders and other groups unfamiliar to the original inhabitants of Rome. The great deities such as Jupiter and Mars were not originally Roman, but made their appearance at a stage when Rome was developing and changing from a small local community to a city with world-wide connections. But still later, that is to say around the commencement of the Christian era, another development of Roman religion was of perhaps more fundamental importance. That was the coming in of 'mystery religions', which, in contrast to those which, as it were, sacralized the affairs of daily life, whether agriculture or whether trade, directed the attention of the believer away from the affairs of the world to the hope of redemption offered by saviour deities.

The Hellenistic age—by which is meant the period roughly from the death of Alexander the Great to the end of the second century A.D.—was a period in some ways not unlike our own. It was an age of international political change; of the rise and decline of states; a time when the traditional local loyalties to city-state and to tribe were losing their meaning. It was an age for many of anomie. As a consequence of this Roman society witnessed the importation of creeds from elsewhere which provided a solace and refuge for many people for whom the traditional religions no longer retained their customary force. Among such religions were those of Isis, of Orpheus, of Attis and of Mithras. What these cults had in common was firstly that they appealed to the individual rather than to the group. They were something which the deracinated individual could join, rather than something to which the only way of belonging was through the fact of birth into a social group. They therefore appealed to the anomic townsman of Alexandria or of Rome. In the second place they involved a personal relationship between the individual worshipper and the deity. They were cults of a particular god or goddess to whom the individual worshipper owed a loyalty and attachment. Thirdly, the mode of entry was through ceremonies of initiation, by which the devotee's attachment to the cult was signalized. Fourthly, they were religions of redemption. The devotee, by becoming initiated as a follower of the deity, received the promise of redemption from sins, and rebirth into a new life. A famous story written in the second century A.D., the *Golden Ass* of

Apuleius, tells how the hero, Lucius, is magically turned into a donkey as a consequence of rash behaviour. After enduring a series of miserable adventures, of a sort all too likely in the situation, he manages to appeal to the goddess Isis. Immediately he receives back his human shape, and thereafter becomes a devotee of the goddess. Clearly the story has an allegorical purpose, pointing to the function of the mystery religions of delivering from misfortune and sin.

During the Hellenistic period the proliferation of cults was due in part to the psychological and social needs brought about by conditions of rapid social change. But they were made possible by a particular attitude on the part of the state. It is permissible here to say 'the state', although the religions covered a large area of the Mediterranean and Near East, because the one effective political power at that time was that of Rome. Now the attitude of the Roman state towards religion was essentially at this time a *laissez-faire* one. Religions were permitted of all kinds, provided they were not hostile to the minimal requirements of the Roman state. That is to say, provided a religion rendered unto Caesar that which was Caesar's, it could teach or profess anything it liked in regard to the things with which Caesar was not concerned. Christians were persecuted, not precisely in Rome's view for being Christians, but for refusing to give the necessary minimal recognition of the divinity of the Roman Emperor. Most of the other mystery cults did not refuse, and they were therefore accommodated with negligent hospitality by the Roman government.

It is important to see that all of these faiths were the outcome not only of a particular set of conditions in the countries to which they came, but also the outcome of a process of diffusion over wide areas. None of them were really original in the Western Mediterranean basin. Mithraism came from Persia, the cult of Isis from Egypt, Christianity from the near East. It is a moot point whether any religion at any time has set itself up for being original. Certainly only a minority can have so represented themselves, and it may well be held that at the age we are speaking of the antiquity of a faith, like that of a law, may have been a characteristic necessary to its popularity.

III

Religious Roles

Religion is a field in which role differentiation appears to be found in almost all societies. It is true that in certain respects simpler societies show a certain degree of role diffusion. Thus to take examples, in simpler societies the father of a family is often its religious head, and interceder with the Powers on its behalf; and kings have often been, either themselves divine, or else in some special relationship with the divinities.

The main genus of role may be described as that of intermediary between man and the 'other'. Religion, it was implied earlier, involves an attempt on the part of man to get into some sort of right relation with non-human powers. But this operation is one which in most societies is regarded as peculiarly difficult. There are no rationalized, no simple, easily learnt, means of doing so. Consequently, the need is recognized in most societies for the existence of certain human beings with either specialized powers or specialized training or both. The precise duties, functions, powers, status, and nature of such beings differ from society to society, varying with such factors as the level of technological development, political democracy and class structure, as well as with the nature of the religion.

1. The first group to be considered are those who are variously known as medicine men, shamans, diviners, or seers. The characteristic of such people is that they are deemed to be possessed of superhuman powers to foresee events, to see at a distance, and to work cures by magical means upon other human beings. Further, through the powers they are believed to possess of overthrowing the work of evil witches and sorcerers, they may effect real social healing. These powers they may sometimes be born with, but more often some form of initiation is a necessary preliminary to their exercise. The powers may be regarded in some cases as hereditary, or more correctly it may be said that there is with some a hereditary predisposition to the possession of such powers. But where this is so usually the individual has to be given, or to seek, initiation into his

role. Thus with the shaman the individual receives a superhuman command to go apart somewhere and to undertake a journey which is attended by dangers and perils. Characteristically he undergoes visions in which he is killed and cut apart and put together again—as it were a symbol of a rebirth. He sees visions, and during this quest he attains his magic powers, after which he returns to his tribe as essentially a different being.[20]

The shaman and other people in this class give evidence of being what might be described as dissociated personalities. Yet the dissociation does not appear to involve what we would call psychosis or neurosis: indeed many students emphasize the highly stable character of the individuals. Perhaps it may be that, as Emmet suggests,[21] the society in which they live has a recognized place for such people, and consequently their own psychologies are stabilized by being able to occupy a role which is socially respected.

2. The second role is that of the prophet. Essentially the prophet is one who proclaims a new message. He is 'filled with God': a charismatic person, to use Weber's term (that is, someone who appears to possess superhuman personal qualities); he regards himself, and is regarded by his followers, as one who has a duty to proclaim to mankind, or to some of mankind, a message from the Deity, concerning reform of creed, of cult, of moral conduct or of political action, or indeed concerning some new dispensation. Thus prophets are characteristic elements in the revitalization of religious movements.

The example presumably best known to us is that of the Hebrew prophets; and it is worth while examining these in somewhat greater detail.

Lindblom[22] asserts that there were three classes of Israelite prophets. In the first place there were what he calls 'cultic prophets' who were attached to the sanctuaries of the god as members of the ordinary staff attending upon him. They received their maintenance from the income of the sanctuary, like priests and other cultic functionaries. They were, so to speak, essentially professional people who were organized in professional associations. Secondly there were non-cultic prophetic guilds living in communities under the guidance of a father. In the third place there were prophets working privately in virtue of their ecstatic endowment and the ability to deliver divine oracles. Lindblom's view, which seems to be that of most modern writers upon the Hebrew prophets, stresses the professional and vocational aspect of their role. Prophecy as an activity was influenced not merely by general social factors affecting that particular society, but also by the more specialized influences of training and of a primary group.

To what extent their charismatic activities were routinized as a result of this organization, it is difficult to say. No doubt this was so to a certain extent, but it can by no means have been so completely. The characteristics of Israelite prophets were firstly that they were individuals having a special power of ecstasy; secondly, that they were looked on as vessels of inspired revelations, visions, auditions: having been admitted to the councils of Yahweh, they felt themselves to be the bearers of his divine word. They were conscious of being under a divine constraint, called and sent to their people by God. They were conscious also of the effective power of the divine word in influencing the events in human society.

The prophets had a significance, both social and political, which made them the objects at once of honour and of contempt. They were honoured as being the apparent intermedairies between God and man; they were held in contempt as being all too frequently the bearers of ill tidings and of messages which were unpopular. They came to hold this ambivalent position largely as a consequence of a change about the sixth century B.C. It has often been pointed out that this change had almost contemporary parallels in the other great centres of world religions. Confucius and Lao Tze in China, Buddha in India and Zoroaster in Persia, were making of religion no longer a way of life which supported the traditional values of society, but one which questioned them, and pointed to something higher. It was no longer only a social ritual; it was to be a personal morality. So, too, the later prophets were still ecstatics, and still regarded as people with the gift from God to work miracles as signs of His power; but at the same time these miracles were designed to point morals for the conduct of the Israelite rulers and people.

The prophet, as it were, exemplifies a sort of political

dichotomy. He is as often as not a critic of the political ruler, and may often bring about the overthrow of that ruler through divine intervention.

Founders and Exemplars

The term prophet may also be held to include founders of new faiths. But the distinction is for us a minor one. All prophets regard themselves as having, in some sense, a new message. And few leaders of historically important groups have ever been (and still fewer have ever regarded themselves as being) the propounders of utterly new religions. Jesus and Buddha regarded themselves rather as reinterpreters of the older faiths. Consequently the distinction between founders and other prophets is difficult to make. Moreover, the growth of what turns out to be a new religion, such as Christianity, depends upon adventitious factors which often come into existence after the death of the person to whom its origin is attributed. It may be said that typically the prophet is one who, to his followers, not only has a message but is a message. The position which he occupies in his faith depends upon a variety of factors. The saints of the Catholic church are regarded as in no way the equivalent of, or even as resembling, the Christ: they are different in kind. Yet they have in various degrees an element of personal transcendence of ordinary human nature which renders them charismatic. In the same way, to take another example, the leaders of the Jewish Hasidic cult in east Europe of the eighteenth century were persons who were not only the exponents of a religion, but also by their own nature exemplars of something which transcended ordinary human nature and ordinary everyday religion.

Hasidic societies[23] were groups consisting of loosely organized bands of families, scattered in various cities, who travelled to and followed the guidance of a spiritual master called a *zaddik*. The members of the society brought voluntary gifts to the *zaddik*, who maintained an establishment where his followers could visit him as guests. People contributed according to their means, and received financial help and guidance from the *zaddik*. There was something which resembled the relationship of a feudal lord to his knights in this sort of society. But the real characteristic of it was that the follower attached himself in unquestioning adoration to the *zaddik*, and this became the primary duty of the hasid.

In the sense we have suggested above, the *zaddik* was the true religious intermediary. As Agus says, 'since it is the purpose of life to worship God with every ounce of one's energy, only the saints can fulfil this purpose. The common people, however, share the merit of the saint by their "attachment" to him.'[24] It is significant that the stories in which Hasidism is so rich stress the personal charisma of the *zaddik* or religious leader. Scholem in his book *Major Trends in Jewish Mysticism*[25] cites a remark made about one of the most famous of those *zaddikim*: 'I did not,' said one of his disciples, 'come to hear the Maggid of Meseretz preach, but to see him tie up his bootlaces.' In other words the mere nature and actions of this holy man were themselves something transcendent and exemplary.

But again it is the function of the prophet and his group to change social relationships. Sociologically, Agus says, Hasidism was in the first place a revolution against established authority within the Jewish community. It was a revolt by the common people, with their own chosen leaders, against the formal authority of the established Rabbinic organization, and its emphasis upon formal learning and formal obedience to law. Secondly, Hasidism was a messianic movement: 'The driven and distraught masses composing the landless and rootless Jewish proletariat saw in the mere appearance of the wonder-working *zaddik* an assurance of the eventual advent of the Messiah'. Sometimes the social constraints within which a religion struggles prove too strong for it: this was the case with Hasidism, which during the nineteenth century itself relapsed into lifeless formality. Sometimes the prophetic group continued within the parent religious movement as a kind of perpetual leaven. This may be the case with the Islamic religious orders, the dervishes. As Lindblom says, the activities of the dervishes are one of those ways in which Islam satisfies the need for a more intimate communion with the Deity than the public religion offers. The dervishes or religious orders are, again like the hasidim, small ecstatic groups each under a leader or sheik to whom they owe the greatest loyalty and devotion, who engage in mystical and ecstatic practices: dancing, hymn singing and the like.

Prophetic leadership is, of course, essentially a personal and impermanent relationship. On the death or senescence of the original leader, there is the tendency either for the group to break up, or for it to change fundamentally its character when it comes under the leadership of another charismatic individual; or thirdly there is the possibility of what Max Weber[26] called the routinization of charisma: that is to say, the settling of the group under some system of recorded administrative rules which provide machinery for authority, succession, discipline and so on, and perpetuate it as a 'formal organization'.

3. It will be convenient here to introduce a third role which may be called that of the evangelist. The evangelist is not a religious leader as is the prophet. He may perhaps be better described as a lieutenant. Many good examples are provided by the early history of Methodism. As is well known, Wesley himself travelled the length and breadth of Britain preaching in isolated localities, and passing on. In these circumstances much depended for the continuance of the Methodist groups on the activity of local people who would continue to preach, to gain converts, and to keep the faith alive. The devotional literature of early Methodism is full of accounts of local worthies of this kind. They were people who itinerated within their areas, led classes, encouraged their fellow believers, and generally acted as minor saints within their own localities. They laid no claim to originality of ideas or of approach, but nevertheless fulfilled an essential function in the development and spread of this sect. There is little doubt that the evangelistic religious movements such as Methodism or the Salvation Army owe a great deal to the players of roles of this kind. As with other forms of message, Lazarfeld's Two-step Hypothesis has a certain validity here: the existence of a second-stage intermediary not only increases the efficacy of the communication, but also warrants its relevance.

4. In formal contrast to the role of the prophet is the role of the priest. While the prophet is ecstatic and innovating, the priest is someone charged with a specific and formal set of

duties. Essentially a performer of rituals and ceremonies, he has 'delegated' to him certain sacred powers for the specific performance of these duties. Thus in the Catholic church the priest has the duty of hearing confessions and the power of remitting sins. These powers he is charged with for the purpose of his sacred office. While the prophet is regarded as being personally and individually something more than ordinary humanity, the priest is, as an individual, no more than an ordinary human being. His powers are the powers of his office and not of himself. The distinction of individual and of office is important. In the Middle Ages, as Ullmann[27] tells us, the powers of the Pope to bind and to loose, and his sovereignty over earthly rulers, were valid quite independently of the individual goodness or otherwise of the holder for the time being of that office.

The prophet and priest are of course types of role. There may be certain religions or certain societies in which the roles are united. There may also be individuals who combine in themselves the activities both of a priest and of a prophet or evangelist. Nevertheless there are typical differences between the two roles.

5. The role of priest is characteristic of an authoritarian type of religious organization. By virtue of his special powers with which he is endowed in virtue of his office, he is in a position of authority over the ordinary members of the flock. Historically in times of religious or of social change, this has, as is well known, aroused hostility, and as a consequence a new sort of role of religious officiant has developed. In various Protestant, particularly Nonconformist faiths, this role has been one devoid of sacred transmitted powers, and of one who is only *primus inter pares*—the *pares* in this case being the leading lay members of the religious congregation (who, as for instance in Calvinistic sects, might have considerable powers of discipline).[28] We may give the name of minister to such roles.

The role of minister is typical of Protestant, and particularly of Nonconformist groups. It is a role apt to be found in organizations showing a democracy or at least an oligarchy to which people come by achievement, not ascription, rather than in those exhibiting a hierarchical autocracy. It is also characteristic of religions in which the ultimate source of religious dogma lies in something which is accessible in principle to all the congregation. This is, for example, a sacred writing such as the Bible. In the priestly organizations, on the other hand, the religious authority is something which is esoterically transmitted.

These comments will show that the differences of roles are connected with differences firstly in religious creeds, secondly in religious organization, and thirdly in different types of society.

6. The roles discussed are those of direct intermediary between the ordinary person and the source of superhuman power. But we also find what may, for want of a better term, be called indirect intermediaries. By this phrase is meant such roles as that of the monk, especially in the Roman Catholic church, the hermit and the mystic. The characteristic of all such activities is that they are not immediately concerned with the teaching or leading of ordinary people but rather with the worship and service of the diety, and the search for one's own Salvation. In this there are, however, degrees. The Catholic monk is characteristically a member of a community of monks. His exercises are certainly for the glory of God, and certainly for his own salvation, but also they are exercised within the body of a monastic community, and the activities of the individual monk are designed, in part at least, for the benefit of the whole brotherhood. It is of course also true that both in fact and in intention the work of many monastic bodies has been for the direct benefit of the society in which they lived. Many monks such as Benedictines have engaged in educational activities. Furthermore, the prayer and worship of the monks have been intended as means of conveying grace to the whole human community of which they were a part: still, this work is carried out as it were indirectly, not 'within' the general society. On the other hand, the individual hermit is not part of a community either religious or lay. The early Christian eremitic communities of the Egyptian desert were, at the most, extremely loosely associated collections of hermits who performed their religious duties primarily as individuals. It is true that some degree of association took place amongst them, and it is also true that they received visits from the faithful, and

indeed engaged in teaching. They were not however in any sense truly groups—organized bodies of faithful. With the mystic we reach in a sense an even greater degree of individual activity. Essentially the search of the mystic is indeed in Plotinus' words a Flight of the One to the One. It is a transaction between the individual soul and his God: the effort to reach a peculiar and unique relationship between himself and the ultimate ground of existence. Nevertheless, of course, mystics have engaged in work in the world; but this is indeed only an ancillary part of the religious activity.

7. Lastly amongst religious roles we may note what can be called hostile roles. By these are meant the roles of the heretic and of the infidel which certainly are essential roles in any religious system of belief or in any religious organization. The sociological aspects of heresy or of unbelief are of very great importance.

Neither heresy nor unbelief can exist without the existence of belief, of organized belief, and of belief organized upon particular lines. In the United States today there is no possibility of heresy, at least in a religious sense; and if it exists in the United Kingdom, it is certainly a crime without content.

Both heresy and infidelity help to define a religion. They force its leaders often to an examination of its tenets, and in any case to make affirmations and denials. They involve conflict-situations and therefore give rise to action which is political as well as religious. But the effect of heresy tends to differ from that of total infidelity. The latter, being the rejection by some group of the religion *en bloc*, means that the faithful can retain it as a total, undamaged system; but the heretic only partially rejects, partially retains and reinterprets, consequently is more difficult for the ordinary person to deal with, more challenging to the sophisticated, and hence more dangerous to religious authority.

IV

Wherever religion is a living belief, it permeates all other fields of social relations. It does so for a variety of reasons. In the first place, a religious belief held in common provides any social group with a focal point, with a feeling of social solidarity. In the second, a religion is often a symbol of the values and the unity of the group. In the third place, religion provides a moral and a cosmological meaning and warrant for action.

The interpenetration of religious with economic, political, and other spheres of behaviour is, of course, a major sociological theme. Marx's view, referred to in an earlier chapter, appears to have been that changes in the technologies of production, with the attendant changes in class-relations, constituted the determining factor in changes in the other elements of society; although both Marx and Engels appear sometimes to accord the latter a certain degree of automony. Max Weber, in *The Protestant Ethic and the Spirit of Capitalism*[29] set out to demonstrate that, sometimes at least, theological beliefs and attitudes could themselves help to determine the course of economic development. His well-known theme was that Western capitalism, as it developed in the sixteenth century and onwards, was unique in that it was based upon a rational and systematic organization of work. This rational and systematic organization was brought about chiefly by a change (which was initiated in certain Protestant sects) in mental attitudes towards work: by the development of the idea of 'vocation': of the *duty* of a man to labour ceaselessly and systematically in his calling. Finally, the need so to employ one's time issued from the theological beliefs of Calvinism: the need to show proof, by the appropriate conduct, that one had been elected by God for a future state of blessedness. A theological belief induced, initially in certain groups, a mental attitude, which resulted in a system of organization of activities, that endured after the theological beliefs themselves had lost their original vigour.

Weber's book aroused much controversy, which chiefly concerned the questions, whether he had correctly interpreted the theology of Calvin, and whether he had correctly understood the historical links in the development of Calvinism and Capitalism.[30] However, his book remains a seminal work, a most important revitalizing of the theme.

Of course, the rules and precepts which any given faith professes concerning work, the rewards of labour, the amassing or distribution of wealth and like matters, may well be exemplified in its practice. The socialistic ideals of the Hutterite

Anabaptists were in fact reflected in their dealings.[31] But it is equally likely that when the daily life of the followers of a religion, or of any section of them, is carried on in large organizations, the very necessities of the organizational structure may overcome the values of the faith. Buddhism, for instance, places the ideal of non-attachment to earthly things high among what is required of its followers—it is necessary to deliverance from the round of existence—yet, as Lien Sheng Yang and Gernet show,[32] in medieval China the chief form of Buddhist organization, the monasteries, were highly adept money-making concerns, with an especial penchant for pawnbroking. A religion of any size has to organize, and organization brings needs, and opportunities which it seems necessary for the existence of the faithful to take advantage of.

A comparison of the major religions shows very wide differences between them in their propensity for organization. The Christian *Church* was based on a pastoral system[33]; and the traditions of Roman and Byzantine administration within which it had to grow up, helped to develop in it this character of a pastorally-organized hierarchy. This would seem to be unique among the major religions of the world (though in some respects it may be true of Judaism) and, both directly and indirectly, has been the cause of the importance of Christianity as a missionary religion: for example, such permanent influence as Christianity has had in Asia or Africa has been due, not to its theological message, but to the hospitals and still more the schools which its missionary bodies have founded. It is no exaggeration to say that these have been a major political factor in the modern world.

Christianity has, in general, shown great capacity for effective organization, both ecclesiastical and lay. Counter-Reformation Catholicism set great store by organization (e.g. the Jesuits) as also Reformed groups such as Calvinists, Moravians, Methodists, Mormons, Shakers: the causes would be difficult to identify fully, but the fact is clear. Largely on this account it has always taken a lively interest in political and economic questions and the practical regulation of social relationships. Its sacred scriptures have been formed into a body of practical morality; and their frequently contradictory nature has given Christian ethics its peculiar richness. Further, it has always shown an intense (though generally disapproving) inquisitiveness about other faiths; and an intense conviction of the importance of the world, as the place for the transaction of God's dealings with mankind. Thus, for the Christian, the political and the religious have frequently been two sides of one event.

In all these respects, Hinduism is almost the exact contrary.[34] It has virtually no ecclesiastical organization: no congregational worship, no organized clergy. Apart from a traditional connection of the Brahmin caste with the post of administrator —not always maintained in practice—there is little connection between religious and political roles. The Hindu belief that Ultimate Reality is without name, form or qualities necessarily makes Hinduism tolerant of other beliefs both in principle and in practice. It is virtually impossible for Hinduism to become a missionary religion not only because of its philosophy, but because the religion is an aspect of the totality of its culture: one could not become a Hindu in religion save by becoming a Hindu in every other sense; it might be termed an 'ascribed' rather than an 'achievable' religion. Hinduism certainly acts as a rallying symbol for communalistic movements; but apart from this, lacks both the philosophy and the organizational basis to support political activity. In so far as it is concerned with social organization, it is a family- and kinship-centred religion, sacralizing family and household relations, duties and conditions, rather than one which gives meaning to public or political relations.

Islam, like Christianity, has been an aggressively missionary religion; and to an even greater degree than with Christianity, there is a close inter-relation between religious and political activity. Indeed this is an inaccurate way of describing their relations: traditionally there is no distinction between the religious and the secular. Islamic law, which minutely regulates the life of any member of an Islamic nation, must be in accord with the provisions of the Koran. And yet, although Islam knows a clerical role (ulama), there is little of the complex hierarchical organization of priestly offices found in Christianity. It is tempting to see this characteristic as related—whether causally or as a sympton—to the apparent lack of continuous political organization in many present-day Islamic countries. Buddhism, finally, differs in various ways from each of the other three. Having been founded by an historical personage who, as his followers believe, discovered the one path to perfect enlightenment, it is both a missionary religion and a religion for which History possesses significance; yet neither of these factors is of such critical importance as with Christianity or Islam. Further, although it would be untrue to say that Buddhism is *indifferent* to political issues, there has traditionally been less systematic interpenetration of religious thought and practice by political concerns. Lastly, in the order of monks Buddhism possesses the basis for a high degree of institutional organization, at both local and national level. In these senses, the organization of a faith itself is a major factor in its political relations. One other factor, however, requires notice.

Buddhism, above all other religions, lays stress upon respect for all forms of life. The Buddha's teaching appears to be, on this issue, far more uncompromising than that of Christianity. It is, therefore, at first, surprising to find the historian de Groot discussing the records of Buddhist monks in China over the previous millennium, who 'freely indulged in carnage and butchery, and took an active part in military expeditions of every description, thus leaving no room for doubt that warfare was an integral part of their religious profession for centuries'.[35]

De Groot points out that although the Buddhist scriptures make murder one of the greatest of sins, they also issue the commandment that one should 'save all living things . . . from death'; these naturally included other Buddhists and Buddhist monks; and to do so, in the lawless conditions of tenth- to nineteenth-century China, meant being prepared to inflict death on their oppressors. Thus, in this instance the Buddhist scriptures accommodated conflicting interpretations, and this degree of accommodation was presumably necessary for the survival of the faith, or its votaries.

It is a common accusation that the religions of the 'developed' societies—and Christianity in particular—are full of moral inconsistencies. But, since religions are social institutions, it is necessary that they be inconsistent, in order to maintain themselves as continuing systems, not only against their enemies, but against their followers. They are ladders, and a ladder must have two ends. An expressive institution requires to be inconsistent, in order that it shall possess symbolic richness and cogency.

To maintain its vigour, it should embrace, but not seem to compromise; not lean too far towards the 'un-worldly' nor too far to the 'worldly'. In the Ceylonese General Elections of 1956, S. W. Bandaranaike was elected as Prime Minister largely through the efforts of a Buddhist religio-political group, the 'United Monks Front'; but when he seemed to be too dilatory in rewarding them with policies favourable to Buddhism (and with more individual favours) they had him assassinated.[36] This was, perhaps, carrying non-violence too far; but it is not yet clear whether Buddhism in Ceylon has suffered thereby. In general, however, it may be said that if Western religion has declined in influence (and the issue is still somewhat unclear) it is not from political vigour, but from lack of conviction: not from doubts as to the location of the lower end of the ladder but as to the location of its higher.

V

Religious Groups

The most important organizational distinction in the field of religion is naturally that between those religions which have been embodied in social systems with a high degree of formal organization, and those which have not. This was discussed earlier. The Christian Church developed in the former manner, and since its organizational character has been studied in some detail, the present discussion will be confined to it.

A fundamental contrast is that between Church and Sect. This distinction reflects a basic incompatibility in the mission of a religious group: it is both to welcome, and to reject; to save the world, and to escape it. This antithesis of Church and Sect has been treated in a well-known passage in Troeltsch's *Social Teaching of the Christian Churches*.[37] These two types are, for Troeltsch, distinguished by multiple differentia. In the first place the Church is universal while the Sect is exclusive. In principle the Church is universal, that is to say it desires to cover the whole life of humanity. It is conservative and accepts the secular order. It desires to come to terms with it in order to preserve its universality. It dominates the masses. On the other hand, the Sect is comparatively small. Its members aspire after personal inward perfection, and aim at direct personal fellowship between themselves. Therefore, they are forced to organize themselves into small groups and to renounce the idea of dominating the world. Since it cannot dominate the world, the Sect needs to avoid the world and the state in order to preserve its moral and religious identity. Accordingly, membership of a Sect is voluntary.

From the above it follows that the Church utilizes the state and the ruling classes, and 'weaves these elements into her own life'; the Church becomes an integral part of the existing social order. It is therefore dependent upon the upper classes. On the other hand, the Sects, according to Troeltsch, are in general connected with the lower classes.

The Church as an organization mediates between its individual members and their ultimate religious goal. 'The Church', says Troeltsch, 'relates the whole of the secular order as a means and a preparation to the supernatural aim of life, and it incorporates genuine asceticism into its structure as one element in this preparation, all under the very definite direction of the Church. The Sects refer their members directly to the supernatural aim of life, and in them the individualistic directly religious character of asceticism, as a means of union with God, is developed more strongly and fully; the attitude of opposition to the World and its powers, to which the secularized Church now belongs, tends to develop a theoretical and general asceticism.'[38] That is, for the Church asceticism is virtually sacramental, while the asceticism of the Sects is 'the simple principle of detachment from the world'. Troeltsch points out the importance of sacraments for the Church, and the importance of personal effort for the Sect.

The Church-Sect antithesis, to which Troeltsch has drawn attention here, is one which continually appears in the history of the more complex religions. Typically, the Sect is the earliest form of a new religion, and emerges through criticism or denial of the Church type of religious organization in which it is born. Sects as a later stage in their development, tend to become more inclusive and to take on the Church form of organization. Since universality is the mark of the Church, the latter therefore tends to become a supra-national body, like Christianity.

Universality also appears to involve the naturalization of a variety of beliefs and practices which have been taken over from earlier cults. Islam in most of the countries to which it has spread, has in effect had to accommodate itself to the existence of beliefs in nature spirits, in magic, and so forth. A number of the Christian saints are probably the descendants or later forms of animistic entities. Lastly, a universal Church tends to have more or less formal grades of membership. Thus most Christian churches distinguish between persons who attend divine service more or less regularly, and those who have undergone the ceremony of Confirmation and thus are in a sense 'full members' of the Church.

However, it is equally a characteristic of the universal Church that it deliberately proselytizes. Not very much has been written up to the present upon the sociology of missionary activity. Among the questions which such a study would seek to answer are, what is the political environment of a universal Church? It would also seek to analyse the sociological variations between the missionary activities of Buddhism, of Christianity, and of Islam. To what extent were these deliberate efforts to promote the spread of the faith, or to what extent did they come as side effects of either military, or political, or trading relationships? It seems certain that all these elements occurred, and it is possible that there was a different emphasis in the case of Islam, either in Africa or in South-East Asia, from the spread of Christianity in those areas, and that of Buddhism in China or in Tibet.

Another important aspect of the question of missions is that of the selective acceptance of the message. The latter has never been something which has been passively swallowed. The motivations for acceptance are various and not all of them by any means purely religious. Therefore the way in which the faith has been presented has sometimes been modified in order to attain results. One of the most interesting instances of this is the Jesuit missionary activities in Ming and Manchu China (sixteenth to eighteenth centuries). In order to make Christian beliefs acceptable to a cultured and sophisticated people, the Jesuits felt obliged to incorporate some of the more firmly held

Chinese traditional ideas into the corpus of Christianity. Thus they allowed it to be held that Christianity was not inconsistent with the worship of ancestors. This involved the Jesuits in continual and damaging controversy with the Pope, and was one of the factors in the suppression of the Jesuit order.

Missions have, as is well known, often been unsuccessful or only partially successful. There has been often a reaction against universality. The political aspects of this counter-religious movement are interesting. Often the extent to which the universal religion has proved successful has depended upon the nature or extent of the demands which it makes upon its converts. Islam appears to have been the most successful in terms of arousing the least reaction because the requirements for becoming a Muslim are very light. Another aspect of the reaction lies in the existence of religions of the oppressed, which have been mentioned earlier. Imperialism arouses revolt, and religions such as cargo cults or the Peyote cult in North America are expressions in religious symbolic form of the desire to regain an original freedom by throwing off the oppressor. In another form the Bantu churches of South Africa express the Negro's desire for autonomy by postulating a group or cultural leader: a black Christ, or the like.

Other classifications of religious groups have been proposed, but in the main these are essentially refinements upon Troeltsch's, and are based upon similar general criteria. Thus Howard Becker proposes a fourfold division, into what he calls ecclesia, sect, denomination, and cult.[39] The characteristics of the ecclesia are firstly that its members are born into it rather than recruited by conversion. Secondly, and partly as a consequence of the first characteristic, it is a predominantly conservative institution, which is not in open conflict with the secular aspects of social life, and which is professedly universal. It is a sacramental body: it attaches high importance to the means of grace which it administers, to its system of doctrine, and to the official administration of its sacraments, and the teaching of its clergy. Also, it is closely allied with economic and national interests, and it is committed to the adjustment of its ethics to those of the secular world, for it must represent the ethical morality of the respectable majority. Lastly, the ecclesia may be either a national or an international body.

The sect, by contrast, is relatively small. It has abandoned attempts to win the whole world over to its doctrines, and is typically confined to an elect minority. Thus it is an elective body which one joins voluntarily on the basis of one's religious experiences. Typically it does not have a separate and specialized priesthood, but rather believes in 'the priesthood of all believers'. It has a separatist attitude towards the world, which it regards as a place of sin from which the believer should keep aloof. Thus it seeks isolation from the world rather than compromise with it. In contrast to the church, the sect tends to be a temporarily transient body: its fervour is greatest in the first generation, and tends to disappear in the second or later generations.

The typical pattern of development is from sect into denomination. The denomination is again a transient body. It is one which originated in a sect, but over the course of time the values and moral attitudes, as well as the organization of the sect have become adjusted to the world, and to the existence of other faiths. One might say that the denomination is a sect which has become adjusted to the demands of organizational continuity.

Finally the cult is an amorphous, loose-textured, uncondensed type of social structure. It has less of the sociological characteristics of a group than has the sect. In Becker's view one does not join a cult, but simply chooses to believe its teachings or to follow its practices. The goal of a cult is the purely personal ecstatic experience, salvation, comfort and healing.

J. M. Yinger[40] makes a further refinement upon Troeltsch's classification, and bases his typology upon two main criteria:

1. The degree of inclusiveness of the membership of a society;
2. The degree of attention to the function of social integration, as contrasted with the function of personal need.

On the basis of these criteria, Yinger proposes a sixfold typology.

1. *The universal church.* The universal church is relatively successful in the achievement of both of these criteria. Thus for instance one of the best examples of the universal church is the Roman Catholic church of the thirteenth century in Europe. This organization was clearly virtually co-extensive with the whole

of the population of western Europe. At the same time it fulfilled relatively successfully both of the functions of social integration and that of providing for the personal needs of members of the church. It did so presumably because the European society of that time showed an unusual degree of uniformity. In heterogeneous societies, says Yinger, the universal church is generally a short-lived institution.

2. *The ecclesia.* The ecclesia is an established church within its society. It is one which designs to accommodate all levels of society. But on the other hand it tends to be so much adjusted to the dominant elements of the society, as it reinforces existing patterns of social integration, that the needs of many adherents, especially from the lower classes, are not met by it.

3. *The class church or denomination.* This group may, like Becker's denomination, retain some sectarian tendencies, but generally it has compromised considerably with the secular power.

4. *The established sect.* This differs from the denomination in that its opposition to the basic patterns of society still remains.

Yinger suggests that while in the denomination attention is given to personal needs without presenting any serious challenge to established social structures, in the sect the social opposition still remains important.

5. *The sect.* This with Yinger has broadly the same meaning as it has with Troeltsch and Becker. Yinger however suggests three sub-types of sect. Firstly, there are those which are characterized by an acceptance of the situation in which they are, because of the belief that personal sins rather than evil society are the key problem. This type of sect appears to resemble or to be in process of becoming, a denomination. The second sub-type is that kind of sect which is marked by aggression against the society. In such sects the worldly society is regarded as evil, and it is the religious duty of members to fight against it. An example would be the Anabaptist sects of the sixteenth and seventeenth centuries. The third sub-type of sect is that in which its members seek to avoid the world.

6. *The cult.* The cult is usually a small group, often built round a charismatic leader and generally short-lived. Its concern is almost exclusively with the problems of the individual rather than of the social order.

These typologies are as useful as most typologies: they should be handled with care, but without reverence. They are like all classifications: actual examples tend to straddle more than one class, and to develop over time from one class into another.

Furthermore, the concept of the denomination is a somewhat unsatisfactory one. There is certainly a transitional stage often found between the sect and the church; but it tends to be merely transitional. Where there is a truly national church (as was the case in later Stuart England) all other faiths become sects. Where there is only a nominal national church (as in mid-twentieth-century England), or not even nominally one (as in the U.S.A.), there is no significant difference between the denominational type and the church type.

Some difficulty may also be found in the distinction between a sect and a cult. As we have seen them in history, sects have generally been historically defined by persecution. A sect is often a body which rejects, because it has been rejected by, the national church. But a sect today is less concerned to reject the creed and practice of a church, than to reject irreligion or secularism (a cause of the contemporary popularity of the sect-type) and in this it is nominally at one with both church and cult.

Nevertheless the church-sect antithesis is one of great importance in the study of religion: it is the institutional or organizational aspect, of the important, though well-known paradox that (assuming that we think it best to speak of 'Religion' rather than 'Religions') the goal of religion is both to be embracing and to be exclusive. It requires to be embracing because a message needs hearers; a leader needs followers. But it requires to be exclusive, because it requires only hearers who will really hear, and followers who will really follow.

This consideration itself however derives from another sociological or existential characteristic of religion—that, if we accept Wach's definition of religion as a total response of the total being to what is apprehended as ultimate reality—then we must say, first, that by no means all men are fully capable of what must in the circumstances be regarded as an adequate response; and, secondly, that, apart from the intensity or the wholeheartedness of the response, opinions differ as to the *kind* of response which is appropriate. And these opinions, these social attitudes, will be affected by social factors.

As a consequence, a necessary organizational characteristic of religion is that it develops a tendency towards the organization of training for uncertainty; or of rationalizing the irrational. Consequently, fundamental social aspects of religion are those of leadership, and of professional training, as has been shown in the earlier discussion of religious roles.

Certain other important sociological facts about religion are not well brought out in the typologies referred to above.

In the first place, it is very well known that religious movements arise within the bodies of ecclesias or universal churches; or indeed, within denominations. Whether these become 'sects', that is to say, groups which have broken away from the main body, repudiating and repudiated by it, will depend in part upon the attitude of the church or other parent body within which they arise.

As an example we may contrast the fate of the religious orders such as Dominican or Franciscan friars within the Roman church with the fate of Methodism in the eighteenth century.

John Wesley, the founder of Methodism, was an ordained priest of the Church of England, and wished to remain within that church. There was no fundamental difference of doctrine between him and it: any differences of emphasis in Wesley's teaching could easily have been accommodated in the hospitable pastures of Anglicanism. Where the two differed was largely in questions of organization and policy. The Methodist manner of preaching—itinerance and the use of lay preachers—went against the parochial system and against the social and political prejudices of the eighteenth-century Anglican establishments. This led to maltreatment of Wesley, his preachers and followers, by mobs incited by local rectors and magistrates. The consequent hostility to the Church of England seems to have been felt more by Wesley's followers than by Wesley, who here was an example of a leader more moderate than his followers, perhaps because he was of the same social class as his opponents. Wesley was ecumenical, many of his followers sectarian. The lack of tolerance on the part of the Church of England led in due course to a separation probably damaging to both sides, and probably avoidable.[41]

In contrast, the medieval popes saw the Dominicans, the Franciscans and other Orders as usefully supplementing the diocesan and parochial establishment of their time: and what might be called a wise political decision determined that these Orders became movements within the church, and not heresies. The typologies referred to above give no place to such bodies, despite their obvious importance. In fact, adjuvant groups like these—'arms of the Church'—have played an enormously important part in the history of the Catholic Church, and also, it seems likely, in modern Islam. In the case of the former, it would appear they receive a wide practical discretion in return for intellectual obedience. A study of this official policy, and its possible function in promoting the harmonious working of a generally authoritarian body, would be of interest.

From the foregoing discussion there arises a second consideration. Where a church has the power to prevent breakaway movements, distinctive religious movements will be found within the fold of the church. For example in the case of medieval Catholicism, religious movements had to evince filial loyalty and obedience to the mother church, if they wished to continue and to develop without persecution. Thus in medieval Europe the proliferation of religious ideas had to be accompanied by protestations of obedience to Catholic ideas as a fundamental characteristic of each movement. On the other hand where there is no such power held by any one church, groups tend to take the form of separate sects or separate churches, as is found in the contemporary United States or Great Britain.

VI

'*Secular Society*'

A popular British Sunday newspaper, *The People*, in its issue of 7th September 1969, carried, between an article on 'Sex-Crazy Britain' and another entitled 'Three in a Bed', a third article, longer than either of these, quite well informed and decidedly sympathetic, upon the preliminary procedures for the canonization of Pope John XXIII. The event exemplifies some of the difficulties in the topic now before us.

No contemporary discussion of religion could fail to discuss the question of its decline. Is Western society (or let us say, that of Britain and the U.S.) a 'secular' rather than a religious society? The term occurs in the title of Bryan Wilson's excellent book[42]; but clearly the title itself depends on an assumption which should be looked at.

The trouble is, of course, in defining operationally, and measuring, 'religious' and 'secular' behaviour and attitudes. One means might be through statistics of attendance at regular places of religious worship. Wilson quotes a number of these, from British sources, and they appear to show a pattern of decline. In 1895, 641 infants per 1,000 live births in England were baptized into the Church of England; in 1962, the comparable figure was 531. In 1895, out of every 1,000 persons in England aged 15 years, 339 were confirmed into membership of the Church of England; in 1960, 315. In 1895, out of every 1,000 persons in England, 298 attended Church of England Sunday Schools; in 1960, only 133. In 1899, out of every 1,000 marriages in that year, 850 were solemnized according to the rites of some religious group, and only 150 were civil marriages; in 1962, the figures were 704 and 296 respectively. In 1885, out of every 1,000 persons in England aged over 15 years, 84 attended Easter Day communion in an Anglican church; in 1962 the figure was 63.

A considerable decline is evident in English church-going over the past seventy years; though on the face of it, the figures are far from suggesting the existence today of a purely secular society. Probably the decline has been greater amongst Nonconformist groups; but probably less among Catholics: reliable figures are unavailable. To Wilson, the figures 'suggest that the church still plays its part in the lives of many, more as a service facility than as an evangelistic agency, more as the provider of occasional and reassuring ritual than as the disseminator of vital knowledge or the exemplar of moral wisdom'. But this is not a conclusion which one can confidently derive from the statistics themselves; nor can we easily make time-comparisons along these lines. The figures which Wilson quotes are from the Church of England only. While they do not show up the probably still greater decline in Nonconformist attendance, they also fail to show the probable increase in Roman Catholic attendance. Further, they are aggregated for the whole country, and overlook considerable differences between different regions. The biggest towns seem to have suffered the sharpest decline; but, as Dr Martin[43] points out, this is partly due to emigration of Anglicans from those areas, where Catholics have tended to replace them. Geographical mobility, as well as changes in heart, are factors in the situation.

Indeed, the statistics of religious practice are extremely unhelpful. What we should like, by way of comparison with today, are not the figures for 1895 (which, in a sense, is still 'today') but for 1850 (pre-Darwin) or 1800, or 1600. For the most part, these don't exist.

If we had them, what should we learn? We should be likely to find that in 1600 nearly every one in England went to Church on Sunday: they were prosecuted and punished if they didn't. A census taken on a single Sunday in the mid-nineteenth century showed an attendance (all Churches together) of some 40 per cent of the total population. (The only comparable figure for today shows an attendance at Church of England churches of about 18 per cent of membership.) It was believed at the time that these attenders were chiefly from the middle-class, and that hostility and ignorance kept the workers away. Non-churchgoers in the England of 1851 would not have been fined; but non-churchgoing might well have been bad for their social status or businesses (missionaries abroad use the term 'rice-Christianity'); and the alternatives to church-going were on the whole monotonous. Was this 'outward and visible sign' the sign of an 'inward and spiritual grace'? Was the 'English Sunday' evidence of a 'religious' society? It is clear that we have to distinguish the nature of religion as a public means of social control (or indeed as a conventional means of conceptualizing social issues—a familiar way of thinking about things) from religion as an individual conviction.

Statistical data on attendance need to be supplemented by qualitative evidence. Wilson and Martin both quote such evidence, but appear to draw rather different conclusions from it. There seem to be at least two main difficulties. First, any notion of a 'decline' must have reference to some starting-point. In this case, the more or less implicit reference seems to be to some period of the nineteenth century. Unfortunately, as Kitson Clark[44] shows, the amount that is known about *popular* religion in the nineteenth century is not as great as could be wished. If it is true that the prestige of the Protestant clergy does not stand high today, there is no sound evidence on which to discuss whether it was in general higher during Victorian times: such evidence as there is does not point one way. Or again, if one used the names of John Henry Newman, Matthew Arnold, Maurice, Simeon and the like as evidence of the intellectual prestige of religion, among the population then, it would have to be shown that they reached any more than a small minority: *ceteris paribus*, are the 'readerships' of Martin Buber, Simone Weil, Teilhard du Chardin, or Bonhoeffer any smaller? It is probable that the comparison, to be convincing should be with an earlier period: 1650 rather than 1850.

The second difficulty is to know precisely what one is to mean by religious attitudes or behaviour. Martin summarizes a considerable body of recent evidence about attitudes, beliefs and opinions of English people today. The conclusion which seems to emerge is that the ordinary Englishman entertains a collection of beliefs and attitudes which, though mostly bereft of theological system or logic, have a large content of diffuse Christian belief, and of morality which, though not distinctively Christian, is in this case largely derived from Christianity: as Martin puts it, 'moral evaluations broadly follow the lines suggested in the fifth to the tenth commandments, with stealing and cruelty regarded as more heinous than lying or adultery'. With all this goes a considerable admixture of superstition. Such collections of beliefs and attitudes may tend to be labile, easily eroded in parts, and not reliable indicators of action in particular circumstances.

Probably the most striking feature of present-day religion in Britain is the development of sects (many of them of course, importations from the U.S.) which appear to differ from the sects of the seventeenth and eighteenth centuries in the smaller place given to theological argument and the greater part given to expressive action, including of course, the acting-out of 'belonging': this is part of their function in an age of anxiety.

These trends do not seem to be peculiar to Britain and the U.S., among Western countries. They appear, for instance, to be taking place in France. France, indeed, offers in this respect an interesting field of comparison with Britain. In each there is what may be termed an Established Church—Anglican and Roman Catholic respectively—and in both cases the organization of this Church in the country goes back to early medieval (or pre-medieval) times. It is, that is to say, organized on the basis of the rural parish and the parish in the small traditional country town. Both nations became conscious of the problem of the urban worker in the nineteenth century—Britain perhaps earlier, because the problem itself emerged earlier there—and in both cases the organizational character of the Church has prevented it from successfully solving its problem.

But the difference is equally noteworthy. In Britain the Church of England has nothing like a monopoly of religious adherence; the opposition to the Church of England is diffused among a number of other Christian Churches, denominations or sects. In France, the important antithesis is still between Catholicism and atheism.

With the lines of battle apparently so clearly drawn, one would have expected of Catholics a significantly greater awareness of the meaning of the faith. But (so far as information goes) this does not seem to be the case: the French mind seems to be as confused as the English on these matters. A recent opinion-survey[45] revealed for instance that 17·9 per cent of those Frenchmen who did not believe in the Trinity said they believed in the divinity of Christ; and 26 per cent of those who did not believe in the doctrine of original sin, believed in the divinity of Christ. Now of those who so replied to these questions, the great majority must, according to the replies given to the rest of the questionnaires, have declared themselves to be 'Catholics'; yet here they were denying fundamental dogmas of the Catholic faith. The fact appears to be that, even in the case of a faith with an explicit dogma and a well-organized system of religious instruction, membership may be quite independent of any clear and appropriate system of belief. One may, as it were, be a Catholic by ascription; indeed, 21 per cent of those who declared themselves convinced atheists also said they were Catholics.

It is therefore interesting and perhaps significant to find[46] that there has been in France a perceptible growth of sects similar to those in Britain—indeed, in many cases identical with them. Although the sects are Protestant ones, it does not appear that doctrinal issues are important: the sects are joined by people who are still nominally Catholic. Presumably their action is a sign that the message of the established cult no longer satisfies them: the sect provides them with the much-needed opportunity of expressing themselves by participation.

Sociological discussions of the nature, extent and intensity of religious beliefs and attitudes enter upon a field of great difficulty, and run the risk of being naïvely dogmatic. Accepting the risk, we may perhaps say that, apart from the obviously small number of theologically skilled persons, for the majority of people today, clear and consistent religious belief and religious duty are not important, but that religious practice, in the form of participation in hymn-singing and the like, is by no means without importance. Apart from reference to the contemporary sects, the B.B.C. TV programme, 'Songs of Praise' may be put in evidence so far as Britain is concerned. It is suggested that what is derived from participation is not so much 'occasional reassurance' (Wilson's words) as enjoyment: the activity is enjoyed for its own sake. It is virtually identical with what used, at various times, to be called community singing or choral festivals. (Incidentally it is interesting to note the very broad age-range in the 'Songs of Praise' congregations.) Naturally, this enjoyment will vary in intensity, according to the church or sect, and the psychology of the participant; but in general we may speak of it as expressive activity.

Religious activity, like artistic, may be either instrumental or expressive. It is the former when it is explicitly undertaken by the religious person as a means of placing himself in a right relation with the Other in whose existence and relevant power he clearly believes. Theologically, this is its proper purpose. But it is also expressive: doing it itself brings satisfaction.

This expressive activity bears a resemblance, which is worth noticing, to the family rituals discussed by Bossard and Boll.[47]

Both in the Anglican and Nonconformist services, and in the modern Western family, there are 'rituals' which are valued both for their own sake, and as a sign of the endurance of certain traditional elements of society; they also have a significant sentimental force. But they lack the institutionalized and normative character, and the symbolic complexity and richness, and the intensity with which they are believed in, which characterize, for example, the great traditional Christian rituals, such as the Mass. They are labile, and quite readily permitted to undergo change, as the discussion by Bossard and Boll, and as the recent practices of Ecumenism (as distinct from the debates on its principles) show.

It is suggested that both share the common characteristics of expressive activity in 'modern' societies: they lack symbolic complexity and richness, and the normative and compulsive character possessed by such forms of activity in societies which have not effected the transition to modernization.

The gist of the foregoing discussion is that religion, in England and apparently elsewhere to some extent, is valued today, where it is valued at all, largely as an expressive activity. It is tempting to see here a relation between it and art. Needless to say, this relation cannot be a close one; the artist is a person of exceptional powers and skill; participants in religious services mostly are not. Still it is worth noting that one of the striking contrasts between the art of the present century and that of earlier periods has a certain parallel with the contrast in religious practices: it is what might be called the 'permissiveness' of the later period—or, better phrased, the emphasis placed upon the right and the duty of the artist to express whatever is in him by any technical or stylistic means. This is certainly in contrast with the canons of earlier centuries, which emphasized the necessity of abiding by certain orthodoxies—those of perspective, 'representational' painting, and so on. Now, while the contemporary artist still has to live by the sale of his work, and in that sense it is instrumental for him, nevertheless the instrumental character of it is less restrictive, and therefore less important: the market is wider; a wider range of variation in kinds of work is acceptable; works are less restricted to particular kinds of use or display. In this sense, it would perhaps be true to say that the expressive character of artistic activity is preponderant at the present time; and in this respect there is at least an interesting comparison with religion. The levels of achievement are of course different; but this is irrelevant: each person creates within his range of capacity. What is important is that there appears to be a definite resemblance in characteristic types of activity in these two spheres.

C. H. Waddington, in a recent article,[48] develops the theme that the contemporary scientist's analysis and interpretation of reality is not restricted by the need to accommodate itself to any dominating theory or model (such as the theory of Evolution, in the nineteenth century). He is free to choose from, or to construct, any sort of model of reality that he deems suitable. This 'epistemological permissiveness' (the term is not Waddington's) in science is reflected, he says, in a similar range of choice in art, which is not today limited to a narrow range of modes of interpreting existence.

The market-situation of art, referred to in the last paragraph but one, and the climate of culture, have widened the possibilities for the *professional* pursuit of art as an expressive activity. Or, in other words, the boundary between what is conventionally 'Art' and what is not conventionally Art is blurred. The situation of Religion is basically the same: the structure of the modern world is such as to make available a large number of 'models' of explanation of Ultimate Reality: the Christian, Buddhist, Vedanta, positivist, Marxist, psychoanalytic, psychedelic . . . these are equally accessible and have, in general, equal prestige. They may be chosen, and relinquished, at will, and thus possess the values of experimental religion, but lack the symbolic richness, and the propaedeutic quality, of a traditional and institutionalized one.

REFERENCES

1. Henningsen, G., 'Fatalism in Systematic Aspect and Fatalism in its Functional Context' (in Ringgren, H., *Fatalistic Beliefs in Religion, Folklore and Literature*, 1967)
2. Tylor, E. B., *Primitive Culture* (2nd Edition 1873), Vol. I, Chapter XI, see pp. 424, 427
3. Durkheim, E., *The Elementary Forms of the Religious Life*, trans. Swain (reprinted Collier Books, 1961), Book I

4. Durkheim, E., *op. cit.*
5. Durkheim, E., *op. cit.*
6. Durkheim, E., *op. cit.*
7. Geertz, C., 'Religion as a Cultural System' (in *Anthropological Approaches to the Study of Religion*, 1966, p. 4)
8. See, e.g. Turner, V. W., *The Drums of Affliction: a study of Religious Processes among the Ndembu of Zambia* (1968)
9. Spiro, M. E., 'Religion: Problems of Definition and Explanation' (in *Anthropological Approaches to the Study of Religion, ut. sup.*, p. 96)
10. Nock, A. D., *Conversion* (1933)
11. Festugière, Alain, *Personal Religion among the Greeks* (1954)
12. Wach, Joachim, *The Sociology of Religion* (1947)
13. King, W. L., *Introduction to Religion: a Phenomenological Approach* (Revised edition, 1968)
14. Sundkler, B., *Bantu Prophets in South Africa* (2nd Edition 1961)
15. Fortes, M., 'Totem and Taboo' (*Proceedings of the Royal Anthropological Institute of Great Britain and Ireland for 1966*, 1967)
16. Fortes, M., *op. cit.*
17. Middleton, J., 'The Yakan or Allah Water Cult among the Lugbara' (*Journal of the Royal Anthropological Institute*, Vol. 93, 1963)
18. Lanternari, V., *Religions of the Oppressed*, trans. L. Sergio (1963)
19. On Cargo cults, see *inter alia*: Worsley, P., *The Trumpet Shall Sound* (1957) and Burridge, K., *Mambu* (1960)
20. See Eliade, M., *Shamanism: Archaic Techniques of Ecstacy*, trans. Trask (1964. For another instance: Elwin, Verrier, *The Religion of an Indian Tribe* (1955)
21. Emmet, Dorothy, 'Prophets and their Societies' (*Journal of the Royal Anthropological Institute*, Vol. 86, 1956) and *Function Purpose and Powers* (1958)
22. Lindblom, J., *Prophecy in Ancient Israel* (1962)
23. The most copious treatment of Hasidism in English is to be found in the books of Martin Buber: e.g., *The Origin and Meaning of Hasidism* (1960), *The Legend of the Baal Shem* (1956). The best is perhaps Scholem, G., *Major Trends in Jewish Mysticism* (Revised edition 1961), Lecture 9
24. Agus, L., *The Evolution of Jewish Thought* (1959), Chapter 11
25. Scholem, G., *Major Trends in Jewish Mysticism* (1961), Lecture 9
26. Weber, M., *The Theory of Social and Economic Organisation*, trans. Henderson and Parsons (1947), Part III (5).
27. Ullmann, W., *Principles of Government and Politics in the Middle Ages* (1961), Part I, Chapter 2

28. See Cox, J. T., *Practice and Procedure in the Church of Scotland* (5th edition ed. Longmuir, 1964), especially pp. 110f
29. Weber, M., *The Protestant Ethic and the Spirit of Capitalism*, trans. Parsons (1930)
30. See Green, Robt. W. (ed), *Protestantism and Capitalism: the Weber Thesis and its Critics* (1959)
31. Klassen, J. P., *The Economics of Anabaptism, 1525–1560* (1964)
32. Gernet, J., *Les Aspects économiques du Bouddhisme dans la Société Chinoise du Ve au Xe Siècle* (1956)
Lien Sheng Yang: 'Buddhist Monasteries and Four Money Raising Institutions in Chinese History' (*Harvard Journal of Asiatic Studies*, Vol. 13 (1950)
33. Carrington, P., *The Early Christian Church* (2 volumes, 1957. See Vol. I, Chapter 14)
34. Smith, Donald E. (ed), *South Asian Politics and Religion* (1966)
35. De Groot, J. J. M., 'Militant Spirit of the Buddhist Clergy in China' (*T'oung Pao*, Vol. II, 1st Series, 1891)
36. Smith, Donald, *op. cit.*
37. Troeltsch, E., *The Social Teaching of the Christian Churches and Groups*, trans. Wyon (1931)
38. Troeltsch, E., *op. cit.*
39. Wiese, L. von, *Systematic Sociology*, adapted by Howard Becker (1932)
40. Yinger, I. M., *Religion Society and the Individual* (1957)
41. See *Journal of John Wesley*, ed. N. Curnock (8 volumes, 1909) (For persecutions etc., see especially Vol. III, for separation, Vols. IV to VIII, *passim*)
42. Wilson, Bryan, *Religion in Secular Society* (1966)
43. Martin, D., *A Sociology of English Religion* (1967)
44. Kitson Clark, G., *The Making of Victorian England* (1962), Chapter VI
45. Maitre, Jacques, 'Les Sondages sur les attitudes religieuses en France' (*Revue française de Sociologie*, Vol. II, 1961)
46. Ségny, Jean, 'Le non-conformisme sectaire en France' (*Revue française de Sociologie*, Vol. VI (1), 1965)
47. Bossard, J. H. and Boll, E., *Ritual in Family Living* (1950)
48. Waddington, C. H., 'New Visions of the World' (*Leonardo*, Vol. I, 1968)

8.

Conclusion

Societies may be seen as structures, that is, as composed of parts more or less adapted to one another for the fulfilment of some function or functions. Or they may be seen as processes: that is, as systems which are in course of change; changes in roles, groups, programmes and so on are related to the existence, in the societies, of conflicts, contradictions, incompatibilities which are as much part of the nature of societies as is functional harmony. Both of these manners of viewing social reality are models, neither of which will be exclusively, or completely, true. Perhaps it would represent the position best to say that the structural-functional is the basic model for a society, since without some assumption of mutual adaptation the concept of society itself could hardly exist. But in itself this model cannot deal with the emergence of incompatibilities, contradictions, conflicts among individuals, sub-systems and the whole system.

Models of society must at some point also take into account the effects of the diffusion of social elements from one society to another. The analysis of such processes as these encounters problems of definition and of fact. Of fact: can we lay bare the actual process of diffusion, when, where, how, or what? Of definition: what is 'a society', so that we may speak of diffusion between societies? These are questions which connect with the field of historical study, showing that history and sociology are ways of looking at the same reality, and therefore must overlap.

This book has been concerned with issues of correlation or co-variation between elements or sub-systems of societies. In the foregoing chapters, an attempt was made to support the proposition that societies showing a higher degree of technological development are, in general, characterized by a greater degree of role-differentiation, and a greater degree of specialization of groups, than are found in 'simpler' societies. This is not a startling conclusion, for increasing specialization has, of course, long been recognized as a feature of 'development' or 'modernization'. But it is well to remember that the degree of specialization differs in different institutional fields. It has developed rapidly and far in the economic and the legal; less rapidly or far in the religious or artistic. Evidently this is connected with the nature of the respective activities.

It is connected with a fact about these activities, or relationships, which may be put by saying that economic and legal activities are primarily means to ends: means of organizing the supply of various satisfactions to various people or categories of people. Economic activity is in pursuit of satisfactions which are not themselves part of the activity. In this respect, religious and artistic activities differ from economic or legal. Prayer or praise is not itself a means to a relationship with God, but *is* itself the relationship; the creation or contemplation of a work of art is not a means to an experience, but is itself the experience. This is what is meant by saying that the former pair are 'instrumental' activities, while the latter pair are 'expressive' activities. But some complications in this relationship require to be noted.

It was suggested in foregoing chapters what differences in degrees of modernization involve changes in the relations between the instrumental and the expressive aspects of activities: 'a greater differentiation between the instrumental and the expressive purposes of programmes; a greater degree of rational organization of instrumental programmes, and a greater degree of informality and simplicity of expressive ones'[1] are characteristics of technologically developed societies. What this means may be illustrated from the theme of religion. Throughout the majority of societies other than 'modern', the rituals and ceremonies, the prayers of the religious suppliant, not only, so to speak, 'act relationships', but also act, or symbolize, the consequences of relationships: they invoke benefits, protection from misfortune, salvation for the believer. *At one and the same time*, the rituals have a double significance. Sometimes this combination of the instrumental and the expressive has its result in behaviour patterns of great complexity; Lienhardt[2] speaks of Dinka religion as giving 'the possibility of creating a form of experience they desire, and of freeing themselves symbolically from what they must otherwise passively endure'.

In simpler societies, ritual thus tends to have a twofold significance—or rather, the distinction between instrumental and expressive is less clear.

But the development of the various sciences and technologies, which is an aspect of 'modern' societies, means that man can to some extent rationally control the influence of his natural environment, and to some extent have a rational understanding of the causes of his own behaviour, and of the behaviour of societies. Consequently the idea of a supernatural being—or, at least, of a supernatural being who 'does things' in any intelligible sense of the phrase—is losing its significance. And therefore the idea of religion as an instrument for procuring benefits likewise becomes divested of meaning. But in a climate of opinion which holds the belief that the Universe, including society and the individual, is 'profane', and that God, if existent, is either incomprehensible or otiose, it is also the case that a person can, or, if he is to have any at all, must, choose or invent his own religion, whose propitiatory, piacular or apotropaic significance, and its weight of meaning, and the norms directing it, become obviously lessened.

Foregoing chapters have suggested that, in different ways, similar processes are to be seen in the fields of kinship relations and of art: activities in each of which both instrumental and expressive aspects have traditionally been of importance. The family, and not only in the West, but in other societies which are 'modernizing', is becoming mainly a place for the free expression of personal relationships; and, say Bossard and Boll,[3] the 'rituals' or patterned activities in which these are expressed are marked by a lessened dependence on tradition or prescription, by more spontaneity, greater simplicity, less formality. And this is so because many of the instrumental functions which the family once performed: the inculcation of formal, clearly defined, traditional moral precepts or standards, besides lineage-perpetuation and so forth, have greatly declined in importance.

What would require, at this point, to be answered, but cannot so far be adequately answered, is the question what common factor, if any, underlies the following characteristic aspects of Western society: first, the relative absence of norms of stylistic orthodoxy in art; secondly, an informal, experimental and dogmaless religion; thirdly, permissive and experimental family-relations; and fourthly, an economic system marked by the increasing development of rational organization—and where, indeed, operational research is now being applied to the socio-psychological problems of industry. Further work on the general sociological principles underlying the co-variation of sub-systems is among the most important tasks of comparative sociology.

REFERENCES

1. See above, Chapter 1
2. Lienhardt, G., *Divinity and Experience* (1961), p. 170
3. See above, Chapter 5

Select Bibliography

Almond, G. A. and Powell, G. B., *Comparative Politics: a Developmental Approach* (Little, Brown and Co., 1966)

Bailey, F. G., *Stratagems and Spoils* (Blackwell, 1969)

Banton, M. (ed), *Anthropological Approaches to the Study of Religion* (Tavistock Publications, 1966)

Political Systems and the Distribution of Power (Tavistock Publications, 1965)

The Relevance of Models for Social Anthropology (Tavistock Publications, 1965)

The Social Anthropology of Complex Societies (Tavistock Publications, 1966)

Beattie, John, *Other Cultures* (Cohen and West, 1964; Routledge, 1966)

Bell, N. W. and Vogel, E. F., *A Modern Introduction to the Family* (Routledge, 1961)

Belshaw, C. S., *Traditional Exchange and Modern Markets* (Prentice-Hall, 1965)

Blalock, H. M. and A. B., *Methodology in Social Research* (McGraw Hill, 1968)

Bohannan, P. and Dalton, G., *Markets in Africa* (Northwestern University Press, 1965)

Cohen, P., *Modern Social Theory* (Basic Books, 1968)

Dewey, Alice, *Peasant Marketing in Java* (Free Press, 1962)

Durkheim, E., *The Elementary Forms of the Religious Life* (trans. Swain; (reprint) Collier Books, 1961)

Epstein, T. S., *Capitalism, Primitive and Modern: some aspects of Tolai Economic Growth* (Manchester University Press, 1968)

Etzioni, A., *Modern Organisations* (Prentice-Hall, 1964)

Firth, Raymond, *Elements of Social Organisation* (Watts & Co., 1951)

Firth, R. (ed), *Themes in Economic Anthropology* (Tavistock Publications, 1967)

Firth, R. and Yamey, B. S. (eds), *Capital, Saving and Credit in Peasant Societies* (Allen and Unwin, 1964)

Fortes, M. and Evans Pritchard, E. E. (eds), *African Political Systems* (Oxford University Press, 1940)

Fox, Robin, *Kinship and Marriage* (Penguin Books, 1967)

Frankenberg, R., *Communities in Britain* (Penguin Books, 1966)
Freedman, M., *Chinese Lineage and Society: Fukien and Kwangtung* (Athlone Press, 1964)
Friedmann, W., *Law in a Changing Society* (Stevens, 1959)
Geertz, C., *Peddlers and Princes* (Chicago University Press, 1963)
Gluckman, M., *The Judicial Process among the Barotse* (Manchester University Press, 1955)
Gluckman, M. (ed), *Essays on the Ritual of Social Relations* (Manchester University Press, 1964)
Gulliver, P. H., *Social Control in an African Society* (Routledge and Kegan Paul, 1963)
Hall, Jerome, *Theft, Law and Society* (Bobbs Merrill Co., 2nd Edition, 1952)
Harris, C. C., *The Family* (Allen and Unwin, 1969)
Hart, H. L. A., *The Concept of Law* (Oxford University Press, 1961)
Hoebel, E. A., *The Law of Primitive Man* (Harvard University Press, 1952)
Lanternari, V., *The Religions of the Oppressed* (MacGibbon and Kee, 1963)
Le Clair, E. S. and Schneider, H. K., *Economic Anthropology: Readings in Theory and Analysis* (Holt Rinehart and Winston, 1968)
Lenski, G., *The Religious Factor* (Doubleday, 1963)
Mair, Lucy, *Primitive Government* (Hutchinson, 1962)
Marsh, R. M., *Comparative Sociology: a Codification of Cross-societal Analysis* (Harcourt, Brace and World, 1967)
Martin, D., *A Sociology of English Religion* (Heinemann, 1967)
Middleton, J. and Tait, D., *Tribes Without Rulers* (Routledge, 1958)
O'Dea, T. F., *The Sociology of Religion* (Prentice-Hall, 1966)
Parsons, Talcott, *Societies: Evolutionary and Comparative Perspectives* (Prentice-Hall, 1966)
Polanyi, K. Arensberg, C. M. and Pearson, H. W., *Trade and Markets in the Early Empires* (Free Press, 1958)
Smelser, N. J., *The Sociology of Economic Life* (Prentice-Hall, 1963)
Weber, Max, *The Protestant Ethic and the Spirit of Capitalism* (trans. Parsons; Allen and Unwin, 1930)
Weber, Max, *The Theory of Social and Economic Organisation* (trans. Henderson and Parsons; Free Press, 1947)
Wilson, Bryan, *Patterns of Sectarianism* (Heinemann, 1967)
Religion in Secular Society (Watts and Co., 1966)
Sects and Society (Heinemann, 1961)
Worsley, P., *The Third World* (Weidenfeld and Nicolson, 1964)
Yinger, J. M., *Religion, Society and the Individual* (Macmillan (New York), 1957)

Index